ANTICLERICALISM:
A BRIEF HISTORY

Anticlericalism:

A Brief History

JOSÉ SÁNCHEZ

UNIVERSITY OF NOTRE DAME PRESS
NOTRE DAME   **LONDON**

Library of Congress Cataloging in Publication Data

Sánchez, José Mariano, 1932–
    Anticlericalism; a brief history.

    Bibliography: p.
        1. Anti-clericalism—History.   2. Anti-Catholicism—History.
I. Title.
BX1766.S25   282′.09   72-3504
ISBN 0-268-00471-4

Manufactured in the United States of America by
NAPCO Graphic Arts, Inc., New Berlin, Wisconsin

CONTENTS

A certain man went down from Jerusalem to Jericho, and fell among thieves, which stripped him of his raiment, and wounded him, and departed, leaving him half dead. And by chance there came down a certain priest that way: and when he saw him, he passed by on the other side.

Luke 10:30-32

PREFACE

Napoleon: *You realize, Eminence, that I can destroy*
the Church.
Consalvi: *Emperor, not even the priests have been*
able to do that.

Anticlericalism is a word laden with meaning. To some it
conjures up the idea of a wealthy, tyrannical, and self-serving
clergy under attack from the protagonists of democracy,
decency, and freedom. To others it brings to mind a noble,
long-suffering, and selfless clergy enduring persecution at the
hands of a cabal of willful conspirators bent upon destroying
God's representatives on earth. These images are the extremes, of course, and between them is a complex spectrum
of anticlerical thought and action.

Ultimately, anticlericalism and the struggle with clericalism
rest upon the notion of power, specifically, the power of the
clergy, and the attempts to limit or destroy that power. In
some ages and in some countries there were no attacks upon
the clergy's power; in others the attacks were a constant
factor, shaping history and influencing ideas, men, and institutions. So powerful did the force of anticlericalism become
that it entered the mythology of tradition, and long after the
clergy's power was destroyed, the attacks continued.

Catholic clergy have been viewed, in anthropological
terms, as the magic-men, the shamans of the culture. Representatives of God, they possessed enormous power over men.
They, and they alone, held the keys of salvation. They interpreted God's will and God's aims. They could bring down
the wrath of heaven, or they could open the gates of
Paradise. To the extent that men believed in the validity of

this argument, the clergy had power. When men ceased to believe, the clergy lost their power.

Not all of it: during the years of belief, the clergy had gathered many of the secular accoutrements of power—political, educational, economic, and social. They were loath to give them up, even though they had lost their dogmatic hold. Indeed, it was no small problem, for the legal and social interweavings of clericalism were many and complex. In many countries it appeared that nothing short of a revolution would break the structures of clerical power.

The way of the anticlericals was made immeasurably smoother by the secular revolution. In those areas where the secular revolution came early and was most successful, in northern Europe, and by transference, North America, there was little anticlericalism after the clergy's dogmatic power was destroyed. The Protestant Reformation marked this event in northern Europe. In Latin Europe and Latin America the secular revolution was less successful; the Protestant Reformation made fewer inroads, and the power of the clergy lasted into modern times.

The main anticlerical struggles in northern Europe took place from the twelfth through the sixteenth centuries. There —chiefly in England and Germany—the interweaving of clerical with social and civil power was not as complex or intensive as in the older and more Romanized areas of Europe. The clergy were less reformed and less able to challenge the Protestant reformers. The entire struggle was relatively uncomplicated by mass political and social ideologies.

In Latin Europe and Latin America the anticlerical struggle came in the nineteenth and twentieth centuries. Stimulated by the secularism of the Enlightenment and the French Revolution, the new liberal and socialist ideologies clashed head on with a Tridentine reformed clergy. The struggles of this era were more protracted, more violent, and left bitter legacies. Social fabrics were torn asunder, and political progress was stifled. The struggles subsided only after the secular revolution penetrated deeply into these countires.

Anticlericalism flourished in certain climates. A majority Church and church-state tensions helped produce an overweening clergy and fertile ground for clericalism. Where there was no tradition of religious pluralism or toleration, the dissenter found no safety valve for his views and expressions. In the United States and northern Europe after the Reformation, the dissenter was free to join another sect or to practice no religion at all. In Latin America and Latin Europe he had to protest within the framework of the predominant religious institution; to have done otherwise would have exposed him to social ostracism and civil danger.

This study, therefore, will concentrate on anticlericalism and its expressions primarily in Latin Europe and Latin America in modern times and in northern Europe before the Reformation. It will deal only with anticlericalism within and against the Roman Catholic Church; Protestant anticlericalism is another area entirely.

To chronicle the history of anticlerical thought would be a task beyond any one historian's powers. Therefore, this study will consider only those thinkers who had a major effect upon the general development of anticlericalism, or whose ideas found practical application of more than local importance. The practice of anticlericalism—generally on the political plane—is easier to discover and document. Although there have been universal trends, the practice of anticlericalism, like the practice of Catholicism, characteristically has been national in context.*

Something should be said about the unique nature of the

---

*In a work of this sort, covering as it does the span of the Church's history, I have necessarily relied heavily on secondary sources. Aside from the impossibility of finding primary sources for all the facts and ideas contained herein, it appears to me that easily available secondary works will be more useful to the student of anticlericalism and hopefully will stimulate research in more specialized aspects of the topic. Furthermore, secondary interpretative works are more valuable for a brief survey of anticlericalism, which is all that this work aspires to be.

Church. It is an institution with all the advantages and defects of an institution and thus bears comparison with other institutions. It frequently has, however, resources that go beyond those of most institutions. It can command intense spiritual allegiance even in its weakest moments. To a great extent, it thrives on persecution, whether justifiable or not. Generally speaking, no institution has had so many competent and devoted servants and bureaucrats as the clergy have been; their devotion to their profession far transcends that of any other professionals.

Susceptible to many institutional laws, the Church defies most of them. It has served Western culture longer than any other institution. Its very existence twenty centuries after its founding, in a world radically different beyond comprehension from the pastoral society of its Founder, proves something about the Church's adaptability.

*

I first became interested in the study of anticlericalism when I began researching the origins of the Spanish Civil War; but my introduction to the subject came much earlier. My father was a life-long anticlerical (in the finest sense of the word), and my mother, who has lived almost eighty years literally and figuratively within the shadow of the Cathedral, once remarked to me when I was very young, "Priests learn everything in the seminary except manners." To both of them I dedicate this book with gratitude for years of generosity.

I owe a great deal to Professor Joseph A. McCallin, S.J., of Saint Louis University. For the past decade in sometimes daily discussions we have thrashed out ideas and concepts; he has provoked, perplexed, and intrigued but never exasperated me. Professor Joan Connelly Ullman of the University of Washington read portions of the manuscript, and Professor Joseph N. Moody of the Catholic University of America read the entire manuscript twice. Both made many valuable comments and suggestions. Miss Betty Prevender did a superb job of editing the work. Of course, I bear sole responsibility for its contents.

Saint Louis University

November, 1972

PART ONE

CHAPTER 1

The Meaning of Anticlericalism

*What? Always these human witnesses, always men who
report what other men have reported, always
men between God and myself!*

Jean Jacques Rousseau

ONE OF THE MOST WIDELY PROPAGATED LEGENDS OF THE
late nineteenth century was the myth of clericalism. Published in dozens of journals, the theme of numerous books,
the mainstay of countless pamphlets, it was a favorite topic
of anticlericals and was frequently accepted by clericals
themselves.

The myth was not new. Elements of it could be found in
the writings of the humanists of the fifteenth-century Renaissance, and it was commonly heard in the salons of the
Enlightenment. Advances of the industrial revolution and the
development of mechanized printing made the myth a stan-
dard element of nineteenth-century liberal culture.

It was partly truth, as all myths are, partly historical exag-
geration, and partly conspiracy theory. Its chief tenet was
that the clergy were a self-seeking group, usually an obstacle
to progress, constantly fomenting superstition, obstructing
knowledge and human well-being, and not above plotting civil
rebellion to maintain themselves in power.

In its broad outlines, the myth went something like this:

The clergy were originally humble folk, practically
indistinguishable from and devoted servants of the laity. In

the primitive Church they were chosen by the laity and had no pretensions to political, social, or economic power. When the Church triumphed over the Roman Empire, the clergy became state officials, a privileged caste; they lost their evangelical simplicity and made themselves the absolute possessors of the keys to salvation. After the fall of the Empire, the clergy were the only educated men, the only professionals in an age of nonprofessionalism. They established rigid requirements and rules for entry into their fraternity and deliberately kept the laity ignorant, instead teaching them superstition. They felt secure in their roles as medicine men, agricultural agents, and civil servants.

With the rise of the competitive dynastic state, the clergy attempted, successfully in most cases, to limit the power of the civil governments, mainly by infiltrating the bureaucracies of the new states and obtaining pledges that bound the princes to ecclesiastical jurisdiction. But by the late Middle Ages they had begun to lose the battle. They became defensive. Unable to cope with the growth of an intelligent laity, they founded the Inquisition to suppress dissent.

Meanwhile, the clergy added to their already considerable economic power. Protected by their self-devised laws of mortmain, they came to control much of the landed wealth of western Europe. When confronted with the new economic doctrines of capitalism, they eagerly embraced them, overlooking their earlier strictures against usury. By the fifteenth century, the clergy were a class answerable only to themselves. Corrupted by power and wealth, they fought all attempts at reform.

Despite their power, they could not prevent the Protestant Reformation. They regrouped themselves in the Council of Trent. With uniform education, standardized training, strict discipline and dogma, they conspired to form the Fortress Church, hurling anathemas at all who deviated however slightly from pronounced dogma. The Jesuits became the spearhead of counter-reform and were themselves examples of militant Trentism, perfectly disciplined robots sent into every Catholic court in Europe and into every Asian palace to exert papal influence.

The clergy, the myth said, stifled the new learning; humanism and scientific curiosity were snuffed out. Erasmus criticized the clergy for their attitudes; Galileo suffered because of them; Bruno was put to death by them. The progress of the scientific revolution and the Enlightenment occurred in spite of the clergy, as Voltaire so well demonstrated.

The French Revolution marked the turning point. The clergy's land was taken from them, their schools were closed, and many were led to the guillotine. In Spain and Italy their power was threatened. As a result, after the Napoleonic defeat the clergy became more defensive, more obscurantist, and more determined to restore their power. They fought every bit of progressive legislation in the nineteenth century, from land reform to public education. They fomented civil rebellion when they could not have their way. But the masses were no longer with them, and the forces of liberalism were too strong.

The climax of clerical defensiveness came in 1864 when Pope Pius IX, later the self-styled prisoner of the Vatican, condemned religious freedom, toleration, progress, and "modern civilization." In 1870 he proclaimed the dogma of papal infallibility, attempting to replace the clergy's declining political power with the spiritual force of coercion.

Thus the myth to 1870. After that it became two. One was a continuation of the old, with proletarian overtones: according to this account, the clergy, now allied with the upper classes, remained defensive, opposed to social reform, paternalistically reminding the working classes to humbly accept their lot in life. The new myth, on the other hand, viewed the clergy as supporting social upheaval and identifying with the proletariat (in Europe) and minority groups (in America) to the exclusion of the middle class in both. The clergy were aligning themselves with the new power groups, certain proof that they were interested only in ingratiating themselves into power wherever they moved.

This was the myth of clericalism. Meanwhile, the clergy
had their own legend, the myth of anticlericalism. They believed that anticlericals had hatched a diabolic plot to weaken
the Church by striking at the clergy. The humanists, the
scientists, and the Freemasons had formed a conspiracy
against the clergy. Usually based in Paris, the anticlerical
conspirators sent agents throughout the Catholic world to stir
up antagonism against the clergy. With the rise of the
proletarian movements, the socialists and communists linked
with the movement to deprive the clergy of their rights.

*

The circumstances that gave rise to the myths of clericalism and anticlericalism were shaped by a number of factors, chiefly the variable relationships between clergy and
laity. There had always been tension, a fact noted by Pope
Boniface VIII in 1296: "Antiquity teaches us," he said in the
opening phrase of his bull *Clericis Laicos,* "that laymen are
in a high degree hostile to the clergy."[1] This hostility had
given rise to expressions of discontent from the laity that
were markedly different from those of the early Middle Ages.
Before the twelfth century, dissent had focused on doctrine.
The heresies of the early Church had dealt with the problem
of evil, the nature of Christ, or the role of Mary; with the
exception of some aspects of Pelagianism and the thoughts
of the Montanists, they did not concern the clergy. After the
religious revival of the twelfth century, dissent turned upon
the clergy with increasing intensity until, by the middle of
the nineteenth century, it was called anticlericalism.[2]

Anticlericalism came to be a catch-all phrase. Anticlericals
included those atheists and agnostics who criticized the clergy
as a way of criticizing organized religion. They included practicing Catholics who felt that clergy were abusing their
power. Among them were those who had little quarrel with
the clergy but who objected to certain of their attitudes.
Finally, they included a small number of persons who were
truly bent on the destruction of the Church.

The tendency was to label as anticlericals all who criticized the clergy and the Church, whatever their motives and whatever their line of criticism. It was simplistic to label as anticlericals such different people as the priest Felicité de Lamennais, who criticized the Pope for not supporting democratic governments; the statesman Camilo Cavour, who wanted no clerical influence in his new Italian state; the anarchist Pierre Proudhon, who felt that a just society could include no priests; the intellectual politician Manuel Azaña, who believed that the regular clergy had long since outlived their usefulness to Spanish society; and even that master of *realpolitik,* Otto von Bismarck, who objected to Roman spiritual influence in his Germany. To lump them all together under the common term anticlerical begs for definition and distinction. Each practiced a different form of anticlericalism.

*

In the broadest sense, anticlericalism can be defined as opposition to the power of the clergy. Conversely, the possession or use of power by the clergy can in the same sense be called clericalism. Most definitions of anticlericalism are stated in negative terms, i.e., opposition to clericalism. C. A. Whittuck's definition of clericalism is one of the earliest and best: "Clericalism is the outcome of a professional bias or rather of a perverted *esprit de corps,* prompting the clergy to make an immoderate, or illicit, use of their legitimate privileges for the benefit of their own class."[3] But this definition begs the question somewhat, for it depends on the meaning one reads into the terms "immoderate," "illicit," and "legitimate privileges." Indeed, the concept of clericalism is elusive, and studies of definition easily turn into exercises in semantics.

But the definition can be narrowed by looking at anticlericalism as it has been expressed in history.[4] Particular anticlericals have had specific grievances against the clergy, despite the rather wide variation of these expressions over the centuries. One of the simplest refinements of the definition is to label anticlericals according to the specific powers of the clergy they attack: there are dogmatic anticlericals, political anticlericals, social anticlericals, economic anticlericals, educational anticlericals, etc. From this point of view intellectual anticlericalism does not exist by itself; it is simply the rationale of an opposition against specific clerical powers.

What many call intellectual anticlericalism is actually an ideological kind that has more to do with motivation than expression. Determining motivation provides as much insight into the problem of definition as do the means used by anticlericals, or the specific powers they attack. According to motivation, then, all anticlericals can be characterized as being either ideological or pragmatic.

Ideological anticlericals are convinced that the powers of the clergy are inherently abusive, no matter to what use they are put. Clerical power is of itself wrong and destructive of whatever values the ideological anticlerical has, whether these values concern the state, society, or the Church. Ideological anticlericals object to the *right* of the clergy to power. Much like Acton's aphorism that power corrupts, the premise for the ideological anticlerical is that clerical power corrupts, no matter how little it is used. Nevertheless, this notion need not be applied to all clergy. For instance, an ideological anticlerical may be anti-Jesuit, convinced that the Jesuits are an inherently destructive congregation and that, no matter how lightly the Jesuits wield their power, in the long run this use of power will corrupt not only the Jesuits but society or the Church as well; but the same anticlerical may have no objection to the right or use of other clergy's power. Or, the ideological anticlerical may believe that all clerical political power is destructive of the stability of the state, even if that power is used only infrequently. In any case, intellectual or moral conviction underlies the attitude and action of the ideological anticlerical.

Pragmatic anticlericals, on the other hand, have no fundamental premise and do not base their thoughts or actions on rigid conviction. They attack clerical power because that power happens to interfere with their aims at the moment. They do not feel that clerical power, any more than that of any other group, is inherently wrong. Pragmatic anticlericals frequently attempt to justify their attacks on ideological grounds, but their practice betrays them, for they express their anticlericalism in a specific action to solve a particular problem. Thus, a ruler may confiscate Jesuit property not because he argues with the right of the Jesuits to possess property, but because the Jesuits have property that he needs at that moment. In different circumstances he would not attack Jesuit properties; indeed, he might use them to bolster his own power. Pragmatic anticlericalism is limited in motivation, whereas ideological anticlericalism is unlimited.[5] Motivation can change, however, and often, under the pressure of circumstances, pragmatic anticlericals become ideological anticlericals. The line between the two is often difficult to find.

It should be kept in mind that anticlericalism is a form of dissent—ideological anticlericalism in particular has a transitory nature—and dissent has always been as varied as human beings themselves. What is tolerated in one age is not in another. Consider the gulf of toleration which separates the sixteenth-century Inquisition from the modern Church. What passes for anticlericalism today would have merited burning at the stake in the Spain of Ferdinand and Isabella. Each age has its own demands and interests, and anticlericalism varies accordingly.

Ideological anticlericalism is therefore dynamic and relative. Its opposition to the possession or abuse of clerical power, status, and authority varies, as does the conception of these clerical attributes and activities in any particular age. As a result, its presence is largely determined by attitudes, actions, and reactions of clergy and laity. Tension between the two is heightened in times of crisis and by the tendency of both antagonists to assert principles to bolster their arguments, the clergy using the principle of authority and the anticlericals the principle of freedom. Frequently the struggles are over these principles alone.

Other kinds of opposition and dissent are often called anticlericalism but are actually something different. One of these is antisacerdotalism. Whereas anticlericals oppose the clergy's powers or abuse of those powers, antisacerdotalists are opposed to the clergy themselves. Often, antisacerdotalists begin as ideological anticlericals and then drift into antisacerdotalism. They tend to view the clergy as symbols or representatives of an opposed institution. Since the clergy usually wear distinct garb and have common training, antisacerdotalists find it easy to focus their opposition on the individual priest, whatever his personal attitudes may be.

Another kind of dissent or opposition commonly labelled anticlericalism is what may be called antiauthoritarian-legalism. This is opposition to attitudes usually held by most of the clergy as well as by many of the laity. Antiauthoritarian-legalists concern themselves with attitudes towards the basic questions of authority, progress, human nature, values, and the institutional structure of the Church. They generally contend that man has progressed and therefore needs less authority than in the past.[6] They emphasize the value of things secular and temporal, criticizing the clergy's stress upon the overwhelming importance of things spiritual and eternal.[7] They want greater freedom within the Church and usually a larger role for the laity. To an extent, antiauthoritarian-legalists are ideological anticlericals as well, for most feel that the clergy are abusing their authority (although the rise of social activism among the clergy in the twentieth century has tended to mitigate this ideological aspect.)

It is obvious that most kinds of anticlericalism are not mutually exclusive. Nor do clear distinctions always emerge. Furthermore, some varieties of dissent share anticlerical attitudes and approaches, yet belong to a different type of movement in their main thrust: laicism and secularism are examples. To add to the confusion, anticlericals tend to center their opposition not upon the clergy in general (although frequently implying that they do), but rather upon specific groups within the clergy. Antipapalism, antiepiscopal-ism, antijesuitism, antimonasticism, and antipastoralism are all specific manifestations of anticlericalism.

Anticlericalism varies between the extremes of mild criticism and violence. It is exhibited in many ways, from the burning of churches, prohibitions upon the number of clergy, and the expropriation of clerical property to restrictions upon the wearing of clerical garb. The laity who support the clergy are also subject to anticlerical attack, from the banning of processions to prohibitions against the wearing of ornamental religious jewelry.

There is no question that in many instances the clergy have been scapegoats for those who have lacked a more convenient target. The distinctness of the clergy, their exposed moral position (in having to live up to the standards which they preach), and their alleged unnaturalness (committed to celibacy and lacking a family life) have made the individual cleric an outsider, separate from the rest of society, but at the same time easily identifiable. In this aspect, anticlericalism shares many of the attributes of other "anti" ideologies, such as anti-semitism, antimilitarism, and anticommunism: the individual is identified mainly as a member of the group, and whatever individuality he has is submerged in the characteristics of the group.

All of these facets of anticlericalism can be seen more clearly in historical context. History is made by individuals, and movements such as anticlericalism are expressions and reactions of individual human beings to the circumstances of their environment.

CHAPTER 2

Anticlericalism:
The First Thousand Years

*The clergy have been long acquiring, and have often
refunded, and still there is no end of their
acquisitions.*

Montesquieu

THE MOST SIGNIFICANT HISTORICAL PROBLEM IN ATTEMPTING
to understand the first thousand years of the Church's existence is that we know so little about it. We have some idea
of the legislation, the thoughts of the few great writers, the
dispositon of some trials, and some occasional commentaries;
but press reports, statistical estimates, and the productions
of the printing presses—the stuff of modern research—did not
exist. At the level on which popular anticlericalism operates
all that we know is negative: that the laity did not generally
hate or dislike the clergy, at least not strongly enough to leave
a record of that fact.

The characteristic determinant of the Church's development during this period was growth in a hostile environment.
That the Church triumphed over society and established a
virtual theocracy by the beginning of the high Middle Ages
is an eloquent testimony to its vigor. The struggle was not
easy. For the first three centuries the Romans persecuted
both the clergy and laity. Then, while riven by doctrinal
heresies, the Church had to contend with the barbarian
invaders in the north and the Moslems in the south. Finally

stabilizing itself against these pressures, the Church had to survive in the hostile world of feudalism and the primitive economy of manoralism.

So great was the force of this pressure that there was no room for the growth of internal anticlericalism. Clergy and laity had to work together to maintain the existence of the Church. They could not afford dissension. There was plenty of persecution from non-Christians, but it was directed against all Christians, clergy and laity alike. Every act of persecution, every fear of the invader served to create unity and harmony. Christians were a minority group, first in Rome and then in the larger world of Europe and the Mediterranean. They were drawn together by circumstances.[1]

Nor did the conditions for ideological anticlericalism exist, because there was no belief in either the possibility or goodness of change. The prevailing intellectual atmosphere was one of moderate pessimism. Plato, Seneca, and Augustine dominated the age.

Plato was a firm believer in order; he felt that any deviation from an established ordered society must be for the worse. Seneca's Stoic philosophy likewise did not endorse any attempts at radical change: it was better for man to nobly suffer the misfortunes of this world than to attempt change. Augustine expounded the idea of Providence: God's governance of the world, not to change it, but to provide spiritual relief and salvation. The world was a vale of tears at best, he felt, and man was helpless—insignificantly helpless —to change it; in any event, man's goal was not material progress but spiritual salvation. Augustine's implication was that, considering man's helplessness and his need for salvation, the clergy, as possessors of the keys of salvation, were the most important people on earth. Paradoxically, Christianity's dynamism for temporal change was ignored.

Under Rome, until the fourth-century decree of toleration, the Christians suffered persecution. They had good reason to believe that the world was filled with sorrow, which indeed it was for them. They were furthermore convinced that the

Millennium was at hand and that any change would come from God. In addition, most of the laity were from the lower economic classes, and so were the clergy. There was no class conflict between the two; furthermore, the clergy were persecuted along with the laity. Anticlericalism in this atmosphere would have been strange indeed.

What division occurred came in the form of heresy. The heresies of the early Church, however, were different from the dissensions labelled anticlerical in modern times. The early heretics were concerned with doctrine, and few had anything to say about the clergy. Of course, they criticized the clergy for holding the theological positions they did, but with few exceptions the heretics did not criticize the structure of clerical-lay relations, nor did they envisage a different relationship within their own heretical sects. The early heretics were more interested in the nature of Christ, the role of Mary, and the problem of evil than they were in matters concerning the clergy.

There were three exceptions that could be called quasi-anticlerical: Montanism, Donatism, and Pelagianism. The Montanists, from what we can gather from their spokesman Tertullian, were a pentecostal sect, opposed to the hierarchy, proclaiming the priesthood of all believers. Their influence was slight, and in their views on human nature they were even more pessimistic than the Augustine-oriented Christians.[2]

The Donatists flourished in that hotbed of heretics, North Africa. They claimed, among other things, that sacraments administered by unworthy priests—clergy in a state of mortal sin—were invalid. Their view was essentially elitist and only coincidentally reformist, for it struck at two of the key points of Christian doctrine, namely the forgiveness of sins and the permanence of Holy Orders. Despite the sect's decline, Donatism remained an essential facet of all later anticlericalism; the unworthiness of the clergy had been observed and criticized.[3]

The Pelagians were the first potential ideological anticlericals. Pelagius, the British monk who formulated the heresy, denied original sin and its effects, claiming that man was capable of salvation by his own work. The Church's mission was to help man achieve salvation, mainly through counsel and good example, but man had within himself the natural power to achieve salvation. Had Pelagius carried these ideas through to their logical conclusion, he would have found himself denying the need for clerical powers.[4] Perhaps the prevailing pessimism of the time was too much for this sort of conclusion. In any event, so vehement was Augustine against Pelagianism that in combatting Pelagius' free-will doctrines he leaned dangerously in the direction of predestination, thereby exacerbating the pessimistic mood of the age.

Changes in the structure of lay-clerical relations began in the fourth century. Following the end of official persecution and the beginnings of establishment, the clergy were recognized by law as a distinct juridical entity. Then, the demise of the Empire in the fifth century made possible almost complete clerical control of society. The Church was the only strong institution left in western Europe, absorbing all of the social and political functions of the defunct structures. In this way, the clergy came to take on many tasks outside their traditional sphere of authority. They were, in fact, the only managerial class in the Western world. Primitive barbarians and despondent Romans looked to them for much more than spiritual guidance, and the clergy soon managed society.

The clergy operated the primitive medieval schools and hospitals. They were the chief dispensers of public charity, performing all of the social services necessary to the age. In northern Europe, the land of small villages and rudimentary political organizations, the clergy monopolized all professional functions. While all were not competent professionals, they had at least the smattering of an education, and they were called upon to give advice on such matters as planting crops, healing the sick, and settling legal disputes. The priest became all things to all men.

It would not be true to say that the clergy did not desire

this power. In most cases they were probably pleased by the regard and attention that their positions gave them. It would be equally untrue to say that the laity opposed them; if any-thing, the laity wanted, indeed demanded, the extension of clerical power. There is no recorded opposition to the clergy's newly acquired functions. It might even be said that had the clergy not taken over the management of early medieval society, the secular fabric would not have withstood the destructive elements of the age.

There appeared to be no alienation of the clergy from society. Recruited from the laity they served, the clergy were an integral part of society. Many were married and many shared the familial problems of their parishioners.[5] They were generally unreformed, and although the gap between precept and practice was wide, it was either not noticed or else simply accepted by the laity.

The danger was that once having assumed all these tasks, the clergy would be loath to give them up, even when a competent lay professional class appeared. Attitudes were solidified, approaches were hardened, and the Church as a rural institution, using rural metaphors and images, would not find it easy to adjust to the demands of an urban society.

For over a thousand years—more than half its existence —the Church was a rural institution. However miserable life may have been at the time, later ages constructed the myth of a society perfectly ordered, perfectly disciplined, aboun-ding in clerical-lay harmony. The romantic clericals of the nineteenth century glorified this age and perpetuated the legend, apparently unaware that the relationships of the Mid-dle Ages had little reality to nineteenth-century society. Insti-tutions do not readily adjust to change, and for centuries after the rise of an urban society, the clergy lived in this romanticized medieval past; they became a broad target for anticlericalism.

*

By the eighth century the growth of the civil state began to pose a threat to the Church's institutional predominance.

The theory governing church-state relations was the Gelasian two-swords concept, positing two separate jurisdictions with theoretically no conflict between the two. Of course, there was conflict. It would be easy to label it an ideological clerical-anticlerical struggle; but it would be misleading to do so, for neither jurisdiction, Pope Gelasius notwithstanding, had its sphere of authority clearly defined. In later years, political and canonical theorists would define the bounds of authority. But in the empire of the Franks, the Spanish Goths, or any of the other newly formed states, this was not the case. Rather, the conflict was one between rivals, over ill-marked jurisdictional boundaries.[6]

One of the first instances of practical anticlericalism occurred in medieval France. Charles Martel confiscated some of the clergy's land and openly distributed it among his followers in order to obtain military support. Perhaps he was more honest—or less sophisticated—than the nineteenth-century anticlericals who justified their expropriation of clerical lands on the basis of utilitarianism, liberalism, and progress. Charles confiscated, but never denied the clergy's right to own land.[7]

Another aspect of this church-state relationship was the regulation of clerical discipline, a practice extending back to Roman times. From the Theodosian code to Charlemagne's capitularies, emperors, kings, and princes had promulgated legislation regulating and ordering clerical life. These laws not only restricted the clergy in certain activities; they also confirmed clerical authority in others. The Church hierarchy generally supported and enforced the legislation. Because it was established practice and because the hierarchy did not object, it would be difficult to call such practices anticlerical.

The clergy were the bureaucrats of the new states. In crown administrations they monopolized the jobs; they were the only literate and competent class available. Furthermore, their personal immunity (it was considered a sacrilege and grounds for excommunication to lay hands on or imprison them) made them doubly useful as bureaucrats. In the eighth and ninth centuries as western Europe succumbed to the new wave of barbarian invasions, the force of feudalism was felt, and the clergy as professionals were even more in demand. Whether in response to this breakdown of the state, or simply to extend their power against the time when the state should rise again, the clergy gathered more power and authority.

They came to have control over oaths and vows, both fundamental to the feudal contractual society. They strengthened their system of separate political jurisdiction, partly as a safeguard against the barbarism of feudal justice. They firmly established the right of mortmain in the possession of their lands.[8] The obverse of this extension and solidification of clerical power was that in many instances they came under the control of the laity, in the form of lay patronage. The laity controlled the papacy for over a century, while in every diocese throughout Western Christendom some layman had control over some cleric. Regarding lay-clerical relationships, all that can be said about the era of feudalism is that the confusion of jurisdictions, power, and authority makes it impossible to discern either clericalism or anticlericalism.

The confusion over jurisdictions, the growing immorality, and disciplinary problems among the clergy had important consequences. One was an authentic anticlerical movement within the ranks of the clergy, the Cluniac reform. Originally a monastic reform group, the Cluniacs began to criticize the bishops for abusing their authority by allowing their sees to come under the control of the lay lords. Although primarily antiepiscopal, the Cluniacs attacked the lower clergy when necessary. Set into motion, the Cluniac reform soon influenced the entire Church; eventually it came to control the papacy.

The reform papacy of the eleventh century began to implement canonical legislation against lay patronage and to attack clerical immorality. In their condemnation of episcopal and lower clerical abuses, the reform popes were certainly practical anticlericals. On the other hand, they did not hesitate to extend papal control over the laity. In a number of extreme statements, Gregory VII maintained the right to depose emperors and to release subjects from their oaths of fealty to unjust rulers, a position strengthened by later popes such as Innocent III and Boniface VIII.[9] This extreme measure was necessary for the creation of a strong lay anticlerical movement. Before this movement could be set in motion, the clergy had to take their stand; they had to provide something for the anticlericals to criticize.

One result of the papal reform movement was another kind of dissent, reactionary ideological anticlericalism, expressed by those clergy and laity who criticized the reforms, particularly those against simony and clerical concubinage. Claiming that the popes had no authority to rule on such matters, they were by definition ideological anticlericals, the first in a long line to oppose clerically sponsored reforms.[10]

By the tenth century, the pressure of the hostile environment was beginning to ease. The ninth-century barbarians began to be absorbed into the new kingdoms. In those areas of Europe that were safe from Moslem attack, a new breed of anticlericals appeared. Before the twelfth century these were mainly itinerant eccentrics who frequently gathered large followings. Whether the popular response is indicative of widespread popular anticlericalism or simply that these eccentrics offered a form of popular entertainment in that somewhat gloomy age is a matter of conjecture.[11] In any event, little is known of these men, and the enthusiasm they engendered died when they did.

The earliest recorded instance of this breed of anticlerical was Aldebert, a native of Gaul in the eighth century. Probably insane, he toured the countryside near Soissons preaching against papal authority and extolling the apostolic simplicity of the primitive church.[12]

Other itinerant eccentric anticlericals are recorded in the eighth and ninth centuries, but it was not until the latter part of the tenth century that another important one appeared. Leutard of Châlons also preached against papal authority, but he struck closer to home in attacking the corruption of the clergy and in denouncing their authority in the matter of tithe paying. He also found widespread sympathy and support.[13]

These anticlericals had in common more than just a protest against clerical authority and clerical corruption. While they too flourished during the papacy's most corrupt days, before the papal reforms began, a unique characteristic distinguished them from the Cluniac reformers, the reform papacy, and even the reactionary ideological anticlericals. They no longer differentiated among the clergy. The Cluniac anticlericals and the reform popes criticized only those bishops who had allowed themselves to come under lay control, or only those clergy who were practicing simony or concubinage. The reactionary anticlericals were opposed only to the reform popes and their supporters. But the eccentric anticlericals, Aldebert and Leutard, focused their anticlericalism on all of the clergy. Therein lay the secret of their popularity among people who liked nothing better than to be offered simple answers to complex problems. "Throw the rascals out," whether all or just a few be rascals, has been one of the most popular rallying cries in history. It became an important facet of the history of anticlericalism.

One last disturbing note, presaging the anticlerical revolution of the twelfth century: in 1057, the Patarini, a group of townspeople in Milan, rose up against the archbishop, claiming that episcopal administration was ruining the city and, indeed, questioning the right of the clergy to rule the city at all. They also criticized clerical immorality and disciplinary abuses.[14] This politicosocial ideological anticlerical movement was not only the first one not led by an eccentric; it was also the first successful one. The era of internal harmony within the Church had ended, and the anticlerical revolution had begun.

CHAPTER 3

The Anticlerical Revolution of the Twelfth Century

Antiquity teaches us that laymen are in a high degree hostile to the clergy.

Pope Boniface VIII

IN 1119, A YOUNG STUDENT NAMED ARNOLD RETURNED from Paris to the Lombardy town of Brescia, the area where the revolt of the Patarini had occurred a half century earlier. Arnold had studied under Abelard at Paris and had become obsessed with zeal for the ideal of clerical poverty. The Church, he maintained, was in danger of perdition if the clergy continued to own property and live in luxury. The townspeople of Brescia were receptive to Arnold's ideas, for they were attempting to wrest their political freedom from Bishop Manfred, the ruler of Brescia. Arnold soon found himself at the head of an anticlerical revolt against Manfred, who was ironically himself a reformer of clerical immorality.

In the course of the struggle, Arnold came to believe that the problems besetting Brescia could best be solved by eliminating both the wealth and the temporal power of the clergy. In fact, this solution could be applied to the problems of the entire Christian world.

The communal movement of Brescia was successful, and in due time the papacy took note of Arnold's ideas; in 1139

Pope Innocent II condemned both them and Arnold at the
Second Lateran Council. Arnold left Brescia and wandered
around France and Italy preaching clerical poverty, declaim-
ing against all clergy who owned property, for whom, he said,
there could be no salvation. In Bohemia, he founded a group
of followers who became known as the Band of Poverty.
Eventually he ended in Rome, where he led an insurrection
against Eugenius III and drove the Pope from the city.
Eugenius' successor, Hadrian IV, was able, with the aid of
Emperor Frederick Barbarossa, to recapture Rome. Arnold
was imprisoned and executed.[1]

Arnold of Brescia is probably the best known anticlerical
of the twelfth century, and his life was typical in many ways
of the ideological anticlericals of that age. He was concerned
with restoring the clergy to a state of pristine, evangelical
poverty. He was popular with the people, who used him for
ulterior political ends. He started out as an anticlerical and
ended up as a heretic. And finally, many of the clergy,
reformers themselves, were sympathetic to his ideals. One
of the tragedies of the twelfth century was that the reform
papacy and the anticlerical reformers could not move in step
with each other.[2]

*

The factors that made possible an eruption of anticlericalism in the twelfth and thirteenth centuries resulted from the
end of the medieval stalemate. The Moslems were being
pushed back in Spain and the Balkans. The Crusaders were
breaking the Moslem stranglehold on the Mediterranean Sea.
In the north, the barbarian Norsemen were being absorbed
into England, France, and the Empire. The pressure was
easing and Europe was becoming secure.

The new security effected great changes. Most of the
people of Europe underwent a psychological transformation
and lost their defensive mentality. A great many other things
gave way also.

Feudalism was one of the first to weaken. Essentially a
defense against a hostile world, there was no need for it when

the hostility diminished. With the beginnings of the commercial revolution, towns grew up along the trade routes. A numerically insignificant but powerfully dynamic class, the bourgeoisie, appeared. Agrarian and rural values gave way to those of a monied and capitalistic society.

In most cases, the new townspeople were antipathetic to the higher clergy. They were suspicious of the clergy's demands for money, and they balked at the clergy's contention that usury was sinful. Many of the new towns were founded under episcopal control, and the struggle for communal freedom was by its nature anticlerical, as the Patarini and Arnold had demonstrated. Not that the townspeople were antireligious: indeed, the great medieval historian, Henri Pirenne, has shown that the towns were dominated by the spirit of religion, but it was a more rigorous and demanding religious spirit.[3]

Another potential source of anticlericalism, class struggle, also appeared in the towns. Frequently the bourgeoisie identified the clergy with the aristocracy, and the class hatreds aimed at the aristocracy were levelled at the upper clergy as well. Moreover, the lower classes joined the bourgeoisie in opposing the upper clergy.

Along with the growth of the towns, there arose the power of the dynastic state. The new countries of England, France, and Spain began to emerge, and the Holy Roman Empire continued to grow. In practically all instances, the growth of the secular power exacerbated the traditional and endemic church-state conflict.

All these circumstances contributed to the general secularization of life in the later Middle Ages. A new spirit of heterodoxy replaced the orthodoxy of earlier times. This was most noticeable in the new universities, where the spirit of criticism of necessity questioned the authority of the clergy and created a new mood for the age. It was no accident that Arnold of Brescia had studied at the University of Paris. In addition, the breakup of Moslem power and the reestablishment of trade routes to the East brought about an influx of

mystical ideas. The appearance of neo-Manichean doctrines
in the twelfth century was largely the result of Eastern ideas
with their emphasis on individualism and that mystical
communion which dispensed with the need for a mediator
between God and man.

The secularization of later medieval life had an immense
effect upon the Church. It intensified the clergy's struggle to
shrug off lay control. From the beginning of the feudal
period, clerical reformers had tried to rid the Church of lay
patronage and lay control. Now the clergy began to close
ranks; all laity were suspect. The reform papacy rejected lay
patronage by centralizing and incorporating the Church.[4]

Centralization increased the papacy's power, so it could
deal effectively with local lay patrons, but in the process the
popes created an awesome clerical bureaucracy. The clergy
took on administrative duties that were difficult to reconcile
with the demands of apostolic simplicity. When anticlerical
reformers called for a return to evangelical poverty, the clergy could respond by pointing out that such a simplistic
approach would once again expose the entire Church to the
evils of lay control. But the anticlericals would not listen.

Centralization also helped to increase class differences
among the clergy themselves. The traditional hierarchical
structure already was, of course, evidence of class difference,
with the upper-class bishops and the lower-class curates, but
a position in the centralized bureaucracy opened the road to
clerical advancement for those curates who had the will and
ability to rise. For every priest who found room at the top,
a dozen stayed in the ranks of the clerical proletariat at the
bottom. Many church funds which had traditionally been collected and kept at the lower levels were now sent to Rome
or to the local bishop to support the clerical bureaucracy. On
the lowest level the curates were impoverished, providing a
sharp contrast to the wealthy and luxurious clerical bureaucrats. As a result, the clerical proletariat provided a fruitful
source of anticlericals.

The incorporation of the Church was another response to

lay control. A system of canon law with restrictions and limitations designed to prevent lay control was established. The reform papacy clearly marked off the boundaries of the Church and set up rigid guidelines for clerical life. Thus, enforcement of clerical celibacy served not only to reform clerical immorality; it also distinguished clerics from laymen in certain disputed areas of jurisdiction. Formulas, rules, and disciplines all became integral to clerical training. In these circumstances it was easy to forget or ignore the demands of apostolic simplicity. The gap between precept and practice was widened.

Other clerical reforms had their effect upon the structure of lay-clerical relations, tending to set the clergy apart from lay society. As is true of any group made distinct and separate, the clergy came to be objects of suspicion and distrust. It is ironic but undeniable that most attempts to reform the clergy simply created a more favorable climate for anti-clericalism.

The new definition of Church doctrine circumscribed the maneuverability of dissent within orthodoxy. Since dissent can be measured only in respect to established norms, when doctrine had been more fluid, norms had been generally ill-defined. Thus, those who would have been considered mild dissenters in early medieval society found themselves branded heretics in the twelfth century.

The result of all these changes was anticlericalism. The reform papacy itself stimulated criticism of the clergy. Gregory VII's early condemnations of immoral clergy smacked of Donatism, and although he denied Donatist implications, the anticlericals were given ammunition for their attacks. Enthusiasm for moral reform was generated, and it could not be channeled into the Church's new rigidities.[5] The Fourth Lateran Council in 1215 forbade the formation of new religious orders (only the Dominicans and the Franciscans escaped this proscription in the thirteenth century), thereby closing another traditional path of reform, which now found its outlet in heresy and anticlericalism.

As in many anticlerical movements, there was the sense of betrayal—so much stronger than if the papacy had never attempted reform at all. Added to this feeling were the apocalyptic tendencies of the later Middle Ages.[6] The belief in the impending resolution of all conflicts was a powerful stimulus to those dissenters who wanted to speak out: they could become the forerunners of the Millennium.

*

The main thrust of ideological anticlericalism in the twelfth century was economic. Toward the end of the twelfth century, increasing in intensity into the thirteenth, political anticlericalism became prominent.

The economic anticlericals wanted a reformed and apostolically simple clergy; they generally felt that clerical wealth was the root of all evils besetting the Church. While it would be easy to read into their actions connotations of a class struggle, it would be misleading to do so. Modern scholars have shown there is little validity to this contention.[7] Undoubtedly there were social overtones to some of their aims, but these were not restricted to a particular class, and the economic anticlericals could be found on all levels of society.

Some of these ideological economic anticlericals were moderates; others can be characterized as radicals. The difference is that the moderates submitted to ecclesiastical authority when the showdown came; they became acceptable and some were canonized. St. Francis of Assisi was one who preached clerical poverty but submitted to the authorities, avoiding condemnation as a heretic. St. Bernard of Clairvaux was another of the moderates. He preached freely against clerical wealth and did not hesitate to criticize Pope Eugenius II for his display of wealth and pomp and for his use of military force to achieve his aims. Even Pope Paschal II believed that the only solution to the Church's problems was for the clergy to renounce all wealth and titles to property.[8]

The radical economic anticlericals had more extreme views. Many held to the Donatist doctrines that the sacraments were invalid when dispensed by an immoral clergy. Most had a puritanically austere view of life, tending to equate holiness with poverty. They emphasized the value of individual judgment and therefore rejected the laws of the Church. But above all, they felt that the cause of the Church's and the clergy's troubles was wealth and worldliness. The brunt of their criticism focused on the clergy's wealth.

When they ran into trouble with ecclesiastical authorities, they became antiauthoritarian, questioning the clergy's right to condemn their views. At this stage they were ideological anticlericals. Then, as the tension increased, they became antisacerdotalists, holding the view that the clergy had no role different from the laity's. By this time they were branded as heretics, and the full force of the clergy was turned upon them. This is why it is difficult to regard these dissenters as simple anticlericals. They were anticlericals, but they were not static anticlericals, and they gradually became heretics.

It would be nearly impossible to list all these radical anticlericals; nor do we know how many there were. We know about those who created enough of a stir to be condemned by the ecclesiastical authorities. Many were prominent because they achieved a following among common folk—in itself an indication of rather widespread popular anticlericalism.

Arnold of Brescia exhibited most of these traits. He had considerably more political power than any of the others, but Arnold was used by the Brescians, whose political motives were not his primary ones. His views on the use of political power and especially his appeal to civil authorities to reform the clergy were more consistent with the political anticlericalism of the thirteenth century.

One of the most important radical anticlericals of the twelfth century was Tanchelm of Brabant. Most probably a renegade monk, he rapidly gained fame preaching against the clergy. The fact that many of his more eccentric ideas—for example, his claiming to be Christ's twin brother—did not antagonize the common folk attests to the popularity of his views. His most popular criticisms were against the hierarchy and against tithe paying. His following was composed mainly of peasants and artisans.[9]

Another apparent renegade monk was Henry of Le Mans. Less eccentric than Tanchelm, he also rejected the authority of the clergy, maintaining in Donatist fashion that they were unworthy and had therefore lost the right to priestly power. He attacked clerical pomp; the true Church, he said, was characterized by apostolic simplicity. He also had a large popular following.[10]

One of Henry's friends was Peter of Bruys, a priest, who likewise attacked the immorality of the clergy and objected to their wealth. He lapsed into heresy by extolling justification by faith alone, thereby rejecting the entire structure of clerical authority.[11]

There were other instances. Clement and Ebrard of Soissons, Albero of Mercke, and the reform dissidents of Cologne all preached against clerical wealth and tithe paying. All evoked strong popular response, an indication that they were not voices in the wilderness.[12]

The largest organized group of radical economic anticlericals were the Waldensians, who appeared toward the end of the twelfth century. They were founded by Peter Waldo, who began preaching against the excessive wealth of the clergy. When he was forbidden to preach by the hierarchy, Waldo rejected their authority, and his views became more radical. Christ did not found a priesthood, he said, and the clergy should not have any rights different from the laity's. He felt that all Christians had the right to preach, and was an early proponent of the priesthood of all believers. His views were very popular and Waldensians appeared all over Europe. Eventually condemned by Innocent III in 1212, the Waldensians were an example of the turn from piety to heresy taken by many of these radical anticlericals.[13]

Another group of radical economic anticlericals attempted to reform the clergy from within. These were the Spiritual

Franciscans and their offshoots, the Apostolic Brethren, the Fraticelli, and the Michaelists. Stimulated by the ideas of orthodox reformers such as Joachim of Fiore and Peter John Olivi, they preached that the clergy had become corrupt through the possession of property and prophesied that the clerical hierarchy was destined to disappear in the near future.[14]

By the beginning of the thirteenth century a host of minor sects, many of them tending toward neo-Manichean ideas, had appeared: the Turlupins, the Adamites, the Paulicians, and others. They were indicative of the change that had come over the anticlerical movement. The neo-Manicheans were not so much concerned with the clergy as they were with dogma. They repeated the stock criticism of clerical wealth and were Donatist, but their main belief was in the dualism of the original Manichean doctrines.

The new dissenters were clearly heretical, so the clergy found it easier to deal with them. The Inquisition was founded in 1184, and the dissenters soon lost their popular support. Apparently, as long as the dissenters confined their attacks to the clergy, the people were willing to support them; once they went beyond this and became heretical they lost their popularity. Furthermore, their appeal faded as the clergy gradually became reformed through the actions of the reform papacy.

If these were reasons for the decline of anticlericalism in the thirteenth century, the rising power of the civil state was another. Anticlericalism appealed to many who were anti-authoritarian by inclination. The state became the new target of attack, siphoning off some of the criticism against the clergy.

Ideological political anticlericals began to appear in increasing numbers by the beginning of the thirteenth century, chiefly as a result of the continuing church-state conflict. These anticlericals were usually advisors to princes, and they aimed their criticism at papal clericalism. The nature of this conflict was essentially no different from that of the eleventh century, but both sides, clericals and anticlericals alike, tended to state their positions in more extreme terms. Again, it should be remembered that neither side had its jurisdictions clearly defined and both were groping for positions of power.

There were numerous pamphleteers among the papal clericals. Giles of Rome, James of Viterbo, Álvarez Pelayo, and Augustinus Triumphus all echoed the idea that the secular authority must be subject to the spiritual.[15] Innocent III, Innocent IV, and Boniface VIII extended the claim of papal power to its limits. The struggle between Boniface VIII and Philip IV of France over the control of clerical property in that kingdom provoked a great deal of controversy. Boniface claimed that all matters concerning the clergy were subject to papal jurisdiction alone. Philip and his advisors upheld the crown's right of eminent domain and argued that the clergy's jurisdiction applied only to the supernatural, that the state could, by applying the principles of reason and natural law, achieve its aims without any supernatural aid.[16]

Boniface responded with three encyclicals: *Clericis Laicos* (1296), *Ausculta Fili* (1301), and *Unam Sanctam* (1302), the latter ending with this broadside: "Both the spiritual and the material sword are under the control of the Church, but the latter is used for the Church and the former by the Church. . . . We therefore declare, say, affirm, and announce that for every human creature to be submissive to the Roman Pontiff is absolutely necessary for salvation."[17]

These encyclicals were said by later popes and theologians to refer only to spiritual affairs; because they had to be revoked, explained away, or defined in such a manner as to pervert the original meaning, such extreme clerical statements were ultimately detrimental to clerical authority. Learned men began to question the authority of a pope who could say such things.

Most of the princes involved in these conflicts with the papacy were practical political anticlericals. They used their advisors and brain trusts to formulate ideological positions, but they themselves were interested only in the practical attainment of power. And certainly they were content not to stir up the radical economic anticlericals. One exception was the Holy Roman Emperor Frederick II. An excommunicate most of his adult life (for political reasons), he used the theme of economic anticlericalism to gain support for his campaign against the papal clergy. He issued a number of "reform manifestos" in which he referred to the clergy as "slaves to the world, drunk with self-indulgence" and appealed to the people: "Arise, arise ye monarchs of the earth! Arise ye princes! Arise ye peoples, open your eyes and see! Endure no longer the disgrace of such enmity! Root out this diseased multitude from the earth who bring confusion and contamination! Reform Holy Church disfigured by such crimes!"[18] These manifestos were quite popular in the Germanies. Frederick, however, persecuted the radical economic anticlericals only when it suited him. He was a politician first and an anticlerical second. And when he died, he was buried in a cowl as a member of the Cistercian Third Order.

*

By the end of the thirteenth century, ideological anticlericalism was beginning to die out. The radical economic anticlericals had drifted into heresy, and although political anticlericals still fulminated against clerical interference in the affairs of state, they had won the battle in practice if not in theory. The papacy was in decline and the clergy were fighting among themselves, presaging the Great Schism. These circumstances created the atmosphere for a new breed of anticlericals in the fourteenth century, the precursors of the Protestant Reformation.

CHAPTER 4

The Success of the Secular Revolution in the North

*In the primitive church the chalices were of wood,
the prelates of gold. In these days the
Church has chalices of gold and
prelates of wood.*

Girolamo Savonarola

AT THE BEGINNING OF THE FOURTEENTH CENTURY THE CLER-
gy appeared to stand at the pinnacle of prestige and power.
Boniface VIII had clearly established the theoretical
supremacy of the papacy. Everywhere princes and emperors
paid obeisance to popes. Kingdoms were held in vasselage
to them. The mendicant orders thrived, fulfilling the needs
of the townspeople to whom they ministered. Clergy were
being educated in the new universities. The centralization of
the clerical bureaucracy had reached fiscal successes beyond
the hopes of any state in past history. The radical economic
anticlericals had largely disappeared from the scene, although
small numbers of Waldensians still wandered about preaching
the ideals of apostolic poverty. The Inquisition had proved
a most effective tool for the suppression of dissent.
Orthodoxy prevailed.

Or so it appeared on the surface. A penetrating observer
could see that the calm was superficial. The very extremity
of papal statements, for example, indicated that all was not

well; a secure ruler does not have to hurl challenges at his enemies. By the middle of the century, disturbing events began to prove how deceptively tranquil the status quo was. The most significant of these events was the Plague.

The Black Death first struck in 1347. Over a third of Europe's population perished, including more than a third of the clergy. The surviving clergy became greatly impoverished. Relying upon smaller tithes and declining rents, they became prey to economic discontent. The small clerical proletariat became larger and more eager to rebel against its bishops. In addition, the clergy's moral and intellectual standards were lowered. So great had been the depletion of clerical ranks that mass ordinations frequently took place, with little or no training for the new priests.[1]

Thus the Church of Abuses came into being. To the growing gap between precept and practice that had been created by the centralization and incorporation of the Church's structure in the eleventh century were now added all the abuses of clergy no longer interested in the care of souls but rather in enhancing their own material position in society.

It would be repetitious to go into the reasons for all the abuses or to discuss them in detail. Suffice to say that from popes down to the lowest curates abuses prevailed. Most frequently mentioned by observers of the time were simony (the traffic in clerical offices), pluralism (the holding of more than one clerical office), and concubinage. Any one of these was sufficient to create dogmatic anticlericalism. Where they touched the laity's pocketbook they created economic anticlericalism as well. Clerical economic and judicial privileges added to the criticism. The upper clergy did not pay taxes on their extensive properties. The clergy were tried in their own courts for all offenses, civil and ecclesiastical, and generally they were given light sentences, usually spiritual penances. Numerous critics complained, preached, and wrote about these abuses; any historical study of the origins of the Protestant Reformation is replete with such examples.[2]

What is particularly relevant is the atmosphere surrounding

these abuses. First, the clergy had never solved the problems which the twelfth-century economic anticlericals had pointed to; indeed they were insoluble. The clergy, forced to live in this world and to maintain an institutional strength to deal with the threat of lay control, would always be concerned with the strength, independence, and wealth of the Church. This posture was increasingly open to criticism in the fourteenth and fifteenth centuries, with clerical abuses so prevalent, the clergy openly seeking wealth and power and ignoring demands for spiritual reform.

Second, the age in which these abuses were so prevalent was an age of particularly rapid change. Growing secularism, the new learning, technological innovations, population shifts, and the new economics made the clergy seem all the less useful.

Third, the clergy were preoccupied with internecine struggles. Practical anticlericalism was rife among them; indeed, most of the anticlerical critics were clerics. The lower clergy envied the hierarchy's wealth, the diocesan clergy had no use for the religious orders, and even among the members of the orders there was endless bickering. Clergy arguing among themselves was a sorry spectacle to the laity, almost certain proof that the clergy had forgotten to put first things first and were fighting with each other rather than attending to their duties.

The most outstanding example of this internecine warfare occurred at the very top. From 1378 to 1417 there were two popes, each vying for and claiming supreme power, each excommunicating the other's followers. The Great Schism brought the whole question of papal and clerical authority out into the open.[3]

Accompanying the decline of the clergy, and in part the reason for it, was the secular revolution. This profound movement had its roots in the growth of urbanization. It struck particularly at the dynamic city-states of northern Italy and at the burgeoning cities of France and the Germanies. It was an upheaval in thought that fundamentally denied religious considerations, or at least relegated them to second place. The secular revolution, whatever its causes, came to be a focal point of many other movements, the most important of which, in the thirteenth century, was humanism.[4]

Neither secularism nor humanism burst upon the Christian world unannounced: both had been in the making for centuries. What gave them a vehicle in the later Middle Ages was the growth of the universities and technological innovations, primarily the invention of the printing press in the fifteenth century, which provided for the widespread dissemination of ideas.

However much humanism might have been Christian in inspiration, its effect was to spread the secular revolution. Humanism emphasized a homocentrically oriented world rather than the theocentric world of traditional Christianity. It elevated human ability and stressed naturalism and individualism. If man's ability was elevated there was less need for a clergy to act as intercessor between God and man. The emphasis upon naturalism and the renewed interest in studying the material world made the clergy less relevant, for they had no special qualifications enabling them to interpret natural phenomena. Individualism stressed the individual's accountability for his own actions, as opposed to the idea of corporate unity in the Middle Ages.

Humanism and secularism led to a critical awareness and a mood of questioning all things. A better educated laity appeared. With the changes wrought by the printing revolution, it soon became apparent that the laity were in many respects as knowledgeable about things as were the clergy; even in the clergy's own field, theology, there were lay persons who knew more than the clergy.

Although the humanists were a minute proportion of the population, their influence was felt strongly among the thinking classes, particularly in the universities. Actually, the masses of laity were influenced more by an antihumanistic movement toward mysticism and other-worldliness known as the *devotio moderna*.[5] This "new theology" stressed interior and noninstitutional Christianity and was in its own way a contributing factor to the rise of anticlericalism.

*

The anticlerical response to the Church of Abuses came on three different yet connected levels. There was an intellectual response, consisting largely of writings and preachments. There was a popular response, primarily in mass movements and crowd reactions. And there was a political and practical response dictated by the actions of governments, generally in the form of limitations upon the clergy's power or in some sort of control upon their activities.

As in the twelfth century, many of the anticlericals became heretics (according to the clergy's definition), and a few founded their own churches. But beyond this no clear pattern emerges. Not all the Protestant reformers were ideological anticlericals, although many were motivated by anticlericalism in their first criticisms of the Church. There were many anticlericals who did not become Protestants. Some arrived at their anticlericalism after they left the Church or joined one of the Protestant sects.

Three basic types of ideological anticlericals appeared: educational-cultural anticlericals (the humanists); political anticlericals (the conciliarists); and dogmatic and economic anticlericals (chiefly, the Protestant reformers).

Humanists tended toward anticlericalism, almost by definition. With their regard for classical lore and the treasures of antiquity, they could not look upon the Middle Ages with equanimity. They tended to see the medieval period as dominated by clericalism, to which they attributed most of the defects of medieval life. Many of the humanists were intensely religious, but they also considered the clergy and the institutional Church hindrances to the achievement of salvation. The humanists were primarily interested in education and the advancement of human knowledge; they looked upon the typical cleric as a fomenter of superstition. Most had plans for the betterment of the clergy, but these generally centered around the improvement of clerical education. Apparently they had no notion of social progress; their main concern was the intellectual progress of mankind.

Among the Christian humanists, it is possible to go as far back as Dante to find anticlericalism, but Dante was more in the tradition of the twelfth-century economic anticlericals than anything else.[6] Most of the earlier figures of the Italian Renaissance held similar views. It is north of the Alps that one finds the chief anticlerical Christian humanists.

Erasmus of Rotterdam stands out as the most imposing and the most anticlerical. In his numerous writings, particularly *In Praise of Folly* he satirized the ignorance of the clergy; monks came in for special criticism. The clergy's formalism, he felt, had helped make a sham of Christianity. Erasmus wanted a simpler form of Christianity, and while he would not have done away with the clergy, he saw no need for a hierarachy and absolutely opposed the clergy's temporal power.[7]

German humanists had similar ideas. John Wimphlening, Sebastian Brant, John Reuchlin, and Ulrich von Hutten were all staunch critics of the clergy and clericalism. In England, John Colet denounced corrupt clerics and clerical celibacy, meanwhile practicing pluralism himself. Thomas More did not stand out as an anticlerical.[8]

South of the Alps the humanists tended to be pagan rather than Christian and introduced the idea of naturalism. Whereas the northern humanists wanted a less worldly, purer, and more devout clergy, the pagan humanists did not care what the clergy were as long as they acted in accord with human nature. They called the clergy hypocrites, feeling that it was unnatural for them to live in celibacy and poverty. This approach marked a most significant shift in the practice of anticlericalism and was the first harbinger of the modern view that the clergy should be more, not less, worldly.

Lorenzo Valla stands out as an exemplar of the pagan humanistic anticlerical. He maintained, in opposition to the clergy's long held contention, that the clerical state was not more perfect than the lay state. There was greater merit, he said, in acting spontaneously and naturally; the vows of poverty and celibacy simply did not allow man to function according to his human nature. Poggio Bracciolini was another humanist anticlerical. His *Dialogue Against Hypocrites* was written with the clergy as his target. In France, François Rabelais wrote *Gargantua and Pantagruel,* a diatribe against clerical abuses, but apparently he was not attacking the clergy with any reformism in mind; rather he was concerned with the absurdity and the comedy of it all.[9]

*

The conciliarists were another group of anticlericals, mainly political in their outlook. Impelled by the Great Schism to seek a solution to the Church's problems, they contended that if the hierarchy was unable to end the division, it was up to the lower clergy and the laity to do so. Thus, they focused on the problem of authority, specifically papal authority, and their solution was found in a rejection or at least a great modification of papal claims. Some hoped that a strong state would have sufficient power to challenge the papacy; others relied on a regenerated clergy; still others saw a lay-controlled (but not lay-administered) Church as the only way out of the morass.

What they had in common as anticlericals was a feeling that the clergy had brought the Church to ruination and furthermore that the clergy were interfering too much in civil affairs. The conciliarists did not feel that the clergy were causing trouble for the state as much as they were ignoring the affairs of the Church. Among the most important of these anticlericals were Pierre DuBois, Giovanni di Janduno, Conrad of Gelenhausen, Henry of Langenstein, Pierre d'Ailly, Jean Gerson, William of Occam, and the most outstanding of all, Marsiglio of Padua.

In addition to his conciliarist views, Marsiglio shared many of the beliefs of the radical economic anticlericals. He held that the clergy had no right to possess material goods; he did not, however, deny their spiritual powers. Presaging the modern anticlericals, Marsiglio said that the clergy should be relegated to dispensing the sacraments and providing the forms of worship.[10]

The third major strain of ideological anticlericalism in this period was a revival of the radical economic anticlericalism of the twelfth century augmented by a strong dogmatic anticlericalism. Most of these anticlericals prepared the way for Protestantism. They did not, however, necessarily follow the progression from anticlericalism to heresy, and many had heretical ideas that were not formed by any anticlerical experiences.

The Waldensians had not died out completely by the fifteenth century. A few continued to preach apostolic poverty and the priesthood of all believers. Eclipsing the Waldensians in importance, however, were two important anticlerical movements of the fifteenth century, the Lollards and the Hussites. The Lollards, followers of John Wycliffe, were critical of all the clergy, holding that there was no scriptural proof for priestly authority. Wycliffe was opposed to clerical possession of material goods. It does appear, however, that Wycliffe used anticlericalism to gain popularity, for it was not an integral part of his religious views. John Hus, the Bohemian reformer, had ideas similar to Wycliffe's, but also used anticlericalism to appeal to Czech nationalism against the German higher clergy in Bohemia—probably the first instance of anticlericalism used in the service of nationalism.[11]

South of the Alps, the Florentine reformer Girolamo Savonarola stands out as an anticlerical in the tradition of the Spiritual Franciscans. Puritanically holy, Savonarola reformed the Florentine clergy and disputed with Pope Alexander VI. Although he was in favor of retaining a reformed and purified clergy, whatever theoretical notions he had about the clergy were lost in the political intrigues of Florence, and it is difficult to untangle the threads of his anticlericalism.[12]

In the sixteenth century, the Protestant reformers dominated the scene. It is a truism to say that the Reformation was anticlerical in many of its aspects, and it could probably be said that it was anticlerical at root. However, to avoid simplistic notions, some distinction should be made between theory and practice. In theory, most of the Reformers were antisacerdotalists, if their ideas were carried through to logical extremes. Martin Luther's priesthood of all believers and his emphasis upon faith implies there is no need for a clergy; man stands naked before God with no mediators, no intercessors, and hence no clergy. In practice, Luther needed a clergy to preach the word. He advocated clerical marriage and the freedom of monastic leave, along with the abolition of the power of the papacy and the hierarchy. Although he held to the priesthood of all believers, he perceived that not all men were able or willing to do clerical tasks, hence there was need for a full-time ministry (but under the control of the civil power).

Luther arrived at many of his views from his experience with clericalism. His visits to Rome and his observations of the German clergy certainly played a large part in the formation of his ideas.[13] John Calvin, on the other hand, apparently experienced little personal anticlericalism. The Genevan reformer stressed the need for a strong institutional church, and his clergy were as authoritarian and puritanical as any Catholic clergy anywhere. But again, there was the difference between practice and theory. Calvin's theories of predestination would, like Luther's emphasis on faith, obviate the need for a clergy.

Lutheranism and Calvinism appear to have been popular anticlerical movements. Both attracted many who did not follow the reformers' admonitions. Particularly in Germany the clerical proletariat supported Lutheranism, and there was much destruction of ecclesiastical property, frequently as a "levelling" effect. These popular movements were often iconoclastic and in many cases violent, presaging modern social anticlericalism. There were overtones of class struggle in the religious wars and in the destruction of churches and other clerical properties.

The other significant group of anticlericals among the Protestant Reformers were the Anabaptists and their various offshoots. Thomas Müntzer, Melchior Hoffman, and Menno Simons can be considered the logical heirs of Luther and Calvin; that is, they carried out the ideas of Luther and Calvin to logical extremes. They wanted no clergy and firmly upheld the priesthood of all believers.[14]

Apparently, anticlericalism was rather rare within the Protestant churches. The same forces that prevented anticlericalism from developing within the early medieval Church operated on Protestantism as well. The Protestants were a minority practically everywhere, and where they were not (in England, for example), they feared the Catholic powers of Spain and France. Thus, there was external pressure to maintain internal cohesion and prevent dissension. In addition, the structure of the Protestant churches and the theology of Protestantism itself were less rigid. Dissidents could simply break away to form another sect.

*

Anticlericalism also existed on a very practical level, in the form of state action against the clergy. One reason for the success of the Reformation in Germany and for the great amount of anticlericalism in Italy was the fact that the state lacked effective control over the clergy in these two regions.[15] Where the state had control, there was less popular and ideological anticlericalism. Thus the Pragmatic Sanction of Bourges (1438) and the 1516 Concordat with the papacy gave the French crown control over the French clergy and resulted in generally successful attempts to reform them. In Spain, the reforms of Cardinal Ximénes de Cisneros and the control which Ferdinand and Isabella came to have over the Church there provided for a reformation of the clergy before Protestantism could take hold. Despite their salutary effects upon the Catholic clergy, these state actions must be seen as anticlerical in nature, the first steps of a practical cismontane (antipapal) anticlericalism that reached its zenith in the eighteenth century.

In England, the Reformation was supported by the crown. Since the anticlerical reforms there consisted of bringing the clergy over to support the crown's actions, which (unlike France and Spain) involved a change in doctrine, the crown's actions were more extreme. In addition, in England there was the struggle between the crown, the nobles, and the middle classes, all interested in appropriating the property of the clergy for themselves. In France and Spain the nobility and the middle classes were not as powerful, and those governments could afford to allow the clergy continued control of their lands in return for political support.

In England there was precedent for crown control over the clergy in the thirteenth-century Statutes of Provisors and Praemunire. In the 1530s, as part of the break with Rome, the crown forced through a number of parliamentary acts which restricted clerical property rights, subordinated clerical courts to civil review, and required the higher clergy to take an oath to the Act of Supremacy, establishing the king as the head of the Church of England.

The most significant act of practical anticlericalism in England was the suppression of the monasteries and the confiscation of their properties. Monastic lands, estimated at more than one-third of the landed wealth of England, were confiscated in a series of parliamentary acts which set a pattern for later confiscations in other countries. Starting in 1536, all monastic houses with less than Ł200 income were dissolved. Many of the monks' tenants protested the crown's actions in the Pilgrimage of Grace, an uprising in the north. In 1539-40 the remainder of the monastic lands were confiscated. In most cases the lands were sold, and a new landed gentry was created. The social and economic effects of the dissolution of the monasteries were far-reaching, and they most definitely ended any hopes of a Catholic restoration. Anticlericalism in England, including a certain amount of iconoclasm in the burning of statues and shrines, appears to have been a movement supported by both crown and people.[16]

*

The Protestant Reformation did more than any other event to create anticlericalism. It was an anticlerical movement itself in many ways, but for the history of anticlericalism, its most important effect was to stimulate a reform of the Catholic Church. This reform, culminating in the Council of Trent, the establishment of the Jesuits, and the consolidation of the papal monarchy, hardened Catholic reaction to such an extent that most of the anticlericalism of the modern age can be seen primarily as a revolt against the new Catholic Church created by the Reformation.

CHAPTER 5

The Clerical Reaction

To a philosophic eye the vices of the clergy are far less dangerous than their virtues.

Edward Gibbon

THE COUNTER-REFORMATION WAS A COMPLEX EVENT, evoking on the one hand a long tradition of reform within Christian history and, on the other, a specific response to the Protestant Reformation. It is of singular importance to the history of anticlericalism because it more directly shaped the clerical temperament than did any other event; and the clerical temperament became the most powerful stimulus of modern anticlericalism.[1]

Where before the clergy had in many cases tried to live with the world and adjust to it—indeed, their compromises had been one of the Protestant Reformers' chief criticism— these efforts were now put aside. Instead, there was now a militancy against the secular world and the urge to dominate it. It was not only a siege mentality that the clergy cultivated, but a militant mentality as well. Their attitude toward secular values was ambivalent. They rated them as of only secondary importance against the overwhelming value of spiritual things; but secular values were also justified, rationalized, and used when they suited the needs of spiritual aims. The threats of torture and corporal punishment were used against heretics, but not by the clergy themselves; instead, they used

47

the convenient fiction of relinquishing to the "secular arm" — the state.

This militant mentality fed itself on a fear psychosis. Everyone not with the clergy was against them. Everything not approved by the clergy was also condemned by God. Any means were justified against the enemy. Because anticlericals were the enemy, they were to be treated as common criminals and heretics with no rights at all. God's Church was in this world but not of it; thus God's clergy did not have to abide by the rules of this world. When danger threatened the spiritual, its guardians were justified in using any means to combat the danger. The principle was: better that all mankind should suffer than one person commit sin; practice followed accordingly.

The enemy lurked everywhere. It was easy to spot the intellectual enemy: his thoughts were heterodox. Among common folk, any deviation from the regularized outward expression of faith was indicative of heresy. The form of worship became all-important; and the conviction was that form would provide substance.

Form became dominant. It was standardized: one dogma, one method of participation, one mentality, one devotional norm. God and God's clergy were supreme; nothing else counted. Salvation could be achieved by following the clergy's rules. Sins were carefully catalogued to fit the rules. Form was institutionalized, and one deviated from the norms only at the risk of eternal perdition.

The rules were made by the clergy at the top of the structure. An absolutist institution long in the making emerged full-blown from the Council of Trent. The pope spoke, the clergy executed, and the laity obeyed. One God, one Church, one mind.

While this is an extreme view—and one that was largely propagated by anticlerical mythmakers—still, it had some substance in reality. Many of the laity liked this arrangement, even if it was more a fond hope rather than the real state of things. It was simple, there was order, and above all there was no difficulty in knowing what to do. The secular revolution posed complex problems, and it was much easier to fight against it than to discern what could be compromised and sort out the values in some secular achievements. It was much simpler to accept the fatalistic argument that evil was at work in the world and that only prayer could triumph over it than to recognize that some evils could be overcome by cultivating secular values. It is, of course, eloquent testimony to the institutional vitality of the Church that the clergy were able to hold on as long as they did in this battle against the secular world. It was not really until the end of the nineteenth century that the clergy began to make the compromises necessary to live in the secular world and not until the twentieth century that the change began to be noticed. With the compromises came the triumph of the secular revolution and with the realization of compromise came the end of the age of anticlericalism.

Three features of the Counter-Reformation helped form the clerical temperament: the decrees of the Council of Trent, which institutionalized the new clericalism, the foundation of the Jesuits as exemplars of the new militant clergy, and the consolidation of the papal monarchy's power, an absolutism that made obedience a virtue.

The Tridentine decrees that most affected the anticlerical struggle were those that standardized the clergy. Seminaries were established in each diocese so that the clergy could be properly trained, and clerical training became uniform. All of the advantages and defects of a centralized school system were created: imperviousness to change (because change had to be instituted from the top), sterile curricula, and learning by rote in order to satisfy the demands of a central controlling agency. While these decrees established a minimum education for all of the clergy and were a necessary ingredient of reform, they had the effect of standardizing the clergy to a degree never before accomplished.[2]

The clergy were more closely supervised than before. Bishops were named by the pope, and enforced episcopal residence was the rule rather than the exception. Bishops were charged with the visitation of all parishes and convents within their jurisdiction, with special attention to be paid to the observance of discipline and the reform of morals. Clerical promotions and appointments were made by the bishops, and the regular clergy were not allowed to use their faculties within a particular diocese without the authorization of the bishop. The bishop was charged with meting out strict punishment for all clerical transgressions.

Within this atmosphere of control, investigation, and supervision, freedom did not flourish. Clerics were more likely to obey rules rather than attempt to change them, no matter how senseless they might seem. Promotion and advancement came to depend upon obedience, outward devotion, and loyalty to the institution.

The most immediate effect of the Tridentine decrees was the intended one, although the long-range results were far different from what the clergy intended. The clerical reformers had wanted the clergy to lead purer and holier lives, untouched by scandal; in effect, to make the clergy superior to the laity. The result was that the clergy became more distinct from the laity. The clergy were clearly marked off, a class responsible only to themselves. With distinction came uniformity and conformity. If one priest said or did something, all priests were held responsible. They dressed the same way, they were trained the same way, and they thought the same way. It became easy to blame the entire group for the actions of one man, just as it was easy to blame the man for the actions of the group. A conspiracy theory was formulated, and the clergy came to be seen by anticlericals as a tightly knit group bent upon the seizure of power and the domination of all facets of life.

Trent also confirmed the triumph of legalism, a trend that had been initiated with the first attempts to incorporate and centralize the Church in the eleventh century. Canon law was formulated, and great texts were written on minute and obscure points of theology and law. To intelligent and educated laymen, these endless disputes over obscure theological and legal points appeared foolish. Controversies over free will or transubstantiation, for example, were important but took up much time and energy that could have been put to better use.

Legalism was partly a reaction to the Protestant Reformation. The Lutheran idea that everyman is his own priest provoked the formation of a priestly caste with rigid rules and requirements. While Protestantism favored laymen as the means of reforming church and society, Trent looked upon the clergy as spearheads of reform.[3] Calvinism made concrete the puritanical attitude toward life, and the Catholic clergy had to become holier than before. After Trent, holiness became equated with piety, and piety came to replace all other virtues.

Not all clergy adjusted to the new disciplined life. In fact, for over a century after Trent, the diocesan clergy reformed hardly at all, for it took that long to put the Tridentine decrees into effect. During this period, it was the men of the new religious orders who set examples of militancy, discipline, and piety. In this regard the Jesuits stood out as the spearheads of the Tridentine reforms.

The Jesuits were the most militant of the clergy. They scored remarkable successes, not only in Europe, but throughout the world. The reconversion of eastern Europe and missionary activities in Asia and America were evidence of their skill, which was due partly to their adaptation of modern techniques (in this sense they were the least clerical of the post-Tridentines), partly to their recruitment policies of seeking and admitting only the most able to their group, and partly to their fame itself.[4] Clericals and anticlericals alike came to believe that the Jesuits could do everything.

If anticlericals believed that the Jesuits could do everything, they also held them responsible for everything. The term "Jesuit" became one of opprobrium, and the Jesuit became the most stereotyped of all the clergy. He was portrayed as a man without a will of his own, a robot performing the commands and whims of an all-seeing papacy. Considered almost diabolically superhuman, the Jesuit was seen everywhere, behind every dire event.[5]

Not only anticlericals believed in the myth of Jesuit omnipotence: the laity believed it also. Jesuits were eagerly sought out as advisors, confidantes, and confessors. Probably the Jesuits themselves came to believe in the myth. There is little doubt that Jesuit casuistry came to be a powerful force in the making of the clerical temperament. The rationalization and justification of the most odious secular means to achieve clerical or spiritual ends was considered to be a Jesuit specialty. Above all, to a mind prepared to accept conspiracy theories, the Society of Jesus was a paradigm.

Furthermore, the Jesuits contributed to the division within the clergy.[6] Diocesan clergy disliked them almost as much as the anticlericals did. The Jesuits drew away their parishioners and exercised political influence far beyond their numbers. The Jesuits had everything; the diocesan clergy had nothing. This division (which was actually a split between a reformed and an unreformed clergy) was perpetuated to modern times.

*

Another feature of the Counter-Reformation was the consolidation and extension of the papal monarchy. The Church, like the secular governments of the time, became an absolute monarchy with all of the trappings. The pope was elected by the College of Cardinals—a self-perpetuating institution—and everything was tightly controlled by the papacy. Bulls, encyclicals, decrees, all sorts of orders were issued from above, with greater authority and tradition than any of the secular absolutists had. All decisions had to be submitted to Rome. Bishops were made and unmade by Rome. Rome spoke and the Catholic world obeyed. While practice frequently lagged behind this ideal, a vigorous group of popes toward the end of the sixteenth century carried the consolidation far.

The prime example of papal clericalism in the post-

Tridentine era was the establishment of the Index of Forbidden Books. This was a most explicit form of clerical censorship. Indeed, only the Inquisition generated more anticlerical criticism.

The Index was an institutional solution to a problem created by the fear that reading heterodox books would endanger one's faith. The practice of censorship had been used by some governments at all times in history; the Index was not unique in this respect. But few governments had published their lists of censored works. The Index was a standing affront to anticlericals. Furthermore, the clergy's promotion of pious tracts of generally inferior quality did little to undo the damage caused by the Index.

*

The first example of the new clericalism in practice was the response to the seventeenth-century scientific revolution. The new scientists based their theories on experimentation and they rejected authority. Inevitably this meant a rejection of clerical authority as well, for during the later Middle Ages the official Church became wedded to the ideas of Aristotle. Like the confusion over jurisdictions which had arisen out of the age of feudalism, there was confusion over the Church's interpretation of scientific knowledge. The scientific issues were not as clearly drawn as later generations tended to make them. The Galileo and Bruno cases were the classic examples cited by later anticlericals of clericalism at its worst, which indeed they were; but it should be remembered that these scientists often appealed to scripture, and the clergy rightly felt that the scientists were trespassing on the clergy's domain.

Galileo was a controversialist by nature; but it is most odd that of all persons who had reason to be anticlerical, apparently he was not. He did not reject the clergy's authority or their right to judge matters of science: he simply wanted them to do so on the basis of facts. He condemned the theologians for invading the field of natural science without proper training and for refusing to look at the facts, but he never condemned the clergy as a class; in fact most of his supporters were clerics.[7]

Giordano Bruno, another scientist, was burned at the stake as a heretic. He had little use for the clergy. In his *Expulsion of the Triumphant Beast* (1584), he contended that the clergy had no right to interfere with the pursuit of knowledge and truth. They should, he maintained, teach an ideal of conduct and morality, but this had nothing to do with truth, for the determination of truth was the task of the scientist.[8] Both the Galileo and Bruno affairs represented a reversal for the clergy. In the pre-Reformation Church, scientific investigation had always been encouraged by the clergy. The scientific revolution provided the first anticlerical martyrs at the hands of a clergy made fundamentalist and fearful by the Reformation.

If some scientific revolutionaries were punished for their ideas, another group of anticlericals managed to stay clear of clerical vengeance, although their writings were placed on the Index. Jean Bodin and Hugo Grotius, known as members of the *Politiques,* toward the end of the sixteenth-century religious wars wrote that no religious idea was worth killing and dying for. They upheld the theory that all authority resides in the state, and the state governs by natural right. The clergy, they said, had no rights other than those delegated by the state; ideally the clergy's function was one of direction and persuasion.[9]

*

In retrospect, it appears that the rise of anticlericalism was more greatly stimulated by the Counter-Reformation than by any other single event in history.

A. G. Dickens points out in his penetrating *The Counter Reformation:* "Wise after the event, we may now perceive that in the long run [Trent's] clericalism was bound to produce a new wave of anticlericalism. Behind Trent there looms the menacing figure of Voltaire, inflated to superhuman proportions by a process of reaction."[10]

One factor stands out: the clergy's attempt to rationalize

their attitudes and behavior as not only an ideal way of life for the clergy, but also a model for the laity to follow as well. That the clergy should be celibate, for example, was one thing; that celibacy should be used as a model way of life for the married laity as well was foolish. And to hold that virginity should occupy a higher place in the scheme of spiritual values than the chaste married state was insulting to laymen.

The anticlericals began to attack the new militant cleric. To be sure, the bumbling worldly cleric who had been the object of attack in medieval times came in for his share of criticism, but it was the new, dynamic, other-worldly priest who now received the major criticism. The new cleric was more dangerous, more skilled, and more clerical than his medieval predecessor. The anticlericals attacked the new cleric, and the clergy found themselves in a dilemma, for while it was relatively easy for the clergy to reform themselves from worldly ways, it was much more difficult to become more worldly and more secularized without doing violence to the clergy's ideals. It was an almost hopeless bind. The anticlericals wanted a more secularized clergy, yet the clergy could offer them only a more spiritualized one. The roots of much of the modern anticlerical struggle can be seen in this tension.

CHAPTER 6

The Enlightenment: Assault on Clericalism

Écrasez l'infâme.

Voltaire

THE INTELLECTUAL REVOLUTION OF THE SEVENTEENTH AND eighteenth centuries broke sharply with the anticlerical tradition of the past. It is true that the philosophes (the enlightened thinkers) made many of the same criticism which had been made ever since the anticlerical revolution of the twelfth century: the clergy were criticized for their obscurantism, their superstition, their greed, and their inability to practice what they preached. The philosophes varied this traditional criticism slightly by offering rational proof, for they were admirers of the scientific revolution. Even so, some new criticisms were made. These aimed at the clergy's other-worldliness, and in these attacks the difference from traditional anticlericalism became noticeable.

The new approach stemmed from the fact that the philosophes were not primarily anticlerical but rather anti-Christian. Although their opposition to revealed religion found expression in anticlericalism, their main aim was the destruction of Christianity. The anticlerical tradition of the past had been chiefly constructive: the twelfth century and Renaissance anticlericals had used their anticlericalism to emphasize the basic truths of Christianity, in an effort to stimulate the clergy and laity to a new awareness of the meaning of Christianity. The philosophes, on the other hand, used anticlericalism to destroy Christianity. Whereas traditional anticlericals had claimed that the clergy and clericalism had ruined Christianity, the philosophes maintained that Christianity had ruined civilization. Their attack was more vehement, more biting, and more pointed: they could criticize without regard to the consequence, for what they wanted was to so weaken Christianity that it would disappear and be replaced by an enlightened deism or atheism.[1]

The philosophes did not attack Christianity itself at first except in an oblique fashion. Only toward the end of the eighteenth century did they become openly critical of revealed religion. As a result, the clergy became their first targets. The state did not frown on these attacks. Indeed, statesmen of various countries used the philosophes' attacks to rationalize their own practical anticlericalism. The clergy were always open to criticism, especially in their support of the church-state relationship, their control of education, and their use of censorship. They were the most visible supporters of the Old Regime and the easiest to attack. The Calas affair, an execution for heresy in France, and the effectiveness of the Inquisition in other countries pointed out the peril, but generally there was little that the clergy could do against the witty, anonymous anticlerical pamphlet or against the reputation and prestige of such a luminary as Voltaire.

The philosophes knew the clergy. Most had been educated by Jesuits or in church schools; they had first-hand experience. They had absorbed all of the education clericalism could offer, and by applying the principles of rationalism to what they had learned, they could make their criticism particularly pointed. It is one of the understandable ironies of the history of anticlericalism that the most vehement anticlericals have been those who were educated in clerical schools: the most vigorous have often been priests themselves.

The clergy were in a particularly poor condition to meet

these attacks. There were reformed and unreformed in each country, those who accepted and those who rejected the canons laid down by Trent. There was also a division between the higher and lower clergy, essentially a class division which tended to widen during the course of the eighteenth century. Indeed, so wide was this chasm that a movement known as Richerism gained many adherents in France and northern Italy. This was a protest of the lower clergy against the hierarchy, against the higher clergy's control of ecclesiastical advancement, against the high incomes of the bishops and abbots, with a demand for a more equitable distribution of clerical income. Richerism was so widespread that in some areas of France the lower clergy banded together to form primitive unions. In France, the century-old feud between Jansenist and Roman clergy contributed to the division.[2]

The clergy were also split between those who defended the Church and those who accepted the criticism of the philosophes and therefore practiced a sort of watered-down Catholicism. Peter Gay in his brilliant work on the Enlightenment has referred to this phenomenon as the "treason of the clerks."[3] It was very pronounced in England among the Anglican clergy, most of whom were deists, and many of the clergy on the Continent also went over to the side of the philosophes. The anticlericals could point to this defection to prove that any reasonable person could see the validity and justice of their criticisms. Many of the best minds among the clergy could not challenge the philosophes' attacks because they agreed with the substance of enlightened criticism. The defenders of traditional Christianity used arguments that ignored rationalist criticisms, and they became even more exposed to attack.

The philosophes' attack on revealed religion was grounded in their adherence to deism, the religion of rationalism. With emphasis upon a rational God, there was no need for a mediator between man and God. The clergy were looked upon as a useless class. Many of the deists left it at that, particularly in those countries where there was no clerical problem. In Latin Europe, on the other hand, the clergy were an ever present threat which had to be countered.

The philosophes' views were also based upon criticism of all existing institutions. If the world was to be reconstructed on a rational basis, no institution was invulnerable. Governments, social groups, classes, and churches all came in for criticism. All restrictions on freedom were opposed. The Church was the easiest institution to attack, and religious freedom was, in many ways, the easiest to achieve; civil freedom was much more difficult to win.

The philosophes also attacked myth. Historical myth was destroyed by the use of new historical method. The historical foundations of Christianity and the classical exposition of ecclesiastical history were subjected to the new rational criticisms, even though "scientific" history had not yet been developed. Historical criticism became one of the philosophes' chief legacies to the history of anticlericalism.

They were, in short, obsessed with religion. As Peter Gay has put it, they attacked religion "as a symptom in hysteria, a device of political management, a mark of illiteracy, or a state in historical development."[4] And they were popular, witty, and prolific about it. France was flooded with anticlerical pamphlets and lampoons, many of which found their way past the censors into other countries. The enforcement of censorship depended largely upon the attitudes of the governments concerned; many allowed books to circulate freely. In any event, clerical condemnation served to increase the popularity of this scurrilous anticlericalism. In educated circles it became popular to be anticlerical, and anticlerical attitudes gave one a social status which allowed entry into the salons of the philosophes.

Despite some individual variations, a few general themes ran throughout philosophe anticlericalism. A constant argument was directed against clerical superstition and intolerance. By fostering superstition, the philosophes argued, the clergy had reduced the level of men's minds and had pre-

vented them from grasping the truths of reason. Church
schools did not teach the principles of reason, but rather the
superstitions of credulity. By intolerance, the clergy had
fomented religious war and had caused endless trouble. The
religious wars of the sixteenth century were held up as proof
of this assertion. In the face of the misery they had caused,
it was intolerable that the clergy continued to preach the
superiority of Catholicism.

The close ties between church and state were another point
of friction. The philosophes argued that by relying upon each
other, both the religious and the secular powers confused
their aims. The state wasted time and resources by supporting
the clergy. And the clergy became so enmeshed in civil affairs
that they could no longer minister to men's spiritual needs.
Humanity was the chief victim of this unfortunate coalition.

The worthlessness of the Middle Ages was another common theme. The philosophes were admirers of pagan antiquity, and they saw the Middle Ages as a period of
obscurantism in which classical learning was snuffed out. Although the medieval monks had actually preserved many of
the classical writings, the fact that some of the early Church
fathers had claimed a dichotomy between classical learning
and Christian truth was enough to prove the point.

*

The French philosophe anticlerical tradition was preceded
by the skeptical anticlericalism of Montaigne and particularly
Bayle in the sixteenth and seventeenth centuries. These early
writers were responding to the Protestant-Catholic conflict
and the religious wars. Both urged toleration; Bayle, however, condemned the clergy, the Church, and Christianity for
subverting mankind.[5] He was the first philosophe anticlerical.

In the early eighteenth century the attack against the clergy
was intensified. Montesquieu admired English customs and
stability (all of the French philosophes did), claiming that one
reason for English progress and stability was the weakness
of the clergy in that country. In the Latin countries, the
other-worldliness of the clergy, particularly that of the reli-

gious orders, he said, weakened the prosperity of the nations, for their clerics were economically useless. Furthermore, clerical celibacy was a cause of depopulation.[6] He used no statistics to prove his point, but he was in fact attempting a "scientific" explanation.

As the eighteenth century progressed, the philosophes became more vocally anticlerical: by the middle of the century they were openly anti-Christian. The most clever anticlerical was Voltaire, certainly the most prominent anticlerical of all time, so much so that his name became synonymous with anticlericalism and later generations called anticlericals "Voltaireans." Voltaire's writings were permeated with his obsession with clericalism. The English were praised for having rid themselves of clericalism, and his interpretation of history was largely a catalogue of clerical crimes. His phrase, "Écrasez l'infâme," came to be the epigraph of anticlericals; at the same time, Voltaire did feel the clergy performed a useful role in teaching religion to the masses in order to keep them in their place.[7]

The encyclopaedist Denis Diderot echoed Voltaire's anticlericalism. With great effectiveness he contrasted the imagined simple and noble virtues of South Sea Islanders with the conniving casuistry of clerical missionaries.[8] Condorcet felt that Christianity and clericalism had been part of a stage in the history of human progress, but that neither had any further contribution to make. He indicted the clergy for their "contempt for humanity."[9] The influence of Rousseau, although he himself was not overtly anticlerical or even anti-Christian, was probably greater than that of all the other philosophes. His stress on the inherent goodness of man and the corruptibility of institutions established the foundations of much of the anticlerical liberalism and socialism of the modern age. D'Alembert, Holbach, and others all enlarged upon the anticlerical theme, until by the end of the Old Regime, the spirit of anticlericalism had spread to all the cities of France. By the time of the French Revolution, French anticlericalism was unmatched in its cleverness, crudity, and popularity.

In England, anticlericalism was directed primarily against the Anglican clergy. The leading English anticlerical was John Toland, an ex-priest who declaimed that Christianity had been ruined by the clergy. Christianity, he said, was a reasonable religion, but the clergy tampered with and damaged it with their superstition and mystical nonsense. Matthew Tindal and Anthony Collins echoed these comments; in general, English anticlericals tended to be Christian deists. David Hume was an exception, but he was not as obsessed with religion as were the others. Even Edward Gibbon, who attributed the fall of Rome to the debilitating spirit of Christianity, lacked the brilliance and wit of the French anticlericals.[10]

In Spain and Italy there were fewer anti-Christians. Criticism in those countries tended to be more traditional and constructive. There was not a strong intellectual tradition of criticism in either country, nor was there a prosperous middle class to support anti-Christian ideas. The masses in both countries were in fact conservatively proclerical. In Spain, the urban mob was dependent upon the clergy for its subsistence,[11] and for all Spaniards, centuries of identification of Catholicism with national aims and goals could not be easily erased.

In northern Italy, under the domination of the Austrian Habsburgs, there was little popular support for anticlericalism, which was looked upon as a foreign import. When the enlightened anticlericals of Austria tried to implement anticlerical reforms in northern Italy, they were met by open popular hostility. The Neopolitan historian Pietro Giannone was a traditional constructive anticlerical. He contrasted the worldly church of the eighteenth century with the pristine primitive church and attacked the Inquisition and the Index.[12] For his efforts he was exiled and imprisoned. Unlike France, the Italian atmosphere was not conducive to anticlerical criticism.

The constructive anticlericals of the Enlightenment—those who attacked clericalism, not the Church or Christianity—were obscured by the brilliance and popularity of the philosophes. On the whole, they concerned themselves with demands for sharing episcopal wealth. Most were clerics themselves. In addition, they felt that the clergy relied too extensively upon the church-state union and by identifying with the state would, in a very prophetic sense, become targets of criticism levelled against the state. They wanted an independent clergy, free to pursue its aims without the taint of worldliness. Many of these anticlericals were opposed to arbitrary state power, and therefore opposed the clergy who upheld the state's authority. Richerism and Jansenism were anticlerical movements of this type. Two French writers, Abbé Reymond and Nicholas Maultrot, both wrote books defending the lower clergy against the power and corruption of the hierarchy.[13]

Except in the cities of France, popular anticlericalism tended toward this constructive type. The chief complaints raised by the populace were directed against the tithing system; many felt it was corrupt, for tithes collected in a particular area might go to someone whom they had never seen —a distant monastery perhaps—while their parish priest received little or nothing. In the cities, the bourgeoisie complained that the clergy competed with them in commercial enterprises, yet were exempt from taxation.

Philosophe anticlericalism had an important effect upon the structure of traditional constructive anticlericalism. Each acted upon the other, frequently adding to the other's effectiveness and sometimes momentarily changing the outlook of the other. The destructive anticlericals continued to rail against the superstition and other-worldliness of the clergy, but at the same time pointed to their corruption and worldliness. Their anticlericalism became more eclectic. The constructive anticlericals continued to complain about the wealth of the clergy, but they also began to see them as "irrelevant" to the world and unsuited to the demands of the modern age.

*

In any event, philosophe anticlericalism set the tone for the partisan anticlericalism of the nineteenth century. The writers and the statesmen of the period following the Enlightenment added little to the themes developed by the philosophes. The politicians used the rationales developed by the philosophes, whatever their real motives. Only the realization that the world was not as rational as the philosophes made it out to be saved the clergy from further attacks—and this realization did not come about until the twentieth century, when the world found out there were worse things than an overweening clergy.

CHAPTER 7

The Practice of Cismontane Anticlericalism

*It is therefore the duty of princes and heads of
republics to uphold the foundations of the
religion of their countries, for then
it is easy to keep their people
religious, and consequently
well conducted and united.*

Niccolò Machiavelli

WHILE THE IDEOLOGICAL ANTICLERICALISM OF THE PHILO-
sophes was capturing the imagination of the literate classes,
a more immediately effective kind of anticlericalism caused
the clergy concern. This was the practical anticlericalism put
into effect by governments of the various countries. It went
by different names: gallicanism in France, regalism in Spain
and Portugal, Febronianism and Josephism in the Habsburg
domain.

In essence, this practical anticlericalism was opposition to
a papal-controlled clergy; hence the name *cismontane*
(*ultramontane*–propapal; *cismontane*–antipapal). It was practiced at the highest levels of government by kings and chief
ministers. Depending upon the country involved, the degree
of popular support for these policies varied.[1]

Cismontane anticlericalism was not new. It had been used
in the Middle Ages, particularly by the Holy Roman Emper-

67

ors in their struggles to maintain control over the clergy in their territories. But opposition to the papacy had diminished during the Reformation when Catholic princes united with the papacy against the Protestant reformers. Clerical enthusiasm for the dynastic cause as the most effective means of combatting Protestantism led to a number of agreements, usually in the form of concordats, which gave the crowns of Catholic countries control over the clergy.

By the eighteenth century the situation had changed. The Reformation had been contained and the new political theory of absolutism posed a greater threat to the papacy. Political reforms designed to centralize power in the crowns clashed with the clergy's traditional rights and privileges. Furthermore, the Tridentine reforms had established rather strict canons for the preservation of clerical and papal independence.

Undoubtedly, the ideas of the philosophes affected the cismontanes. Many of the monarchs and their ministers considered themselves enlightened; certainly the practice of benevolent despotism was an enlightened political theory. The philosophes' reformist ideas, especially in economics, also affected church-state relations, for the clergy were powerful landholders in most countries. The cismontane anticlericals differed from the philosophes in their regard for the dogma and faith of Christianity. They wanted to keep their subjects Christian and had no intention of destroying the Catholic religion; they wanted to control it in conformity with their dynastic policies. Many were personally devout, even pious.[2] They were true practitioners of practical anticlericalism: no ideological impulse drove them; they wanted to control the clergy here and now, recognizing that under different circumstances the clergy could be allowed freedom.

If there was an ideological element in their anticlericalism, it was the concept of "dual allegiance." Because a citizen's primary political allegiance should be to the dynasty, the clergy's allegiance to the pope, who was actually a foreign prince, was intolerable. While both bishops and parish priests had generally been under some form of crown control since the sixteenth century concordats, the members of religious orders were another matter. Their allegiance was to their superior, usually resident in Rome, who in turn was responsible only to the pope. The cismontanes considered this problem particularly acute because of the large numbers of regular clergy and because of their vigor and dynamism.

The Jesuits were especially independent. Most took a special vow of obedience to the pope. They operated the best schools in every country. Their influence had been widespread ever since the sixteenth century. They were confessors to kings, and their network of houses throughout the world provided them with sources of wealth and information possessed not even by the crowns. In brief, the Jesuits were an uncontrolled element in any crown's scheme of things.

All clergy were a disturbing element within most countries. Corruption, confusion over jurisdictions between regular and diocesan clergy, and the privileges of canon law which provided the right of sanctuary in church buildings for brigands and outlaws, all contributed to the disturbance of normality.[3]

A significant motivating force in cismontane anticlericalism was the fiscal crisis of the eighteenth century, when almost all countries, particularly France, were in deep fiscal trouble. Antiquated tax bases and the cost of seemingly endless wars in the seventeenth and eighteenth centuries drained the royal treasuries. As one solution to the problem, the physiocrats, those economists who maintained that land was the basis of all wealth and that for land to be productive it must be free, proposed the confiscation of church properties. The clergy controlled extensive properties in all countries except England (where confiscation had been accomplished in the sixteenth century). Mortmain laws forbade the clergy to sell this land. Some was owned by bishops, some by monasteries, and some by various lay confraternities; most was held under the provision that the wishes of the original donors forbade alienation of the land from the purposes originally intended. The physiocrats urged the crown to free church land by putting it on the open market, thereby improving the national economy and incidentally providing the crown with an immediate solution to its fiscal problems.

In each country cismontane anticlericalism attempted to subject the clergy to stricter state control, to expropriate church property, and to limit the numbers of clergy. The two most common ways of limiting the numbers of clergy were to control the seminaries and to attack the religious orders. Where the cismontanes were successful, the seminaries saw a decrease in the number of graduates. The attack on the regular clergy was based on the argument that since their number was decreasing (in comparison to their heyday in the Middle Ages), those remaining should be consolidated into fewer communities and their vacant houses and properties appropriated by the crown. Decrees to this effect were followed with specific limitations upon the numbers of regular clergy allowed in a particular area or country.

Attempts to gain control of church property were generally unsuccessful. Land was power and the clergy were able to prevent these encroachments upon their principal source of income. The governments were, however, able to prohibit the clergy from acquiring more land without specific crown permission. The tithe was another matter; this was normally collected by the state, which retained a portion of it. Attempts were made by the state to gain larger portions of the tithe, but the clergy usually resisted. In any event, by the end of the eighteenth century, the theoretical basis for the expropriation of clerical lands had been worked out by the cismontanes in practically every country.

Clerical immunities from civil law—the clergy's right to be tried for civil crimes in church courts, and the right of sanctuary for common criminals—were abolished. The cismontanes contended that the clergy were often involved in nonreligious enterprises (commercial, for example) and that criminals and brigands often took advantage of the right of sanctuary to elude arrest.

Control of clerical appointments had been practiced since

before the sixteenth century. In many cases the crowns had also established the practice of controlling clerical communication with Rome. Sometimes the papacy agreed to these privileges, most of which were made formal in the eighteenth century. By the middle of the century, there was no country in which the pope had complete freedom to appoint clergy and, although the clergy were generally free to correspond with Rome, no papal bulls, encyclicals, or other communications were read in the churches without crown permission.

*

In France, by the beginning of the eighteenth century, the crown had already established a high degree of control over the diocesan clergy.[4] By the sixteenth-century Concordat of Bologna, the crown had the privilege of nominating bishops, and in the seventeenth century, Louis XIV had posited the Gallican Articles, which deprived the papacy of any control over the French clergy and established three authorities for the Church: the crown, the pope, and the Assembly of the Clergy. By the eighteenth century, however, actual control had come under the domination of the crown, for the papacy was reluctant to press its claims, and the French clergy, badly split by the Jansenist controversy, were crown appointees.[5]

Thus, cismontane anticlericalism in France was directed largely against the regular clergy. The Assembly of the Clergy was ordered to investigate the problems of the religious orders, and upon its recommendations, the crown decreed that whenever the number of members of a particular monastery or house fell below nine, the house was to be closed, its inhabitants sent to houses with larger numbers, and the property and revenues of the closed house assigned to a special fund used for charitable purposes. In order to limit the number of regular clergy, the crown ordered that no regular cleric could profess vows before the age of twenty-one and forbade any order to have more than two houses in Paris or more than one in any of the other cities. In 1773, the Assembly of the Clergy ended the regular clergy's exemption from episcopal jurisdiction.[6] By the end of the Old Regime the crown had firmly established the rule that no order could carry on any activities without its permission.

As for clerical property, the crown never succeeded in gaining control. Whereas the clergy cooperated in most other activities, they held on to their properties, which in turn gave them the wealth and prestige to enable them to resist the crown's requests. The crown was able to decree that the clergy acquire no further properties without its permission, but this was a weak victory. Finally, in its hour of greatest financial need, in the 1780s, the crown asked the clergy to increase annual donations to the government. The clergy refused.[7]

In Spain, regalism was the theory of crown control over the clergy. It had been practiced in the American possessions since the sixteenth century, when the crown had obtained the rights of patronage in the New World.[8] In the fifteenth century the crown had obtained the right to collect a portion of the *cruzada*, which was a per capita indulgence based on the crusade against the Moslems. Furthermore, in the sixteenth and seventeenth centuries the crown had used the Inquisition to much greater effect than in any other country.

In the eighteenth century, the new Bourbon dynasty obtained great privileges from the papacy in the Concordat of 1753: the crown was given the right to appoint most of the Spanish bishops, the *cruzada* was granted to the crown in perpetuity, and the clergy's right of exemption from taxation for land held in mortmain was abolished.

Charles III, Spain's benevolent despot, practiced the art of cismontane anticlericalism to a degree surpassed only by Joseph II of Austria. His ministers, Aranda, Floridablanca, Campomanes, and Jovellanos, all encouraged the King to restrict clerical property and to take action against the regular clergy. Their decrees forbade the further acquisition of property by the clergy, abolished the rights of sanctuary, removed from ecclesiastical jurisdiction all cases of smuggling involving clerics, and affirmed the crown's control of communication with Rome. A major victory Charles and his ministers won was the right to submit the clergy to the same tax laws as laymen. Although the Spanish clergy continually balked at this law and the decrees were never fully implemented, they remained on the books, ready to be used by the liberal regimes of the nineteenth century.

Charles III had come to the throne of Spain well versed in cismontanism. As King of the Two Sicilies before he ascended the Spanish throne, he had prompted his minister Bernardo Tanucci to anticlerical reforms. Tanucci had arranged a concordat which provided for taxation of the clergy and for a decrease in their numbers to an eventual ratio of one cleric to one hundred laymen.[9]

In the Habsburg domains, the practice of cismontane anticlericalism was based on Febronianism, a theory that denied papal control of the clergy; under Emperor Joseph II the practice was known as Josephism.[10] Although Maria Teresa, Joseph's mother, had placed some restrictions upon clerical property and had ordered state supervision of the seminaries, she did not implement the decrees when Rome protested. Her son put them into effect.

"The state is no cloister," was Joseph's assessment of the situation, and he acted accordingly. The diocesan clergy were brought under stringent control. All bishops had to take an oath to obey all laws without exception. No cleric could receive any office or honor without crown permission. Seminaries were placed under direct crown control, and seminarians were forbidden to go to Rome. Dioceses were redistricted and a layman appointed to consider plans for the lay administration and jurisdiction of the Church in the entire Habsburg Empire. As for the regular clergy, all contemplative orders were suppressed; only those which ministered to the sick or aged or were involved in teaching were allowed to remain ("being useless to the world, they cannot be pleasing to God").[11] Their property was confiscated and used for educational and charitable purposes. As for the remaining regulars, none was allowed to profess vows before the age of twenty-four; all regular clergy were made subject to the bishop of their diocese; no communication was allowed with the Roman superiors. In the last years of his life, Joseph even undertook regulating the clergy's reading material, the numbers of candles to be used during mass, and the size of statues in church buildings. "Brother Sacristan," Frederick II called him.[12]

The Pope protested, even came to Vienna, but Joseph remained adamant. Only the force of popular reaction stayed the implementation of his decrees, and then only in Tuscany and Belgium. In Tuscany, Scipione di Ricci (the nephew of the Jesuit General) was named prime minister. For his efforts to implement the Josephist decrees there, he was made Bishop of Pistoia. But the people of Tuscany would have none of his reforms. They stormed Ricci's episcopal palace, and most of the decrees were withdrawn.[13] In Belgium a general revolt against Joseph's reforms ultimately led to the proclamation of Belgian independence by the Archbishop of Malines in 1789, an independence cut short by the French Revolution and the eventual conquest of Belgium by the French armies.[14] To what extent these popular revolts were directed against "foreign" tampering with customs or were stimulated by genuinely clerical feeling is difficult to determine.

It was in Portugal, however, that the most spectacular anticlerical action was initiated. There the Marquis of Pombal, King John's prime minister, was determined to expel the Jesuits from the Portuguese Empire and to work for the suppression of the Society.[15] Pombal was a cismontane, and most of the reforms were implemented in Portugal: age limits for regular clergy, suppression of some of the regulars' houses, and a prohibition against assigning monies in wills for masses for the dead. Pombal also made Portugal a haven for foreign anticlericals and established a board of censorship which promoted the sale of the philosophes' works but banned clerical writings. His greatest enemy was the Society of Jesus.

By the middle of the eighteenth century, the Jesuits had become the most controversial of all the clergy. For the many who doted on them, there were many who disliked them, including bishops and diocesan clergy. The myth that saw the Jesuit hand behind everything played a large part in the events leading to their suppression: Public reasons advanced for their suppression ranged from their supposed advocacy of tyrannicide and regicide to their business enterprises and their political influence. There was also the Jesuits' intense ultramontanism, the strength of their organization, their widespread influence over the sons of the nobility and the middle class in their schools, and simple jealousy. Nor should economic motives be overlooked; the reputed wealth of the Society invited confiscation.

Pombal was the first to act. After conflicts with the Jesuits over their reductions in Paraguay, he ordered the members of the Society expelled from the Portugese Empire in 1759 and confiscated their property. In France, Louis XV's prime minister Choiseul followed Pombal's example: after the Jesuits were involved in a notorious and public scandal, the Society was suppressed in France in 1764. In 1767, Charles III's minister, Aranda, was able to suppress them in the Spanish Empire. Tanucci in Naples followed suit. Finally under intense pressure from Aranda and Pombal, Pope Clement XIV in 1773 issued a brief suppressing the Society everywhere.[16]

The suppression of the Jesuits was the last action of the eighteenth-century cismontane anticlericals before the great upheavals of the French Revolution. Cismontanism continued to be an important facet of anticlerical activity—although after the Revolution its cause was largely taken over by parliamentary bodies—and much of the liberal anticlericalism of the nineteenth century was simply cismontanism writ large.

PART TWO

CHAPTER 8

Modern Anticlericalism

*I never saw, heard, nor read that the clergy were
beloved in any nation where Christianity was
the religion of the country. Nothing
can render them popular but some
degree of persecution.*

Jonathan Swift

THE COMING OF THE FRENCH REVOLUTION IN 1789 MARKS
the beginning of the era of modern anticlericalism. For the
following century and a half the clergy were primary targets
of criticism, legislation, and violence in most Latin countries.
Modern anticlericalism grew out of the practices and attitudes
of the cismontane and philosophe anticlericals, but it was
shaped by the three dominating ideologies, liberalism, nationalism, and socialism, which surfaced after 1789 to become
the motivating forces of governmental policy and the stimulating elements of public opinion. Two of these demanded an
allegiance to institutions that clashed with traditional ones the
clergy had learned to live with: nationalism promoted the
nation state, socialism the brotherhood of the proletariat. The
third ideology, liberalism (in its purest form), called for the
abolition of clerical influence and the breaking of institutional
restraints so that men could progress.

These ideologies were part of a larger trend toward
secularism. Catholicism was being replaced in men's minds
by a new faith. The secular revolution, which had won over

northern Europe in the sixteenth century, was now penetrating Latin Europe. As the industrial revolution spread, so also did secularism; where there were large numbers of peasants, the secular revolution was less influential. As the clergy lost their dogmatic hold upon men they lost clericalism's chief power. But conflicts arose because the clergy had over the years garnered large amounts of political, economic, and social power. They were loath to give these up, even though (or perhaps because) they had lost their spiritual grip on men. Only the complete success of the secular revolution in the twentieth century brought an end to anticlerical tensions and conflicts.

*

Anticlericals after 1789 fall into two groups: political and social. Political anticlericals were more numerous and more active in the nineteenth century. They believed that the problem of clericalism was amenable to a political solution, either by executive fiat or by parliamentary legislation. Theirs was a moderate view, supported by middle-class liberals who wanted the activities of the clergy narrowly circumscribed.

The political attack upon the clergy was aimed at three targets: regular clergy, land, and education. The arguments against the regular clergy were the same in the eighteenth century, namely, that they were uncontrolled, useless, unproductive, and fostered superstition and ignorance in their schools. The political devices used were the traditional ones: limitations upon the numbers of regulars, confiscation of their properties, suppression, and, in extreme instances, expulsion. In most cases, political anticlericals were satisfied with the legislation alone and did not necessarily demand its implementation. Since suppression of a religious order usually meant only that the order did not have any special recognition at law, its members were otherwise free to pursue their aims, and suppression was not actually as harmful as the clergy made it out to be. That the political anticlericals did not encourage implementation of the suppression laws indicates that they may have had other motives for legislating suppression in the first place.

Clerical property was a target of the political anticlericals in almost every country, for political anticlericals were the chief purchasers of land. Except in France, where some peasants purchased them, generally the properties went to middle-class speculators, who found that the expropriation had three salutary effects: it deprived the clergy of their economic power and forced them into reliance upon the state for their subsistence; it helped solve the government's fiscal problems; it turned the bourgeoisie into men of property.

The process of land expropriation was slow. Usually it took decades, as first the lands of the regulars, then the lands of the lay confraternities and brotherhoods, and finally the properties of the diocesan clergy were each put on the market. The process was complex and involved, and historians have not yet determined the total losses incurred by the clergy in each country. Furthermore, the expropriation led to the problem of a state-salaried clergy. Salaries were originally offered in recompense for the confiscated property, but legislative appropriations seldom kept pace with inflation, and the clergy constantly agitated for increases.

Ordinarily, the expropriation of clerical lands marked the transition of the clergy's political role. When the clergy possessed landed property, they had wealth, control over their tenants, and the political influence that went with these. When their property was expropriated they became dependent, either upon the government that paid them salaries, the wealthy classes that supported them, or the political party that defended their interests in the legislature. Perceptive anticlericals then saw that the way to further diminish clerical privilege no longer lay in attacking the clergy, for this simply gained them more support among the faithful, but in attacking the group—government, class, or party—that supported them. Emotional anticlericals could not see this and continued to attack the clergy.

In extreme circumstances and under unusual conditions, the groups supporting the clergy deserted them. The clergy were then forced to resume an independent political role, despite their lack of practical power. At this point, perceptive anticlericals once again focused their attack upon the clergy. The resulting anticlerical conflict was usually most intense and frequently disastrous for both clericals and anticlericals.

Clerical education was another anticlerical target. With the notable exception of France, where lay schools were established during the Revolution, in the other Latin countries at the beginning of the nineteenth century the clergy held a monopoly on education. They operated most of the schools and taught in what few public or state schools existed. Political anticlericals saw that by suppressing the regular clergy, most of whom were teaching orders, they could indirectly weaken church schools. The anticlericals were then faced with the alternative of constructing a completely new (and expensive) public-school system. They met the problem in most countries at first by allowing the clergy to teach in the state schools but forbidding them to teach religion. This was impractical, and the political anticlericals usually gave up on the problem. The legislation was on the books but it was seldom implemented effectively. The regular clergy, in one guise or another, continued to teach and staff most of the schools in the Latin countries. It was not until teacher-training schools were established late in the nineteenth century that a practical lay-school system was developed. In the meantime, the same political anticlericals who had passed the laws sent their sons to Jesuit schools, and their wives would not consider sending their daughters anywhere but to convent schools.

The political anticlericals often paid only lip service to the ideals and aims of anticlericalism. They did not compromise on the expropriation of clerical property, as they did on the suppression of the regulars and the abolition of clerical education. They could thus stand in good grace with their anticlerical constituents without upsetting the clericals. Political anticlericalism served the demands of politics, and the clergy became scapegoats for problems unrelated to religion.

In the Latin countries, political parties seldom had enough power to rule by themselves. Coalition governments had to be formed. Where cismontane rulers in the eighteenth century might prudently have hesitated to decree anticlerical reforms for fear of clerical reaction, legislatures subject to popular scrutiny could not be as prudent. Anticlericalism came to serve as the bond of the governing coalition in middle-class governments. Whether or not clericalism was a threat, governments found that anticlerical policies were popular; they were the one activity all members of a coalition could agree upon, and, except in rare instances, they were relatively harmless because they were seldom implemented. A government accused of inaction found that a bit of anticlericalism could prove that it was indeed alive and functioning. Political anticlericals used anticlericalism as a dodge, a smoke screen to cover up their inability to solve more pressing problems. More often than not, the clergy did not understand this strategem and reacted as if the laws were really being implemented.

One of the chief vehicles of political anticlericalism was Freemasonry. Founded early in the eighteenth century as a secret upper middle class and aristocratic organization whose aim was to spread the ideals of deism, freedom, and rationalism, Freemasonry had included in its ranks many of the philosophes, cismontane ministers, and even some of the upper clergy. The papacy condemned the movement, and it quickly became the *bête noire* of the clericals in much the same way the Jesuits became that of the anticlericals. Freemasonry became more radical in the ninteenth century, and in most countries it had a distinct anticlerical program. Clericals viewed it as a tightly organized conspiracy determined to destroy the Church, and they saw a Masonic hand behind every anticlerical action. To what extent this view corresponded to reality is difficult to determine, but the idea of a conspiracy does seem farfetched in light of the many tangible reasons for anticlericalism. Certainly Freemasons were anticlericals, but the movement was more a vehicle rather than a motivating impluse; without Freemasonry the anticlericals would have used another vehicle.[1]

While political anticlericals were usually moderate, in times of crisis they could become violent, especially when they lacked popular support or found their opposition too strong. This occurred during the French Revolution and in the early nineteenth century, when the urban middle classes and working classes were inspired by the new ideals of liberalism and nationalism. Nationalism in particular engendered a hostility toward priests because of the issue of dual allegiance. When a nation was threatened by forces which had the support of the papacy, the clergy were attacked as traitors. Sometimes political anticlericals stimulated and promoted violence against the clergy but did not themselves take part in the violent attacks. There are hints that middle-class anticlericals occasionally hired *agents provocateurs* to stir up proletarian hatreds against the clergy, or else subsidized such proletarian anticlericalism.

*

Violence against the clergy and against church buildings and property is more characteristic of social anticlericalism.[2] This differs from political anticlericalism in that it is directed against the clergy's class role, their ministering to the needs of one class in preference to another. There had been social anticlericals in the twelfth century: the complaints against clerical wealth and luxury had social as well as economic connotations. But the special notion of class consciousness and class warfare is a distinctly nineteenth-century phenomenon, appearing with the rise of working-class ideologies. The particular fury of proletarian anticlericalism can be understood only by considering the fact that Christianity is itself a revolutionary force. It constantly demands the spiritual progress of the individual Christian, and its ideal of brotherly love is truly revolutionary compared with almost every form of political and social thought up to the nineteenth century.

With the advent of socialism and anarchism, charity—in the form of the state's more equitable distribution of economic goods—and brotherly love—in the form of the brotherhood of the proletariat—became the concerns of working-class movements. As the clergy had lost much of their revolutionary impetus (whether mythical or actual) they had in a sense disavowed their origins and betrayed their ideals.

For the political anticlericals this made little difference; not so for the social anticlericals. They saw the clergy as heretics to the revolutionary cause. As Gerald Brenan observes, "The Bible, and especially the New Testament, contains enough dynamite to blow up all the existing social systems in Europe, only by force of habit and through the power of beautiful and rhythmical words have we ceased to notice it."[3]

Hence the bitter spirit of social anticlericalism. As heretics are always persecuted with more vigor than are simple nonbelievers, the clergy were persecuted for having deserted the cause of brotherly love. Being proletarians and unable to influence legislation, the social anticlericals took a more direct approach: the unworthy cleric had to be rooted out and destroyed. Violence was the answer.

Social anticlericals were iconoclasts as well. Church incendiarism in particular appears to have been largely their work. They wanted not so much to destroy as to purify. There was no way of purifying the clergy other than by destruction, but churches could be burned and purified by fire. Especially in southern Europe, with its lavishly decorated churches, fire reduced church buildings to shells of simplicity. Fire was handy, and church furnishings usually made splendid blazes. There was something elemental, almost promethean, in this incendiarism.

While proletarian social anticlericalism was more noticeable, middle-class social anticlericalism was felt after the clergy began to preach and practice the new social teachings of the Church in the last two decades of the nineteenth century. Then the clergy were criticized for supporting the proletariat to the exclusion of ministering to the middle and upper classes. This reactionary social anticlericalism was not violent (because the upper and middle classes did not use violence), nor did it have the powerful revolutionary impetus of proletarian social anticlericalism, but it was nonetheless a valid and interesting aberration upon the structure of anticlericalism.

*

In the nineteenth and twentieth centuries, the papacy played a much more important role in the struggle between clericals and anticlericals. Particularly after the accession of Pope Pius IX in 1846, Catholics—clericals and anticlericals alike—looked to Rome. This was partly because of the papacy's more active involvement as expressed through an increasing number of encyclicals and statements, and partly because of more modern means of communication and transportation. The popes came to a more thorough and quicker understanding of events throughout the world, and their statements reached a wider audience. Furthermore, national bishops could be contacted more quickly; visits to Rome, at least from European countries, could be made in a day or two.[4]

Part of the papacy's new prestige stemmed directly from its beleaguered aspect. Condemnation of anticlerical policies created more anticlericalism but it also increased clerical support for the papacy. Furthermore, many heretofore neutral Catholics came to support the clerical view, perhaps feeling sympathy for the popes under attack, perhaps affected by papal condemnations of modern society. Catholics found the changes wrought by the industrial and secular revolutions confusing, and papal utterances promoted simpler, if harsher, points of view on these events. The papal loss of temporal power coupled with the proclamation of infallibility, although provoking anticlericalism, gained more sympathy for the papacy from all Catholics. By the beginning of the twentieth century, the papacy began to enjoy international prestige resulting from its successful efforts at mediation between states and from its humanitarian endeavors.

Catholics generally supported the papacy in its struggles against anticlerical politicians, but there were two controversies which provoked a considerable amount of "internal" anticlericalism from Catholics who otherwise supported clerical policies. These controversies revolved around the demochristian movement and modernism.

The formation of Christian democratic political parties posed potential anticlerical conflicts. The demochristian idea of a mass political party based on papal social teachings and designed to appeal primarily to Catholics was proposed at the turn of the twentieth century, particularly in France and Italy, where new parties were formed. By their nature, however, these parties depended on papal approval or at least neutrality: one word from the pope could make or destroy a demochristian party. Some popes frowned on the idea, favoring instead episcopal or papal control of Catholic votes. Others encouraged the movement as a means to truly implement papal social teachings. The movement played a significant role in creating anticlerical tensions among Catholics.[5]

The modernist controversy, also occurring at the turn of the twentieth century, had to do with new forms of biblical and theological criticism. Modernists contended that interpretation of dogma could be made considerably broader than the narrow confines of Trent. Most of the modernists were priests, and they became theological anticlericals when the papacy reacted strongly against their ideas. The modernist controversy spilled over into politics, for most of the demochristian leaders were sympathetic to the modernists' more liberal spirit of criticism.[6]

For understanding modern anticlerical struggles, it is useful to classify the popes. They can be characterized as being reactionary clerical, moderate clerical, moderate, or progressive, based on how they used and judged the scope of their authority; that is, the more clerical a pope was, the more widely he used his authority and the more narrowly he viewed the judgment of the laity. Keeping in mind that many of these characterizations are generalizations, and that specific instances can be found in which the individual pope does not fit the characterization, the popes can be classified as follows:[7]

Pius VII (1800-1823): moderate. Although he was forced to grant vast powers to Napoleon and was imprisoned by the French Emperor, when restored to power he proved more progressive than most of his bishops. Guided by Cardinal Consalvi, he pursued a moderate course in reforming the administration of the Papal States and resisting attempts by the clerical *zelanti* (extreme clericals within the Curia) to condemn liberal and revolutionary movements.

Leo XII (1823-1829): moderate clerical. Elected by the *zelanti,* he renewed earlier condemnations of Freemasonry, rationalism, and liberalism, although he was a moderate in his dealings with the French and Spanish governments.

Pius VIII (1829-1830): moderate. His reign was brief, and he did not vigorously continue the clerical policies of his predecessor.

Gregory XVI (1831-1846): reactionary clerical. He issued extreme condemnations of the new ideological movements, condemned the Polish uprising against Russia (on the grounds of obedience to constituted authority), and condemned the French priest Lamennais, thereby halting for decades the growth of liberal Catholic movements.

Pius IX (1846-1878): reactionary clerical. At the beginning of the longest pontificate in history, Pius was hailed as a progressive. After the 1848 revolutions, he became reactionary and condemned the movement for Italian unification (which threatened the Papal States). He condemned liberalism and all other progressive ideologies in the Syllabus of Errors (1864), and convoked Vatican Council I, which defined papal infallibility. After he lost the Papal States and Rome in 1871, he condemned the new Italian government and became the self-styled prisoner of the Vatican.

Leo XIII (1878-1903): moderate. Although Leo continued Pius IX's policies toward the Italian government, he was moderate toward the Third French Republic despite anticlerical provocations. He enhanced the prestige of the papacy by his mediation of the Caroline Islands controversy and promoted lay political participation in his encouragement of the demochristian movement.

Pius X (1903-1914): reactionary clerical. He condemned the French and Portuguese governments' anticlerical policies and condemned modernism. He frowned on demochristians and blocked their efforts in France and Italy.

Benedict XV (1914-1922): moderate. He unsuccessfully attempted to mediate between the warring parties in World War I, supported demochristians, and generally relaxed the implementation of his predecessor's restriction of the modernists.

Pius XI (1922-1939): moderate clerical. He was lukewarm toward the modernists, but his diplomatic policy with most nations was conciliatory. He condemned the reactionary *Action Française,* thereby improving church-state relations in France; he contributed to Mussolini's rise to power in Italy and concluded the Lateran Treaty as a solution to the Roman Question. Despite anticlerical provocations, his policy toward the Spanish republicans was moderate, and he condemned Nazi racist policies.

Pius XII (1939-1958): moderate clerical. Although he raised the papacy's international prestige with his humanitarian endeavors during World War II, he came under criticism later for failing to condemn the Nazi regime and its persecution of the Jews. Theological condemnations of modernist trends and support of authoritarian-clerical regimes marked his later years.

John XXIII (1958-1963): progressive. He convoked Vatican Council II; his encyclicals were generally less condemnatory and more positive.

*

To understand papal policy and its transmission through national bishops, it must be kept in mind that bishops do not always reflect papal policy. There are governmental pressures which restrict them. Furthermore, there is usually a "genera-

tion gap" between pope and bishops. With the exception of
the long pontificate of Pius IX, most popes reigned for fewer
than two decades; consequently, the appointees of one pope
served under the next pope, and only toward the end of his
reign did a pope normally have a majority of his own bishops.
In practice, this meant that the French bishops, for example,
who served under the moderate Leo XIII were appointees
of the reactionary clerical Pius IX and therefore did not carry
out Leo's policies with the same degree of enthusiasm as
those of his predecessor. By 1900 Leo XIII had, through
normal attrition, replaced most of these bishops with moderates, who in turn served most of their tenures under his successor, the reactionary clerical Pius X.

*

While there were enlightened middle-class or aristocratic
types of anticlericals, usually with Freemasonic connections
and secularistic views, the degree of anticlericalism varied
considerably in different countries. Latin Europe and Latin
America were racked with anticlerical conflicts which had
profound impacts on almost all facets of national life.

It is tempting to explain these struggles as the flowering
of a unique temperament—the Latin temperament, a paradox-
ical authoritarian-antiauthoritarian, love-hate relationship
with the clergy. However, there are more easily discernible
factors which account for the high incidence of anticlericalism in these countries.

All the Latin countries were in majority Catholic, since
Protestantism had made few inroads during the Reformation.
Although the number of practicing Catholics was often a
variable—in some cases as low as ten per cent—still, there
was no other religion to which dissenters could turn. Dissent
was channeled into anticlericalism, whereas in countries
which tolerated Protestants, the dissenter was free to become
a Protestant or to practice no religion at all without fear of
civil disability or social ostracism.

If the Reformation had little impact on the Latin European
countries, the influence of the French Revolution was great

indeed. All of them were occupied by the revolutionary or Napoleonic armies for long periods of time, and a strong attempt was made to implement the revolutionary reforms. Latin America, although not occupied by the French, was subject to many of the same revolutionary upheavals, essentially the attempts to create both a new state and a new society in brief spans of time. Furthermore, the importation of French revolutionary literature was widespread in these countries despite official censorship.

Clerical landholdings were large in the Latin countries, making the clergy more independent than elsewhere. Simply stated, the clergy had greater power than where the secular revolution had already occurred. They had support among the peasantry, and the urban mob was usually proclerical.[8] The existence of greater class division contributed to social struggles in which the anticlerical conflict became involved. In essence, clericalism was a valid and pressing problem in France, Spain, Italy, Portugal, and Latin America.

Even when the clergy were legislated against, the force of tradition was still strong. Madame d'Agoult, an astute observer of nineteenth-century France, made an observation about tradition that applies to other Latin countries as well: "The Catholic church still rules, not, to be sure, over the mind or heart of French society, but over its habits. In a country in which principles are so weak and passions so changeable, is not command over habits really command over life itself?"[9]

It is true that in northern, central, and eastern Europe there were countries with majority Catholic populations, but they did not have the same kind of anticlerical conflict. In these non-Latin areas there were usually more pressing problems that relegated the clerical problem to a secondary place and prevented the growth of internal anticlericalism. Thus, although Ireland and Poland were both majority Catholic countries, the people were united in their opposition to the English and Russian overlords. Their church was a persecuted faith; the pressure of external circumstances inhibited the development of anticlericalism, although the English and Russian rulers were frequently practical anticlericals.[10] Similarly, Austria with its multinational empire was much too concerned with the preservation of its defensive position in central Europe to provide the conditions for the growth of anticlericalism. In any event, the Josephite practices of the late eighteenth century severely circumscribed the independence of the clergy, and this subservience continued into the following centuries.[11]

Belgium did have anticlerical conflicts in the nineteenth century over educational problems. The country was temporarily polarized between clericals and anticlericals, but these incidents were of short duration, and the anticlericals finally lost out in 1895 when the Catholic party established the principle of state subsidization of church schools. Belgium was too industrialized and too concerned with defending herself first against the Dutch and then against the Germans to allow anticlericalism to become a truly divisive element in her development.[12]

In Germany, Catholics were a minority after the proclamation of Empire in 1871, and there was little internal dissension after Ignace von Döllinger broke with Pius IX over the question of papal infallibility. The Kulturkampf, Bismarck's attack on the Church, was not exclusively directed against the clergy and was in the cismontane anticlerical tradition. There was never any significant parliamentary anticlericalism in the Reichstag. Hitler's persecution of the clergy in the 1930s was purely practical and paled into insignificance when compared to his destruction of the Jews.[13]

Switzerland experienced a brief civil war between the Protestant and Catholic cantons which resulted in the eventual and permanent expulsion of the Jesuits, but little else. The United States, where Catholics were a minority, did not have anticlerical conflicts. The Church—clergy and laity alike —was an immigrant institution subject to pressures from a hostile Protestant majority, and even immigrants from the most anticlerical parts of Europe came to look upon the clergy as their protectors and benefactors.[14]

*

In examining modern anticlericalism, this study will focus upon those countries where anticlerical conflicts created deep national divisions and greatly influenced the development of all aspects of social and political attitudes. In Europe these countries were France, Spain, Italy, and Portugal. In Latin America, virtually every country experienced anticlericalism, but the struggles in Colombia and Mexico were the most intense.

CHAPTER 9

France

Le cléricalisme — voilà l'ennemi!

Léon Gambetta

ANTICLERICALISM RUNS A TANGLED COURSE THROUGH MOD-
ern French history. Less violent than the Spanish, more
serious than the Italian, the French anticlerical tradition was
more philosophical, more self-conscious. The French were
aware that they were acting in the public eye, that they had
a tradition to uphold. The anticlericalism of the French Revolution became a prototype for political anticlericalism in other
countries. As they did not want others to forget this, the
French anticlericals never forgot it themselves. Thus, there
was a certain amount of posturing in their anticlericalism, a
feeling that whatever happened on the floor of the chamber
of deputies was watched by the world. Their anticlerical
literature—and anticlericalism provided a major literary
theme throughout the nineteenth century—reflected this
self-awareness.[1] There was a determined logic about French
anticlericalism which lacked the spontaneous violence of
Spanish anticlericalism or the tragic-comic overtones of
Italian anticlericalism.[2]

*

The French Revolution of 1789 began a period of rapid
change. History was condensed and there was a natural tendency to carry ideas and actions to extremes. The revolutionaries were ushering in a new society, bringing a utopia into

being, and halfway measures would not do. Their anticlericalism as well went to extremes. For their part, the clergy were provoked to clerical extremes. For years they had been preaching against the new trends and the new secularism. The confusion of the Revolution was ample proof of the validity of their warnings. Extreme begat extreme; actions provoked reactions until mercifully, after a decade, both sides had burnt themselves out.[3]

The clergy became the scapegoats of the revolutionaries. They had collaborated with the Old Regime (few anticlericals looked beneath the surface gallicanism to see the real conflicts) and they could be blamed for its defects. As the revolutionaries became disappointed that their new society did not spring into being, they sought something· to blame. Consciously or unconsciously, they fixed upon the clergy, easily identifiable, clearly apart from the rest of society. All the old myths rose to the surface. If the Jesuits had once been reputed to be the conspiratorial hand behind dire events, the entire clergy could be made to fit the mold now. Furthermore, the clergy were the only staunch supporters of the Old Regime who stayed behind to face the revolutionary fury (although most of the bishops emigrated). The nobility fled, the wealthy fled, but the clergy stayed; they were available for persecution.

The dispassionate observer reading the revolutionary decrees and legislation, hearing the speeches, and scanning the pamphlets would think that the French clergy had reached their nadir in 1789, that all priests were scheming, grasping self-servers, and that in all justice the Church needed a thorough housecleaning. In fact, this was not so: numerous modern historians attest to the selflessness of the French clergy and, if one excepts the wealthy bishops and abbots, to their poverty as well. Nor were they all clericals; the spirit of the Enlightenment had affected them as it had the laity. Henri Daniel-Rops notes that "on the eve of the Revolution, there were only seven atheists and three deists among the 135 French bishops." and that one-quarter of all French

Freemasons in 1789 were clerics, who apparently saw no incompatibility between their priestly office and membership in the condemned society.[4]

It is also established that the clergy provided much of the impetus for the early stage of the Revolution. The lower clergy predominated among the members of the First Estate and were instrumental in transforming the Estates General into the National Assembly, siding with the commoners against the wishes of crown and nobility. The First Estate had also made known its desire for clerical reform. In the *cahiers,* lists of grievances and proposals for reform, most of the lower clergy had proposed the election of bishops by the clergy and redistribution of clerical property, so that the lower clergy would come to share in the wealth, and had agreed with the *cahiers* of the Third Estate in proposing reform of the tithing system and the suppression of religious orders.

Despite the lower clergy's revolutionary views, the clergy in general were characterized as reactionary. It was common knowledge that the people of Paris had little use for priests. George Rudé cites at least two instances of this popular anti-clericalism. As early as 1752 the Archbishop of Paris was "mobbed in the streets" after he was condemned by the Parlement of Paris for refusing the last sacraments to a dying nun suspected of Jansenism.[5] In 1789 there was a popular riot against a priest who had refused to bury a carpenter without full payment of the burial fee: the mob stormed the church and forced the priest to say a requiem mass.[6] These instances, before and at the very beginning of the Revolution, are not indicative of popular support for Jansenism or even sympathy for the poor; similar incidents occurred thirty years later during the Restoration, when priests were threatened for denying the last sacraments to persons suspected of holding revolutionary views. They indicate a popular anticlerical view that the clergy have no right to sit in final judgment upon a person's life, but their function is to administer the sacraments to all who ask for them.

Beyond these incidents, there is ample evidence of a more

widespread hostility toward priests. Rudé records that in the fall of 1789 crowds shouted, "A bas la calotte" (down with priests), at processions in the streets of Paris.[7] Aside from such spontaneous hostility (which involved no bodily harm to the clergy and, coming on the heels of philosphe anticlericalism, probably did not even disturb their poise), the common people of Paris tended to a rather harmless anticlericalism. Adrien Dansette sees them as more apathetic than anything.[8] Although Jacques Hébert's anticlerical newspaper *Le Père Duchesne* had wide circulation, the bulk of anticlericalism during the Revolution was political and not social. Undoubtedly popular hostility against the clergy played a role in the Revolution, but at most it was a murmuring undercurrent of approval of anticlerical legislation rather than the soul-satisfying violence of the social anticlerical.

*

When the National Assembly met, the clergy voluntarily gave up all of their feudal rights, including the tithe. Many supported legislation expropriating clerical property, lands which only the wealthy clergy controlled anyway. In the debates on expropriation, the overriding argument was that the sale of church lands would ease the state's fiscal crisis, which had led to the calling of the Estates General in the first place. Mirabeau, one of the leaders of the Assembly, argued that "utility is the highest law." Accordingly, the clergy's lands were expropriated in November, 1789.

The consequences were long lasting. The peasant proprietors who eventually came to own much of this land lent stability to French society throughout the nineteenth century. Immediately in 1789, those conservatives who owned the *assignats* (a form of currency based upon the value of the lands) had a vested interest in the success of the Revolution and thus were generally unwilling to support the clergy later in the extreme phases of the Revolution. The clergy, in recompense for their properties, became salaried and therefore employees of the state, and the loss of economic power inhibited their ability to impose a regime of clericalism upon society.

After dealing with the land question, the Assembly legislated against the regular clergy. Characterized as drones and threats to the security of the state, all orders not engaged in education or social work were suppressed in 1789 and 1790. Monastic vows lost their legal force, and those who wished to leave the orders were offered pensions. Although clerical control of education was not yet the burning issue it became in the nineteenth century, the Assembly removed control of the schools from episcopal authority and turned it over to civil officials.

The Revolution entered a more radical anticlerical phase in 1790. The Assembly passed the Civil Constitution of the Clergy, which regularized the civil status of the clergy, a move made necessary by the confusion of the anticlerical laws. By the Civil Constitution of the Clergy, dioceses were redistricted, the clergy were forbidden to recognize the authority of any foreign bishop (the pope), cathedral chapters were suppressed and replaced by councils of vicars who had the right to veto any episcopal actions, and all ecclesiastical offices, from bishop down to pastor, were made elective by all French citizens (including non-Catholics) under that cleric's geographical jurisdiction. All clergy had to take an oath of allegiance to the government to carry out the terms of the legislation.

The event provoked a schism in the French Church. The Pope condemned the legislation, while the clergy were divided into juring (those who took the oath) and the nonjuring (those who refused). The nonjuring clergy were deprived of both their salaries and their parishes, and the government branded them traitors. Civil war broke out in some provinces between laity who supported opposing sides. In a sense, this division was deeper than any other caused by the Revolution, and it persisted down to the twentieth century.

The Assembly soon ordered all nonjurors to take the oath or be placed under surveillance as potential enemies of the state. By 1792 all remaining religious orders were suppressed (including women's orders, which had not been affected up to this time). Wearing clerical garb in public was prohibited, possibly as an attempt to make the clergy less distinct. As a result, nonjurors began emigrating, thereby adding to the problems of clericalism in the countries to which they moved. Many others went underground.

This was also the year of the September massacres. As the war intensified with the threat of a royalist attack on Paris, a number of royalists and priests were imprisoned. With the populace whipped up to a fever pitch by rumors of the approaching invasion, about 250 priests along with 800 other victims were set upon and murdered. It was the first violent anticlerical action, but it was political in nature, with no indication of the workings of social anticlericalism.[9]

By the year of the Terror, 1793, the campaign against the clergy had entered its most radical phase. Churches in Paris were closed and transformed into temples of reason. The local communes were given complete authority to do as they wished with their priests. Clerical salaries and pensions were abolished even for the juring clergy, and any priest denounced as a nonjuror by two witnesses was subject to the death penalty. The only exceptions to these repressive laws were for those priests who married; indeed, some were given the choice between marriage and death. Anticlericalism also entered a symbolic phase. Many of the most anticlerical communes changed street names from those of saints to classical or revolutionary figures. So intense did the anticlerical fury become that statues were taken from churches and guillotined, an act of iconoclasm that had overtones of social anticlericalism.

After Thermidor (1794), the radical phase of the Revolution was ended, and although the anticlerical legislation was not repealed, it was enforced only sporadically, depending on the needs and circumstances of the various governments. But anticlericalism had done its damage, and one important consequence was an increase in clericalism. The exiled nonjuring clergy began to return to France, much more reactionary and clerical than when they had left. They called for a counter-revolution, and in the more conservative areas of

France, clericals formed bands who roamed the countryside attacking anticlericals and persons suspected of anticlerical leanings. Those clergy who were not clerical in 1789 became so by 1799; they had seen the extremes to which anticlericalism led and they wanted no more of it.

On the Revolution in general, Dansette comments: "[It] was responsible for developing and spreading throughout France an active hostility to the Church that had been merely embryonic outside intellectual circles in the [eighteenth century]." By 1800, anticlericalism had made inroads among the populace. "A member of the Council of State entrusted with the task of inspecting the country explained . . . in graphic terms: 'the people would have preferred church bells without priests to priests without bells.' "[10]

When Napoleon came to power in 1799, his practical anticlericalism replaced the revolutionaries' ideological type. The perfect example of a practical anticlerical, he placed the clergy on a par with everyone else in France: they could be used to further his aims (although he did feel that monks were a lazy and "unprofitable" lot).[11] He wanted to settle the church-state controversy and make the clergy acceptable, if somewhat harmless, servants of the state. The clergy did not object, for he promised them protection from the anticlerical legislation. He concluded the Concordat of 1801 with the Pope: this instrument revoked the Civil Constitution of the Clergy, gave the state the right to appoint bishops, and reinstated clerical salaries. The problem of the divided clergy was settled by inviting all nonjuring priests to return, absolving married clerics, and forcing all bishops to resign so that Napoleon could appoint his own men. Church buildings were returned to the clergy, but the expropriation of clerical lands was not revoked, and the clergy were forbidden to purchase new buildings or property.

Nothing was said about the regular clergy, who remained banned under the laws of the Revolution. In 1804, Napoleon decreed a law which distinguished between those associations having the right to possess property and those not—in effect, allowing the state to decide which orders could resume functioning. He allowed women's orders to return, and certain missionary orders were reestablished.

The clergy became servants of the state. They preached civic obedience and respect for authority (making them open to anticlerical attacks in the future). There were fewer vocations, and the numbers of clergy declined. In order to remedy this situation, the clergy established a system of minor seminaries to promote vocations. The result was two separate school systems, for the bishops had not been allowed to resume control of the state school system, although religious instruction was part of the curriculum.

After the Empire began to decline in 1808-1809, Napoleon imprisoned the Pope, discontinued subsidies to the foreign missions, and made the clergy in some areas subject to military conscriptions. Some of the clergy withheld their support of the regime. In any event, the state controlled them all. As Sturzo comments, "What would survive of the Napoleonic experiment . . . would be on the one hand the laicization of absolute power following upon that of democratic power . . . and on the other hand the achievement of a concordat that lasted nearly a century, and a system of perpetual police control of the Church which future laic-jurisdictionalist governments would find useful."[12]

*

With the coming of the Restoration in 1815, a period of extreme clericalism began. The clergy, lacking the confidence that comes with strength, overracted.

The Church was weak; the clergy were few and were absolutely dependent upon the state.[13] The monarchy was also weak and feared revolution, as did the clergy. Each leaned on the other for support, and the clergy came to think that the trappings of power—establishment, ceremonial presence, etc.—gave them the substance of power. Each stressed the consubstantiality of throne and altar, the clergy presumably unaware that by identifying themselves with the regime they would suffer as the regime suffered.

Despite the insecurity of both clergy and crown, there were some strengths. The aristocracy was clerical, because they found it both fashionable and politic to be so, just as before the Revolution they had found it fashionable to be anticlerical. The atmosphere of romanticism lent support to clericalism in its hearkening back to the past and emphasis on emotion and mystery. Chateaubriand and deMaistre, clerical romantics, were widely read.

In the balance, then, the clergy were clericals because they feared revolutionary upheaval. Having survived the Revolution, they valued the institutional well-being of the Church above all else and exhibited the typically human response of aggressiveness in time of weakness. And if the clericals identified the trappings of power with the possession of it, the anticlericals believed in this myth also.

The anticlericals overestimated the strength of the clergy and supposed that an attack upon them would remove the strongest prop of the absolutist monarchy. Moreover, the clergy were relatively easy to attack (as compared with the government). Actually, the situation was just the reverse: it was the government that supported the clergy, and without its backing the clergy would have had little power. The anticlerical attack led the clergy to entrench themselves with the government and served to rally lukewarm Catholics to the clerical cause. Few anticlericals realized their error until the latter half of the nineteenth century, and by that time clericalism was much more difficult to remove.

*

The reign of Louis XVIII from 1814 to 1824 was marked by reactionary clerical legislation, but without implementation. Neither the middle classes nor the aristocracy were interested in the implementation of measures which might hurt them. As a result, clerical legislation served merely to antagonize anticlericals without actually diminishing their power. Had the clergy possessed the Inquisition or some other effective instrument, they might have eliminated the anticlericals; as it was, their aggressiveness served only to antagonize. A clear example of this was the law directed at the press outlawing "grave offenses against religion." Not only did this offend the anticlericals, but the newspapers brought to trial were never silenced; indeed, censorship made the anticlerical press more popular.

Other legislation prohibited divorce and cut off pensions to married priests (holdouts from the Revolution). Clerical salaries were increased, and the Jesuits (reinstated by Pius VII in 1814) and the other regular clergy returned (although none of the suppression laws was formally rescinded). All forms of petty clericalism appeared in the smaller towns of France. One of the most unpopular was the refusal of church burial to those who had not lived in conformity with clerical standards. Many rural Frenchmen were anticlerical because the clergy threatened to take back the lands lost during the Revolution. In a penetrating essay on private anticlericalism, Theodore Zeldin shows that many Frenchmen became anticlerical because the confessional was used by the clergy to discourage simple and harmless pleasures: vestiges of Jansenism remained alive through the nineteenth century.[14] The clergy, however, believed in their own myth, that rural France was clerical at heart and that the peasants would form the base of a "restoration" of clericalism: this against all evidence to the contrary.[15] Nevertheless, it was true that the clericals were stronger in the countryside, where traditional faith was stronger. In some areas clerical organizations were formed so that one had to be a professed clerical to obtain any kind of government sinecure. In addition, the clergy exercised control over many rural schools.

This clerical reaction was surpassed during the reign of Charles X, from 1824 to 1830. With further limitation of suffrage, Charles attempted to impose a completely absolutist regime. He ordered the death penalty for any person found guilty of sacrilege, in particular, profanation of the Sacred Host. Trials of anticlerical newspapers again occurred with frequency, but most of these were not silenced. The sacrilege law was never implemented.

The anticlerical reaction was predictable. In the schools, an entire generation of students who had clericalism forced upon them turned anticlerical; they were the ones who came to support the anticlericalism of the July Monarchy of 1830. Dansette comments, "The children were inclined [like the clergy] to see a connection between legitimacy and religion [on the one hand] and liberty and irreligion [on the other]— and they preferred the latter."[16]

The Jesuits were the first target, although in fact they hardly represented a threat to anyone (there were only 130 Jesuit priests and 431 seminarians in all of France compared to a presuppression strength in the thousands). Stanley Mellon notes, "The simple truth is that the Jesuits were more of a conservative hope than an actual power: their numbers, strength, and influence . . . were infinitesimal."[17] Ironically, although the Jesuits were even more blindly loyal to the monarchy than any other clergy, the main charge made against them was treason. In 1827, Charles bent to anticlerical pressure and appointed Martignac, an anticlerical, premier. Apparently, even the absolutists were beginning to see that the clergy were fast becoming an albatross around the neck of the monarchy. In 1828, all teachers in France had to declare that they were not members of an unauthorized teaching congregation; this was specifically directed against the Jesuits. Later the same year, Jesuit seminaries were closed by decree, and the number of pupils in all church schools (actually minor seminaries) was limited to 20,000; furthermore, these pupils had to wear religious garb to indicate that they were indeed seminarians.

The intellectual atmosphere as well was becoming distinctly anticlerical. In addition to the enduring literary anticlerical masterpieces of Stendhal and the popular anticlericalism of the press, there were scholarly studies of church-state problems. J. F. Gobeau de la Bilennerie, Abbé Pradt, and Charles Laumier addressed themselves to the problem of Jesuit clericalism. Laumier maintained that men of such ability as the Jesuits simply could not be given power, for they would use it to exalt the aims of their order: they were victims of their historical origins. He admitted that many of the charges against the Jesuits were false, but maintained that history had passed judgment, and it would be folly to allow them to remain in France.[18]

One of the most vociferous anticlerical writers was François de Montlosier. His popular study maintained that hatred of priests was responsible for nearly all of the problems of French history; not the priest themselves, but hatred of them. Thus, he concluded, priests should stay in their churches and not meddle in temporal affairs.[19] Montlosier was a gallican and was bitterly opposed to ultramontanism, which he saw as the root of clericalism.

But the most important and prophetic anticlerical of the entire nineteenth century was the priest Felicité de Lamennais. A prolific writer, he was at first a convinced ultramontane, certain that only undivided allegiance to the papacy could solve the Church's problems. Restoration clericalism, he claimed, was a greater threat to the Church than the Revolution had been. "The Restoration monarchy subsidizes religion the same way it does horse breeding."[20]

By 1828 he came to feel that the Church should embrace democracy and he proposed freedom of worship and disestablishment; he also urged the clergy to interest themselves in the needs of the working classes. Despite (or because of) the opposition of the bishops (whom he called "tonsured lackeys"), by 1830 he was certainly the most popular Catholic reformer in France, and his periodical *L'Avenir* attracted many of the younger clergy and laymen, in particular Lacordaire and Montalembert.

In 1831, he appealed to Pope Gregory XVI to support his democratic ideas. Gregory rejected him and condemned his ideas in the encyclical *Mirari Vos*. After this blow, Lamennais became at first convinced that the Pope, whom he once had upheld as the only hope for mankind, was a prisoner of the *zelanti*, but then he came to realize that Gregory was very much his own man, if anything, the leader of the *zelanti.* Eventually Lamennais maintained that freedom and Catholicism were incompatible, but that Christianity and democracy were consubstantial. He died unreconciled to the Church of Gregory. The whole affair turned many of his followers anticlerical and had a great impact on the Catholic romantics, particularly Lamartine, de Vigny, and Victor Hugo.

*

The Revolution of 1830 and the establishment of Louis Philippe's July Monarchy was partly an anticlerical reaction to Restoration clericalism. In the overthrow of Charles X there was some violent anticlericalism, and seminaries and rectories were attacked and burned. Although resembling social anticlericalism, the attacks were apparently the work of extreme political anticlericals. Philip Spencer cites evidence that the violence, while carried out by the mob, was actually subsidized by middle-class political anticlericals.[21] No priests were attacked, although most prudently stayed indoors for a few weeks. If indeed the bourgeoisie were subsidizing violence, they were setting a dangerous precedent for the social anticlericalism of later times.

With the well-to-do firmly in control of the government, clerical salaries were decreased, religious instruction in the state schools was abolished, along with the military chaplaincy, and the 1828 decrees against the Jesuits were strictly enforced. The Carthusians, Trappists, and Franciscans were expelled from the country.

The clergy were silent. There were no condemnations from either the papacy or the French clergy, who probably wisely realized that their fortunes were tied up with those of the state and complaints would only bring about the complete abolition of clerical salaries. As a result, the government soon ended its anticlerical policy. By 1833, clerical salaries were increased, the expelled religious orders returned, religious instruction was allowed in the state elementary schools, and religious elementary schools were given legal rights.

But this was only a partial solution to the educational problem, for the clergy, rapidly becoming more ultramontane, wanted influence in the secondary schools. The middle class, pleased to have the clergy teach obedience in the elementary schools, was just as determined to keep clericalism out of the upper-level schools, heavily patronized by middle-class children. Thus, the government enforced a law prohibiting graduates from Catholic secondary schools from enrolling in the universities.

By 1845, anticlerical tension was again increasing. The July Monarchy was becoming more unyielding every day, while some of the clergy were beginning to oppose the regime. The layman Montalembert attempted to organize a Catholic political party (which never materialized because of episcopal opposition). The educational struggle and the sensation caused by the publication of Eugène Sue's *The Wandering Jew,* a violently anti-Jesuit novel, impelled the government to action: it decided to implement the never rescinded 1764 law of suppression against the Jesuits. François Guizot, the prime minister, asked the Pope to recall the Jesuits before the government was forced to take action, and Gregory agreed. In one of the last acts of his pontificate, Gregory ordered the Jesuits to close some of their establishments, and the government announced that the Society of Jesus had ceased to exist in France.

*

The 1848 Revolution, which overthrew the July Monarchy, was in marked contrast to earlier upheavals. Aside from the isolated instance of burning a monastery at Bourg, there was no political anticlericalism; in fact, the clergy were eagerly sought as allies by the lower middle-class revolutionaries. The clergy became a powerful factor in the election of a constituent assembly, for they could deliver the rural vote. Furthermore, this political intrusion was not widely resented.[22]

Three factors prevented the rise of political anticlericalism. First, the clergy had not given wholehearted support to the July Monarchy, and by the mid 1840s many of the clergy as well as laity supported the revolutionary forces. Second, the accession of Pius IX as pope in 1846 had greatly enhanced the image of the papacy as a force for liberal reform. In the first two years of his pontificate, Pius showed promise of being a reformer, and his election was widely hailed by liberals and constructive anticlericals.

The most important factor was the rise of social unrest and the realization by both the middle class and the clergy that it would be to their mutual benefit to join hands to suppress radical social dissent. The proletarian movement had grown as the industrial revolution had spread through France. Its force was evident in the 1848 Revolution and in the popularity of the writings of Pierre Joseph Proudhon, the most articulate social anticlerical of the nineteenth century. This prolific writer claimed that justice and religion were incompatible and that the abolition of the Church was a necessary prerequisite for the establishment of a social utopia. He maintained that the clergy taught concepts absolutely incompatible with the aims of a just and progressive society.[23] Proudhon's rage against the clergy was so great that he penned the lines, "Is there a single honest man in France today who does not say to himself: 'Shall I die without killing a priest?' "[24]

Despite Proudhon, social anticlericalism in France never became as violent as in other countries. Rather, the French proletariat simply deserted the established Church. It would be interesting to speculate on this phenomenon: perhaps the French proletariat had become too secularized for the love-hate relationship with the clergy that the Spanish proletariat had, resulting in the latter's violent social anticlericalism.

The clergy were motivated by fear, just as were the middle-class anticlericals. They misjudged the force of the proletariat and the influence the working classes would soon come to have. Some Catholics, such as Lacordaire, Ozanam, and Maret, did attempt a modern approach to social problems, but their efforts received scant support from most of the clergy. A tacit alliance had already been made with the middle class in the name of law and order. The upper middle class dropped its traditional anticlericalism and became

"Christians by fear." Ozanam put it well: "There is not a Voltairean burdened with an income of a few thousand francs who is not anxious to send everybody to Mass, provided he does not have to go himself."[25]

Thus, when Napoleon III established the Second Empire, the clergy wholeheartedly supported his program of law and order, family, and property. Napoleon III, like his uncle, used the clergy to his own advantage. For the first decade of his reign, the Emperor carried out a policy pleasing to the clericals. He sent troops to Rome to protect the Pope against the Italian nationalists, went into the Crimean War ostensibly to protect the Holy Places against the infidel, and allowed the return of the Jesuits to France. The clergy took advantage of his attitude and increased their property holdings.

What cemented the alliance between the clergy and the regime (Montalembert called it a coalition between "the guardroom and the sacristy")[26] was the Falloux law. This provided for the entrance of Catholic-school graduates into the universities and gave the bishops power to formulate academic policy in the state school system. Within a few years the numbers of Catholic secondary schools had greatly increased.[27]

The natural result of the clergy's privileged position was anticlericalism. On the national level, anticlericalism erupted as a protest against the Emperor's Italian policy. On the local level, Roger Magraw comments: "The opportunities for friction [between clergy and local officials] within the villages were infinite."[28] Disputes over the expenses of rebuilding and remodeling churches, the schools, and clerical disapproval of what they considered immoral behavior on the part of local townspeople were more or less constant, adding to the tension that eventually burst out after the fall of Napoleon.

Napoleon was aware of these feelings, and he knew that he had to appease the anticlericals as well as the clergy. In 1861 he began to allow the anticlerical press to operate freely, and he appointed Victor Drury, an anticlerical, his minister of education. Drury established a system of state secondary schools for girls, thereby invading a traditional convent preserve.

Certainly, the main intellectual current remained anticlerical. Michelet, Quinet, Hugo, Renan, and Littré were a few of the great writers who stressed anticlerical themes. The rise of Comtian positivism also influenced anticlericalism by emphasizing scientific investigation that shattered many traditional Christian beliefs. The clergy were unable to answer these critics; since 1814 they had been educated in piety and theology, and scientifically trained clergy were rare.

Freemasonic lodges came to play an increasingly important role by providing secret meeting places for the republican opposition to the regime. The bonds forged in the lodges carried through into the anticlerical atmosphere of the Third Republic.

During the entire period from the Restoration to the fall of the Second Empire in 1870, the great number of anticlerical writings speaks volumes, not only about the machinations of the clericals, but also about the freedom anticlericals actually had.

*

When the Napoleonic regime was toppled in 1870, an anticlerical surge was released that carried through until the Separation Laws of 1905.[29] Practically all of this anticlericalism was political and moderate; the only violence occurred in 1871 when the Parisians established the Commune.

The communards were both violent political anticlericals and social anticlericals. They separated church and state and nullified all of the clerical laws, "because the clergy have been accessories to the crimes of the monarchy against France."[30] They looted churches, turned them into guardrooms and storehouses, and killed twenty-nine priests, including the Archbishop of Paris. It is difficult to call them all social anticlericals, because Paris was besieged by the moderate forces of the National Government, and the communards were reacting to a military situation not unlike that which produced the September Massacre of 1792. Many

of the wealthier Parisians were also attacked and killed.[31]
*

When the Commune was suppressed, a distinctly monarchist and clerical National Government took over power in France. The military chaplaincy was restored, and the clergy were given the right to establish universities. But anticlericalism was still the most dynamic movement in France after 1870. With the removal of restrictions, anticlericals became publicly active and gained seats in the National Assembly. However, it was not until 1876 that the anticlericals won control of the chamber of deputies and not until 1879 that they captured the senate and the presidency.

When they finally came to power, the anticlericals had enough charges against the clergy to last for three decades. The most important of these was the clergy's support for a royalist restoration. Rectories were turned over for use by royalists, and the clergy regularly denounced republican candidates from the pulpit. What particularly bothered the anticlericals was that the clergy were in effect salaried civil servants supporting what the anticlericals considered a treasonable party.

Another reason for the anticlerical reaction was the attitude of Pope Pius IX. His Syllabus of Errors of 1864 had denounced everything the republicans stood for: progress, toleration, secularism, and liberalism. Furthermore, the promulgation of the dogma of papal infallibility in 1870 was a gesture of defiance against all anticlericals. The Pope was telling the world that only he could direct Catholics in their beliefs. This infuriated the anticlericals, and they were horrified by the royalist-clerical proposal in 1872 that the government once again send French troops to restore the Pope to possession of Rome (the Napoleonic troops in Rome had been recalled at the outbreak of the Franco-Prussian War in 1870).

Positivism gave impetus to the ideological anticlericals. Comte and Littré were the intellectual godfathers of republican anticlericalism. The anticlericals came to believe that they were on the threshold of the positivistic age and there would be no need for priests. The popularity of what they considered superstitions, such as the miracle at Lourdes, made them even more determined to eradicate clericalism.

The anticlericals were also inspired by the spirit of nationalism. They wanted a school system permeated with patriotism, and, although there was no evidence that the clergy were less than patriotic, the issue of allegiance to a foreign prince (the pope) was raised. There was also a rather sneaking admiration for the Prussians, who had just defeated them, and the erroneous assumption that the Prussian school system was free from clerical influence.

There were also some nonreligious motives behind republican anticlericalism. It could be used as the bond of the governing coalition. Economic gains could be realized from the confiscation of clerical properties, and the large number of bureaucratic and academic sinecures held by the clergy could be taken by the anticlericals. Anticlericalism was also used as leverage in foreign policy, both as a substitute for the policy of revenge against Germany until the French could be rearmed and to urge the Italian anticlerical government to enter the French alliance system.

Finally, the fact cannot be overlooked that the anticlericals had history on their side. They were reacting to a century of clericalism. In 1848 the clergy had had their chance: they had entered a new era with clean hands and had supported the revolutionaries; but immediately thereafter they had collaborated with Napoleon III to establish a regime of clericalism. The clergy could not be trusted. In 1876 the anticlericals grasped the opportunity to rid France forever of the stranglehold of clericalism.

The Freemasons played an important role in the Third Republic. Every important government minister was a Freemason. There were numerous lodges throughout the country. Acomb estimates that in 1876 there were over 200,000 active Freemasons in France (compared to 30,000 religious clergy and 130,000 nuns in the same year).[32] The

Freemasons conducted anticlerical education programs, distributed anticlerical literature (attesting to a high degree of popular anticlericalism), and generally lobbied anticlerical legislation through the Assembly. Freemasonry was, however, just a vehicle: Dansette notes that "the Republican party and Freemasonry were subject to the same intellectual influences and underwent a continuous process of osmosis and endosmosis. They were, therefore, naturally inclined to adopt the same solutions to problems and there is no reason to assume that they were under a common direction."[33]

*

Moderate political anticlericals dominated the Assembly from 1876 to 1899; the radicals controlled legislation after that. The two differed in that the moderates wanted to maintain the Concordat of 1801 as a means of control over the clergy, because this gave the government the right to nominate bishops, along with the power to increase or dimish clerical salaries. The radicals wanted complete separation of church and state through abrogation of the Concordat. Both aimed to restrict the regular clergy and to remove clerical influence from education.

Léon Gambetta, premier in 1881-1882, was the most active moderate anticlerical. He coined such epithets as "vaticanist," "monkish," and "syllabic" when referring to clericals. He delivered the memorable speech in the Assembly which concluded with the phrase, "Le cléricalisme — voilà l'ennemi!" Supported by the moderates, Jules Ferry, the minister of education; Jules Grévy, the President of the Republic; and Charles Freycinet and Jules Simon, Gambetta led the attack against the clericals.

Most of the moderate anticlerical legislation was passed between 1879 and 1886.[34] The Jesuits were suppressed again, and all nonauthorized male religious orders were ordered to apply for authorization. After a few months, those who had not applied were suppressed and were expelled from their houses, although their property was not sold.

The entire state school system was ordered secularized.

Church universities were deprived of the right to grant degrees. The faculties of Catholic theology in the state universities were suppressed (the Protestant faculties were not). The clergy were removed from the boards of public instruction, and religious education in the state secondary and primary schools was abolished. Primary education was made free, lay, and compulsory. Because large numbers of regular clergy still taught in the state schools, that part of the Falloux law which allowed a declaration of obedience to the bishop as a substitute for the possession of a teaching certificate was repealed, although this was softened to the extent that it did not apply to those clergy over thirty-five. Finally, in 1886, the Assembly legislated the removal of all male regular clergy from the state elementary schools within five years; nuns were to be replaced as the occasion arose.

The clergy protested these laws. When primary education was secularized, the bishops responded by placing all new lay textbooks on the Index of Forbidden Books. The government responded in turn by suspending the salaries of those priests who read the episcopal decrees from the pulpit. Despite such confrontations, the laws were never fully implemented. After the first spate of anticlerical legislation, the government closed its eyes to violations of the laws. The nonauthorized clergy returned to possession of their houses, and in some of the more Catholic areas of France the laws were not implemented at all.

The reason for the government's inaction was the increasing conservatism of moderate anticlericals. Occasionally they had to give in to radical pressure, but as the proletarian forces grew in strength, moderate anticlericals began to view the clergy as a force for stability. Indeed, there was a tacit alliance between the upper middle class and some of the clericals against the radical anticlericals and the proletarians. Gambetta, in particular, was charged with using anticlerical sound and fury, but no action, as a "red herring" to cover up the regime's unwillingness to undertake social reform.

The attitude of the new pope, Leo XIII, was also a factor.

He urged the clericals to moderation, (although, saddled with Pius IX's reactionary bishops, he did not have the success he wanted) and he asked French Catholics to accept the Republic and to form a political union (the *ralliement)* to combat anticlerical legislation within the legal framework of the Republic. His attitude mollified the moderate anticlericals, but he antagonized the radicals, who termed the *ralliement* "clerical liberalism." He also antagonized the clerical monarchists, who became political antipapists (while remaining clericals in every other way). This was the first modern example of the phenomenon of clerical backlash against a liberal clergy. The royalists considered Leo's activities an abuse of papal authority. As Dansette puts it, "They objected to the assumption that the political control of Frenchmen who were Catholic was in the hands of the Pope."[35] Furthermore, Leo had additional problems with many farsighted Catholic liberals who felt that his concept of papal interference might set a dangerous precedent for future reactionary clerical popes who, using the same principles, might just as easily condemn the Republic and encourage a royalist restoration. Leo was the first modern pontiff to experience the pitfalls of clerical progressivism.

*

By 1899 the moderate anticlericals were losing power, and the stage was set for a new anticlerical reaction. This was in part provoked by the clergy's support of the anti-Dreyfusards in the Dreyfus Affair (the Assumptionists played a particularly strong role), and partly by the rise of the socialist party as an influence on parliamentary legislation.

There had been little proletarian social anticlericalism since the Paris Commune. There were plenty of social anticlerical writers, such as Fernand Pelloutier, August Blanqui, and Georges Sorel, whose *Reflections on Violence* was instrumental in shaping the technique of violence in other countries. But the French themselves did not resort to anticlerical violence; the government was avowedly anticlerical and there appeared no further need for anticlerical action. Furthermore, the socialist party was controlled by Jules Guesde, who was opposed to both anticlerical violence and legislation, which he considered a bourgeois dodge to turn proletarian attention away from what he felt to be the real source of France's troubles, the irresponsibility of the middle class. Guesde saw clearly that clericalism was not a threat to the Republic.

In the elections of 1902, however, the socialists lost strength, and Guesde was replaced by Jean Jaurès. Jaurès proposed that the socialists support anticlerical legislation as a means of dividing the middle class: the radical anticlericals could use their support, the moderates would be alienated, and the socialists could thereby drive a wedge between the two middle-class factions. In fact, the moderates had become more radical as a consequence of the Dreyfus Affair and were now willing to support more stringent laws. This accounts for the ease with which anticlerical legislation was passed in the years from 1902 to 1905.

The radical anticlericals differed from the moderates in that they aimed at the abrogation of the Concordat and the actual implementation of the anticlerical laws. The chief radical anticlerical politicians were Émile Combes and Georges Clemenceau ("The clergy must learn to render to Caesar what is Caesar's . . . and must also learn that everything belongs to Caesar").[36] These two were matched in their passion by the reactionary clericalism of Pope Pius X, who replaced Leo XIII in 1903. Pius made absolutely clear his intention to intervene in political affairs whenever they touched the interests of the Church. Both clerical and anticlerical intransigency heightened tension to the breaking point.[37]

René Waldeck-Rousseau, whose ministry lasted from 1899 to 1902, was a moderate anticlerical, but in order to stay in power he had to implement anticlerical legislation. He applied the Law of Associations to the religious orders. Originally designed as a measure of control over labor unions, this law required government authorization for all associations of over twenty members. It was made applicable to the clergy, who were also still bound by the Napoleonic laws requiring government authorization for their legal establishment. Waldeck-Rousseau ordered the Assumptionists dissolved and all other nonauthorized orders (only five male orders had been authorized since 1805) to apply for authorization within three months.

The governmental decree was not fully implemented, however, until Émile Combes, a former seminarian turned physician, became premier in 1902. He ordered the regular clergy to apply for authorization under pain of suppression, and as the requests came in the Assembly rejected them. As a result, schools, hospitals, and asylums all over France were closed. Finally, in 1904, the Assembly took the ultimate step against the orders: all orders, authorized or not, were forbidden to teach in France, in private or public schools. In addition, all houses of the regular clergy were ordered closed within ten years, and their property was to be expropriated. Over the next seven years, this law was actually implemented.

Pius X responded with condemnations, and the French government severed diplomatic relations with the Vatican. In 1905, the government abrogated the Concordat of 1801. Church and state were separated; the clergy no longer had official status, nor were they to receive salaries. Church buildings, which legally had belonged to the state ever since the Civil Constitution of the Clergy of 1790, were to be turned over to associations of laymen and municipal officials. They in turn could lease them to religious associations if application were made. The Pope condemned this law as well.

During the entire period from 1879 to 1905 other anticlerical legislation had been passed. Holding processions required permission from municipal authorities. Cemeteries were secularized. The military chaplaincy was abolished, and seminarians were conscripted into the army. All of the later laws evoked protests from the Vatican, whereas the French bishops, many of them appointees of Leo XIII, acted cautiously.

*

After 1905, political anticlericalism ceased to be an issue. There was little further action the government could take: the regular clergy were suppressed, the clergy were no longer paid by the state, and public education was out of clerical hands. Furthermore, as international tensions increased, the need for internal unity not only overcame considerations of domestic politics, but also gave the government a more valid bond of unity. By 1912 the anticlerical laws had been quietly relaxed, and many of the regular clergy were returning to the possession of their houses and to teaching in the Catholic schools.

World War I probably had more to do with healing the anti-clerical rift than any other single event. The need for internal unity was clear. As soon as the war broke out, the military chaplaincy was reestablished, and as the war dragged on, 45,000 priests who had been conscripted while seminarians were called up with their reserve classes to serve in the French armies. Their actions laid to rest any notions that the clergy were less patriotic than anticlericals. Furthermore, many of these priests formed lifelong companionships with their fellow soldiers, thereby breaking down many of the traditional barriers between clergy and laity. The government suspended the 1904 laws of suppression, and practicing Catholics served in the ministry for the first time since 1876.

The diehards still kept up their verbal attacks. They claimed that the clergy had sent funds to Germany to promote the war so as to weaken the Republic and hasten a restoration. They also contended that the conscripted clergy were assigned to rear-echelon jobs in the army (a charge demonstrably untrue, for 5,000 clergy were killed in action). Diehard clericals retorted that the war was a divine punishment upon an anticlerical nation.

But harmony was more evident than tension. After the war the government reestablished diplomatic relations with the Vatican, and reached a *modus vivendi* with Pope Pius XI on the status of church property. All the other anticlerical laws remained on the books, but the government tempered them with moderation. The regular clergy flourished, and students in Catholic schools, although down in numbers from the 1880s, still numbered one-fifth of the French children.

In 1924 a leftist government under Édouard Herriot took office. Commanding a slim majority in the Assembly, and apparently needing the issue of anticlericalism to hold his government together, Herriot announced his intention of implementing the anticlerical legislation. Protests, especially from veterans' groups, forestalled immediate action, and Herriot's ministry fell before he had a chance to carry out the laws. It was the last concerted attempt to implement official political anticlericalism in France.[38]

Pope Pius XI, who assumed the pontificate in 1922, although a moderate clerical, helped to end the tension. One problem was the *Action Française,* an ultraroyalist nationalistic organization which had long supported the clerical cause. Its leader was Charles Maurras, a gifted journalist supported by many clericals, including bishops, who had repeatedly made extreme statements that the Vatican could not support. So blatant was Maurras' use of religion to further his political aims that the reactionary clerical Pius X had placed the organization's periodical on the Index, although he did not make the decree public. Pius XI publicly condemned the organization in 1926.

The reaction, if predictable, provided an interesting twist to the history of anticlericalism in France. Maurras refused to submit and complained that the Pope was abusing his authority by intervening in political affairs, essentially the same charge that royalists had made against Leo XIII at the time of the *ralliement.* Maurras' periodical, subscribed to mainly by clericals, became the most rabidly anticlerical publication in France, dredging up all of the real and mythical anticlerical cases of the past.[39] The Pope eventually forced one of Maurras' chief supporters, Cardinal Billot, to resign. But the incident took on less importance as international tension developed in the 1930s.

After the fall of France in 1940 and the establishment of

the Vichy regime, Pétain's government formally repealed the 1904 laws against the regular clergy. Although clericals supported Pétain, enough of the clergy helped deGaulle's resistance movement that there was no cause for anticlericalism after World War II. In fact, so quickly did anticlericalism disappear that in 1959, shortly after the proclamation of the Fifth Republic, the Gaullist regime legislated the Debré law, which granted state financial aid to the Catholic schools.

The only significant anticlericalism after 1940 was an outbreak of reactionary social anticlericalism against the worker-priest movement. This experiment, in which priests volunteered to take on factory jobs and live and work along with the proletariat in order to bring these classes back to the Church, was started in 1940. It drew sharp criticism from the conservatives and middle classes, especially after 1945, when many of the worker-priests joined and assumed positions of leadership in the CGT, which was affiliated with the communist party. Following strikes led by worker-priests and anti-American protests in the early 1950s the Vatican curtailed the experiment in 1954 and suppressed it altogether in 1959.

CHAPTER 10

Spain

*In Spain everyone follows the Church: half with a
candle, the other half with a club.*

Spanish proverb

IF FRANCE HAS BEEN CONSIDERED A CLASSICAL ANTICLERI-
cal arena, it is only because the French struggle preceded
those in other countries. Actually, Spain has had a greater
variety of anticlericalism and was the only country where violent social anticlericalism became a more powerful force than
political anticlericalism.[1]

There were no neutrals in Spain. Everyone was caught up
with the religious struggle. There are many reasons for this
preoccupation; certainly, an important factor was the militant
crusading mentality developed during the centuries-long
struggle against the Moslems which carried over into the
discovery and settlement of the New World and into the
Council of Trent.

By the eighteenth century, when the decline of the Empire
had set in (although temporarily stopped by Bourbon
reforms), Spain was already divided into two peoples, the
"two Spains."[2] One was liberal progressive, urban, and anticlerical (and small); the other, conservative, rural, clerical,
and traditionalist (and large). These two factions have
struggled against each other ever since. At times the conflict
exploded into civil war; at others it was simmering beneath

123

the surface. At root, it was a psychological problem: Spain had once controlled the world and now she was a second-rate power. How could her greatness be restored?

Liberal Spain insisted that the nation must pursue a national policy rather than a Catholic one. The Empire had declined because Catholic interests had predominated over Spanish ones. History had proved that the policies of traditionalist Spain had failed. Spain must adopt new ways, modern and progressive ones. Clerical influence must be done away with, and Spain must get into the mainstream of Europe.

Traditionalist Spain viewed the decline of the Empire as the result of the baneful influence of liberals and progressives. Enlightened despotism and cismontane policies had ruined Spain. She must look to her crusading past to recapture the spirit that had once made her great. Marcelino Menéndez y Pelayo, Spain's leading intellectual traditionalist, had summed up this position in the nineteenth century: "In Catholicism is our greatness and unity: there is no other."[3]

Thus, the debate between the two Spains was seen in terms of clericalism and anticlericalism, and the struggle took on much wider dimensions than elsewhere. Exacerbating this tension was the struggle between regionalism and centralism, a conflict with deep roots in the past, with regional interests struggling against governmental attempts to impose centralized administration. In the eighteenth century, centralism took on an anticlerical cast. The crown was cismontane and used the resources of the centralized state to legislate against clerical power. The clergy in response took up the cause of regionalism, and the anti-Bourbon regions became the stronghold of clerical reaction. Until the last half of the nineteenth century, the centralized government of Madrid generally represented the anticlericals, and clerical strength was found in Vasconia, Navarre, and the hinterlands of Catalonia. The anticlerical struggle used and was used by those involved in the centralist-regionalist conflict.

The Spanish Church was a powerful institution. Regalism

was never as powerful in Spain as gallicanism was in France; the clergy retained a great deal of independence. In fact, until the Bourbons came to power the Church was more powerful than the state. There were less clerical abuses in Spain than in most other countries, and there was a strong puritanical element in the Spanish clergy. Nevertheless, decline in ability, character, and prestige was evident in the eighteenth century. Two centuries before, the Spanish clergy had led the Catholic world, not only in intellectual and theological endeavor, but also in the harsh climate of missionary activity. But by 1700 the clergy had become self-indulgent, lazy, and ignorant. They had proliferated to the extent that the Bourbons were concerned about the large numbers of monks and nuns who were not gainfully employed.

The Bourbons took vigorous steps to solve this problem (see chapter 7). Charles IV (1788-1808) continued his father's cismontane policies for a short time, but when the anticlerical excesses of the French Revolution began, he moderated his activities. Strict censorship was imposed upon all anticlerical (and other revolutionary) literature coming in from France, and French clergy seeking refuge in Spain were treated with hospitable suspicion, for fear that they might be tainted with revolutionary ideas. By 1800, however, Charles' new prime minister, Manuel de Godoy, renewed the cismontane policies and decreed the expropriation of the regular clergy's property. Very little of this property was actually taken before the French invaded Spain in 1808, because the regulars were powerful enough to prevent the action.[4]

When Napoleon's troops invaded Spain, the clergy joined the patriots in becoming the leaders of national resistance.[5] They did so partly for reasons of nationalism, as did most other Spaniards, but also because the French brought liberal reforms with them, and the clergy feared revolutionary anticlericalism. Their response and leadership greatly increased their prestige, and much of the strength of clericalism in the ninteenth century derived from the clergy's central role in the greatest moment in Spain's modern history.

The Spanish liberals were another matter. Most of them were patriots and rejected the Napoleonic government, as did the clergy. But they were determined to uproot clericalism. When in 1810 they established a government for Spain in the absence of the King, who was Napoleon's prisoner in France, they formulated an anticlerical constitution. This Constitution of 1812 suppressed all religious communities with less than twelve members and expropriated their property.[6] The liberal government emulated the French regime and abolished the Inquisition. But the liberals' power extended to only a few of the southern coastal towns, and their reforms did not affect most of Spain.

The Napoleonic government began to court liberal Spaniards by decreeing anticlerical reforms. The regular clergy were suppressed and their property confiscated, the Inquisition abolished, and all clergy put under civil law. But their laws had effect only where the force of French arms prevailed; rural Spain was hardly touched by the anticlerical laws.

These anticlerical actions convinced the clericals that the monarch must be restored. Although they had opposed the Bourbons' cismontane anticlericalism, they did not fear the new king, Ferdinand VII. The circumstances in 1814 were quite different from those of a decade earlier. The country had been ruined and the familiar power bases destroyed. There was no money in the treasury and trade with America had slowed to a standstill. Only the clergy had economic power. They had prestige, land, and popular support. Thus, when Napoleon's troops were driven out and Ferdinand restored, he had to base his regime on the clergy's power. They in turn supported him because they could control him.

Ferdinand's regime was in fact marked by clericalism. Unlike the clergy of the French Restoration of 1814, the clergy in Spain were the main power; the King served at their pleasure. Only the transfer of clerical land or an industrial revolution which would create another economic power base could eliminate clericalism. The clergy were opposed to both;

they were determined never to become pawns of the crown again.

All of the anticlerical legislation was annulled. All church property was restored. The Jesuits and the other suppressed clergy returned. Strict censorship was imposed and implemented. The Inquisition was reestablished and became an effective tool in the hands of the clericals.[7] Prominent anticlericals were hunted down and imprisoned or forced into exile. The entire administration of the kingdom was honeycombed with priests; even the prime minister was a priest. It was the most reactionary clerical regime imaginable; even the Papal States, administered by clerics, was not as extreme.

In 1820, liberal revolutionaries with the backing of the army —the other powerful institution in Spain—overthrew the regime, and Ferdinand was forced to take an oath to the reproclaimed Constitution of 1812. Although they still had power, the clericals were frightened and began machinations for a counter-revolution. In response, the anticlericals expelled the Jesuits, abolished the Inquisition again, and carried out numerous acts of violent political anticlericalism. They could not maintain power for long, however, and in 1823 conservative Europe gathered arms and a French army restored Ferdinand to power.

The clericals returned to power, but weaker. The European powers had insisted that the Inquisition remain abolished. The clericals blamed Ferdinand for this, but they were disposed to put up with him because he had no children and would be succeeded by his brother Carlos, a tool of the clericals. They waited a decade for Ferdinand to die, meanwhile losing more of their power as the beginnings of industrialization added to the strength of the middle classes. In 1830, Ferdinand married again and produced an heir, Isabella. With Carlos' succession threatened, the frightened clericals began to plot to overthrow Isabella after she assumed the throne in 1833.

The reactionary clerical movement became connected with this dynastic struggle; its supporters became known as

Carlists.[8] They were extreme clericals, economic pastoralists, and, as their strength was drawn from the northern separatist provinces, they were regionalists. The anticlericals were liberal, urban, mercantile, industrial, and centralists. They supported Isabella because there was political advantage in doing so and because she was subject to fewer clerical influences than was Carlos. In this larger struggle of Carlism against liberalism, all the elements of clerical-anticlerical tensions were present. The liberals were Freemasons and until 1868 supported by the army officers. When the liberals came to power, they tended to divide into factions, which ultimately brought about their downfall. On the other hand, the clericals became involved in the struggle for regional rights, although this was secondary to their chief aim of establishing a theocracy.

Throughout the 1830s civil war raged between the liberals and the Carlists. Two significant events occurred in 1836, both evidence that the Carlists were losing strength. One was an act of violent political anticlericalism: over a hundred Jesuits in Madrid were set upon and murdered. Little is known about this massacre. Apparently, it was touched off by a rumor that the Jesuits had poisoned the wells of Madrid (1836 was the year of the cholera plague); possibly middle-class anticlericals started the rumor and urged the populace against the Jesuits. Certainly it was an indication that the clergy had lost their prestige and that their support of the Carlists was unacceptable to most Spaniards.[9]

The other significant event of 1836 was the beginning of the *desamortización*–expropriation of clerical landed property. Juan Álvarez Mendizábal, an anticlerical premier, effected the passage of the expropriation legislation, which was implemented sporadically over the next three decades.[10] The *desamortización* caused the loss of actual clerical power, because many of the Carlists purchased the property and deserted the Carlist cause.[11] It brought about the same results as the expropriation of clerical property in France in 1789 (except that wealthy men purchased the lands and a peasant-proprietor class was not created in Spain): the clergy, in becoming salaried, were bound to the state and lost much of their vigor and independence. From the time the *desamortización* was finally completed about 1870, there was no longer the possibility of the return of independent clerical power. Liberal regimes, however, whenever they came to power in the following century, still continued to take action against the clergy and pass anticlerical legislation. These actions naturally antagonized not only the clergy, but also lay Catholics who otherwise would have supported the liberal regimes. But liberalism became identified with anticlericalism, and much harm was done to the liberal cause.

The expropriations also forced the clergy into a tacit alliance with the wealthy middle classes, upon whom they now depended for financial support, and they lost the support of the working classes. In the ensuing class struggle, the clergy supported the bourgeoisie, marking the beginning of violent social anticlericalism in Spain.

*

The remainder of the reign of Isabella II was characterized by alternating liberal and conservative coups. Each time the liberals came to power they expelled the Jesuits, restricted the other regular clergy, and continued the expropriation of clerical property. Each time the conservatives came to power they would lift these restrictions, but would leave the expropriated clerical property in the hands of its purchasers. In time, as the power of the Carlists decreased, Isabella became more subject to clerical influence, for she no longer needed the support of the liberals. The royal palace was crowded with such clericals as Sor Patrocinio, the "bleeding nun" (an apparent stigmatic), and St. Antonio María Claret, both of whom urged Isabella to extremist policies. As a result, liberal and anticlerical opposition to Isabella grew.

In 1868, she was overthrown by a liberal coup. During the following six years the country passed through a succession of governments: the politicians sought another monarch (Amadeo of Savoy was selected), eventually established a republic when Amadeo abdicated, and finally restored the

Bourbons in the person of Isabella's son Alfonso XII in 1875.[12] As the various regimes became more liberal and then more radical, they became increasingly anticlerical as well. Anticlerical activity was partly an attempt to unite the liberals, but it was also a reaction against the Carlists, who had once again risen to oppose the anticlerical regimes. All the typical anticlerical actions were taken: expulsion of the Jesuits, restrictions or suppressions of the other regular clergy, and attempts to secularize education—although, in fact, the Spanish educational system was so poor that it needed massive overhauling.

There was also a great deal of violent anticlericalism. Most was extreme political anticlericalism aimed at priests who were considered enemies of the regime. It is not known whether the proletarian classes participated in the violence on their own or at the direction of the middle-class anticlericals, but most of the violence was not markedly dissimilar from other acts of violent anticlericalism earlier in the century.

An exception was the burning of churches. Incendiary anticlericalism was not new; there were numerous examples in other countries during the Reformation and during the attack on the Spanish Jesuits in 1836. But now it occurred on such a large scale and over such an extended period of time—actually lasting (with periods of increasing and diminishing intensity) until the end of the Civil War of 1936-39. Church arson became a typical feature of Spanish anticlericalism.

Although there is evidence that middle-class anticlericals occasionally subsidized such acts, church arson was largely the work of anarchists, of whom in Spain there was a significantly large number. The anarchists were actually romantic rebels; they had more in common with twelfth-century socioeconomic anticlericals than they did with modern anticlericals. Favoring the destruction of all institutions as the prelude to a utopian society, and being both poor men and Spaniards, they singled out the clergy as their chief enemies. They were not antireligious. Rather, they felt that the clergy had betrayed the essence of Christianity with their tacit alliance with the bourgeoisie for temporary economic gain. They felt that there was no solution to the problem other than to get rid of the unworthy priest.[13]

While murder was a capital crime, arson was not. Probably some of the anarchists hoped to convince the clergy that the Millennium was at hand. In any event, their actions were not dictated by strategic considerations: they acted from the heart (which was one reason why they were not very successful). They expressed their anticlericalism in violent fashion because they lived in a violent world and because political action, as they saw it, was neither effective nor open to them.

It is frequently difficult to determine the difference between acts of violent social anticlericalism and violent political anticlericalism. The political anticlericals were not above incendiary acts, and in fact there is little evidence to show who actually burned the churches. Usually the police arrested anarchists, probably because they were the most likely, but not necessarily the most guilty, suspects. Most of the church burnings did occur in areas where the anarchists were numerous.

The violence of social anticlericalism in Spain is indicative, it seems, of a fondness for the clergy in earlier centuries. It would be unusual to have such an intense hatred for the clergy if there had not been an intense attachment earlier. Just as parricide and fratricide are usually more violent and brutal crimes than homicide, so also Spanish social anticlericalism exhibited a violence that could stem only from love.

*

When the upheavals of 1868-1875 subsided, the clergy found themselves in a weakened position, comparable in many respects to that of the French clergy in 1814. Although the governments after 1875 honored the Concordat of 1851, which provided a privileged position for the clergy and paid them salaries, the fact was that the clergy had lost their lands and were dependent upon the state and the wealthy classes for their subsistence. They had the trappings of power: the bishops held seats in the senate of the Spanish Cortes, and civil representatives participated in religious processions, but the clergy had no substance of power. Their dogmatic grip on the people was being loosened; the numbers of practicing Catholics declined rather spectacularly. Nonetheless, the clergy behaved as if they had real power, thereby duping themselves and antagonizing anticlericals.

The violent social and political anticlericalism of the preceding decades had frightened the clergy. They supported the government and the oligarchic classes as bulwarks of law and order. The government likewise favored the clergy as a force for order, and the clergy became identified as the ruling establishment. If the clergy were convinced they could carry out their mission only in an atmosphere of law and order, the lower classes were equally convinced that the clergy had deserted them, for to the proletariat law and order meant oppression and injustice. Each *cacique* (political boss) in every small town was backed by the local priest, upon whom he relied to help turn out the vote in favor of the establishment parties.

Although some of the clergy were clever enough to see that they needed independent financial power, there was little they could do. Rumor claimed the Jesuits were major stockholders in lucrative enterprises, but this allegation was never substantiated.[14] In fact, the clergy's (and particularly the Jesuits') support of the government and the oligarchy disproved the charge of clerical wealth; a financially independent clergy would never have supported the Restoration state.

The clergy had lost their power, but the anticlericals did not recognize this fact. The past half-century had taught them the dangers of clericalism. The defeated Carlists still made noises from their strongholds. The anticlericals found it easier to attack the clergy instead of the oppressive state. The clergy fought back, and Spain became obsessed with anticlericalism. To call a person clerical or anticlerical carried connotations of a whole way of life. As a result, many of the energies of Spain's best minds went into the religious conflict while social and economic problems went unsolved.

Intellectuals and novelists were also obsessed with anticlerical themes.[15] In the late nineteenth century, Benito Pérez Galdós developed them in his novels, and Vicente Blasco Ibáñez claimed that the clergy were frauds and responsible for most of his country's ills. While many of the "Generation of '98" debated national issues—trying to find the reasons for Spain's loss of prestige and proposing various schemes to restore it—intellectuals on both sides of the question were anticlerical. All could agree that Spain's educational system was dominated by an ignorant and superstitious clergy. Joaquín Costa, one of the seminal thinkers of modern Spanish history, urged Spaniards to forget their past if they wished to prosper in the future, and part of forgetting the past was to forget their role as the defenders of Catholicism. Even Miguel de Unamuno, who proposed that Spaniards search more deeply into their past and cultivate those uniquely Spanish virtues that had once made Spain great, had no use for the clergy.

Spanish anticlerical thinkers, however, did not fit into a pattern. Although republicanism and anticlericalism tended to be synonymous. Spaniards were too individualistic to be stereotyped. Pío Baroja displayed radical anticlericalism in his novels, yet he favored the Jesuits and at one time supported the Franco dictatorship. When José Ortega y Gasset wrote that Spain's chief problem was that all of the institutions practiced exclusion without any thought of compromise, he particularly indicted the Church. Certainly, the anticlericals were more dynamic and more widely read than the two chief clerical thinkers, Marcelino Menédez y Pelayo and Juan Vásquez de Mella.

*

The government during the first two decades of the Restoration was controlled by the liberal and conservative parties, indistinguishable except for the latter's more pronounced moderate anticlericalism. The two parties had a tacit agreement to alternate in power, and no significant anticlerical reform was legislated. The clergy prospered under this beneficient system.

By the turn of the century, democratic parties, both middle class and proletariat oriented, had begun to appear. As suffrage was extended, they gained power and clamored for anticlerical legislation. Republican groups also appeared, and anticlericalism became the bond of all reformist parties. The clergy were singled out as the most visible reactionaries within a corrupt and unjust establishment.

Hatred was focused particularly on the regular clergy. Legally, the orders were governed by the wording of the Concordat of 1851, which specified that only three orders were to be allowed in Spain, the Vincentians, the Oratorians, and one other to be named by the pope. The pope never named this third order; as a result, all orders proliferated. Most were teaching groups, which disturbed the anticlericals, who felt that only modern education could pull Spain out of her slump. While the clergy dominated most of the schools, the few lay schools that were established had to face great social and political pressures.

By 1900, the anticlericals had marshalled a large part of informed and influential public opinion on their side. When the decline of Spain became evident, with the loss of empire in the Spanish-American War, the clergy were made scapegoats for all of the nation's ills. The missionary orders were blamed for having caused abuses which had aggravated the colonial revolts leading to the disastrous war with the United States. There were complaints from businessmen that the regular clergy were competing with them; the Jesuits were rumored to be major stockholders in many corporations and were reputed to have control over one-third of the corporate wealth of Spain. Even the working classes were angry with the regular clergy; frequently nuns competed with proletarian wives in the laundering business and the sweetmeat and pastry industries. The workers had direct contact with the regulars, since they dispensed most of the Church's charity, and the clergy usually demanded religious observance as the price for charity; sometimes their sense of *noblesse oblige* antagonized the workers. The union leaders were angry with the regulars for having helped to form Catholic labor unions (which stressed cooperation with employers).

Furthermore, the number of regular clergy had increased dramatically around the turn of the century. Large numbers returned from the former colonies of Cuba and the Philippines. Many more came from France and Portugal, forced out by the anticlerical legislation in those countries. The situation was ripe for a major outburst. (Although the anarchists had frequently relieved the tension with sporadic attacks on churches and processions, these were isolated affairs, generally of little political importance.)

The outburst came in Barcelona in 1909.[16] Stimulated by an antiwar movement against Spanish military activities in Morocco and by an industrial depression, the proletarians in Barcelona attacked and burned churches and convents. During this "Tragic Week" about one-third of Barcelona's religious establishments were destroyed, and two clerics killed.

The destruction of the "Tragic Week" was motivated by social anticlericalism against the regulars. But it was urged on by the members of Alejandro Lerroux's Radical party, a lower middle-class group hoping to attract proletariat support. Lerroux's demogogic appeal to burn the convents and "liberate" the nuns was motivated by his own strong radical political anticlericalism; once the "Tragic Week" began, he used his anticlerical appeals to divert proletarian assaults away from the government—which was the real source of trouble—toward the Church, because he was reluctant to destroy the patronage and power his Radicals had in the government. It was a variant of the bourgeois dodge, and while it is true that the workers were still fundamentally anticlerical and the uprising could never have taken place in the way which it did without their deep-seated anticlericalism,

Lerroux had used it for his own devious purposes.

During the "Tragic Week" an anarchist educator, Francisco Ferrer, was arrested, tried, and executed as one of the provocateurs of the uprising. Apparently, he was made a scapegoat by the clericals and the government, for he was not responsible for what occurred. He became an anticlerical martyr and provided a paradigm of free thought to the rest of the world, an opinion little shared by Spaniards.

Since the results of the "Tragic Week" brought no gains to the workers, the proletarian parties thereafter maintained a discreet distance from the reformist bourgeois parties. Incendiary anticlericalism by anarchists continued, sporadic as before and with little immediate effect. The liberals in the Cortes tried one last attempt to legislate against the regulars. In 1910, José Canalejas, under the pressure of the growing numbers of regulars, introduced the Padlock law, which called for the registration of all orders under a law of associations (originally aimed at labor unions) and required the superiors and at least two-thirds of the members of all orders to be Spanish citizens. Although the law was passed, it was never implemented; the King protested and arranged a quiet *modus vivendi* with the Vatican two years later which completely nullified the law.[17]

After World War I, Spain's government broke down. Rioting and industrial violence in Barcelona, continued disaster in the Moroccan War, and the general inability of the government to solve pressing social and economic problems because it was not willing to consider radical reform measures contributed to the breakdown. Anarchist violence increased, and eventually martial law had to be declared in Catalonia. The end result was a military coup in 1923, when General Primo de Rivera seized power and overthrew the civilian government. During this entire period, the clergy sided with the forces of order. They supported Primo's military regime because it protected them and paid them salaries. The reformist groups continued to remain anticlerical. There was a minor protest and some rioting in 1927 when the clergy managed to obtain concessions in higher education.

By the 1930s, the reformist mood was overwhelmingly anticlerical. The republicans, demanding the abdication of the King, wanted action against the clergy, who had supported the King and had proclaimed the consubstantiality of crown and clergy. Each reformist action, in a long series which led up to the overthrowal of the monarchy in 1931, was touched by some anticlerical incident. The clergy, though fearful, just as resolutely defended the monarchy.

The overthrowal of the monarchy and the proclamation of the Second Republic in April, 1931, began the most intensely anticlerical period in Spanish history.[18] The clergy, aware that this might happen, had supported the monarchy in the elections of 1931, and some had even publicly declared that a vote against the monarchy would be a mortal sin. The Primate of Spain, Cardinal Segura of Toledo, ostentatiously grieved over the King's departure. These actions contributed to a tense situation, and although moderate republicans urged caution and moderate Catholics urged acceptance of the new regime, the anticlericals would not be put off.

The republican-socialist regime grasped the republican experiment as their chance to change the course of Spanish history, to right all the wrongs of the past, and, with varying aims, to usher in the new society. Typically, they were convinced that anticlericalism was a necessary first step. It would provide a bond between widely divergent reformists and would serve to satisfy the populace that some action was being taken. Of course, the clergy were no longer a threat to the state; in fact, they were utterly dependent upon it, and the regime would have been better served to have conciliated the clergy. Nevertheless, despite words of caution from moderate statesmen, the anticlericals acted.

The Church was disestablished, clerical salaries were phased out, the Jesuits dissolved, and provision was made for a law prohibiting the clergy from teaching (in private or public schools) or engaging in any kind of business activity. All of this was written into the constitution.

As time went on, the republican-socialist coalition revealed its fundamental incompatibility, and the only way the coalition could maintain itself in power was through repeated anti-clerical action, the one activity that all could agree on. All of the constitutional laws were implemented, and in the waning days of the coalition a law was passed to implement the restrictions on the regulars, who should be prevented from teaching, Premier Manuel Azaña said, as a matter of "public mental health." Gil Robles, the leader of the clerical party, referred to the coalition's action as taking an "injection of anticlericalism" to keep alive.[19]

Among the constitutional provisions was a law prohibiting the "public display of religion." This was interpreted by different municipal governments as they pleased. In some areas, the wearing of ornamental crucifixes was prohibited; in another, a priest saying mass in a roofless church was fined for a public display of religion. Processions, the lifeblood of traditionalist Spain, were also forbidden.

The frightening spectre of social anticlericalism was also raised. The anarchists, disappointed that the Republic did not immediately usher in the proletarian utopia, began burning churches. They were probably abetted by extreme political anticlericals who were anxious to provoke the clergy to a counter-revolution so that the Church could be crushed. Possibly the anarchists wanted to set the clericals and anticlericals at each other so that they could profit from the confusion. In any event, the first incendiary activity occurred a month after the Republic was proclaimed. In Madrid and in southern Spain over one hundred churches were burned in the space of three days. The new republican government did nothing to protect the churches, although the cabinet had been forewarned. Thereafter, on a much more limited scale, church burnings continued.

The clergy's response was predictable. They condemned the anticlericals and rallied the faithful to defend the churches. They also organized a political party to defend the clergy's interest in the Cortes. Others were not so moderate. In northern Spain, the Carlists began drilling troops to protect the interests of both the monarchy and the clergy. There is no doubt that the vast majority of priests and Catholics in Spain were monarchists and wanted a restoration, but each act of republican anticlericalism or republican inaction in the face of proletarian incendiarism turned them even more against the Republic and made them more receptive to plots to overthrow the regime, whether these plans came from the monarchists, the army, or the newly organized fascist party, the *Falange.* In sum, the republicans' anticlerical policy antagonized not only the clergy but also rallied many lukewarm Catholics to the defense of the Church. Many sincere reform-minded Catholics were won away from support of the Republic.

The elections of 1933 turned out the anticlerical bloc, but the Church's party, the CEDA, did not win a clear majority. The CEDA had enough power, however, to prevent implementation of the anticlerical legislation; the regulars continued to teach and priests' salaries were restored under the guise of pensions. Church buildings were protected and no more arson occurred. But if the CEDA prevented further enactment of anticlerical legislation, it was also beholden to monarchist votes to prevent implementation of necessary reforms. The liberals and proletarians, aided by separatist movements in Catalonia and Vasconia, grew frustrated. In late 1934, the CEDA demanded power in the cabinet, and although the President refused to name its leader, Gil Robles, premier, three Cedists were named. This was the signal for an abortive uprising in northern Spain by anarchists, socialists, and republicans who were afraid that the Cedists would restore the monarchy. In the fighting, which lasted for two weeks, churches were again burned, and some thirty-four clerics were killed, although it is difficult to tell how many were killed because they were priests and how many because they happened to be in the areas where the fighting took place. The government called in the army and the rebellion was crushed with great severity. Thousands of rebels were killed.

Late in 1935, the ministry fell; elections were held early

in 1936. The leftist forces united in the Popular Front and promised implementation of the constitution. They won, and the new government began implementing the anticlerical laws again. Apparently caught between their own frustrations and the fear of anarchist violence, the republicans and socialists allowed the anarchists a free hand against the clergy. Since political amnesty had been an electoral promise, the prisons were opened and anarchists poured out to wreak havoc on the churches. The government was powerless to protect the clergy. By July, 1936, hundreds of churches had been attacked and burned or looted and destroyed.

The clergy quite naturally gave renewed support to the conservative forces, who promised a return to order. When the army rose against the Republic in July, 1936, the clergy wholeheartedly supported the rebellion not necessarily as a means of restoring their long-lost power, but simply as protection against anticlerical onslaughts. When the rebellion lengthened into civil war, the clergy were attacked as political enemies. The anarchists also decided to settle old scores with the clergy. In the terror that lasted from August to December, 1936, some 7,000 clergy were killed, along with thousands of Catholic laity.[20]

It was the most prodigious bloodletting in the history of anticlericalism. Motives were both political and social; the clergy were arrested as enemies of the republican regime, and the anarchist attempt to implement their utopian dreams led them directly to execute priests. Every church in republican Spain was either burned, destroyed, or closed. Among the clergy killed were thirteen bishops. Priests were not just killed; they were mauled, tortured, even crucified.

Some of the clergy supported the republicans, but after the excesses of the terror, few remained in the republican camp. The only area in which large numbers of clergy and Catholics supported the Republic was in the Basque country, where the granting of regional autonomy stirred separatist sentiments and brought the Basques over to the Republic. When the region was invaded by Franco's troops, most of the priests who had supported the Republic were executed. If nothing else, the Spanish Civil War showed that at least as far as the clergy were concerned, there were no neutrals.

When the war was over, the clergy gave the Franco regime unyielding support. Despite their identification with a hated regime, there was little anticlerical activity from the extreme left. The war had apparently produced a catharsis. Spain needed unity, and anticlericalism was divisive. Furthermore, a younger generation of priests began to take the side of the proletarians in the late 1940s and 50s. The regime dealt harshly with them, and they were condemned by the conservative classes, who now became reactionary social anticlericals. Apparently, though, the young clergy served to prevent proletarian anticlericalism; in any event, the coming of the industrial revolution brought the secular revolution to Spain, and anticlerical tensions began to fade into the past.

CHAPTER 11

Italy

You are fortunate, General, in going to fight
the Russians; while I must stay here
to fight monks and nuns.

Victor Emmanuel II

ONE OF THE MOST STRIKING ASPECTS OF ITALIAN ANTI-clericalism is that it was so much more moderate than the French or Spanish.[1] No churches were burned, few clergy were attacked, and generally church-state relations were adjusted without the extreme polarization that occurred elsewhere. That this happened in the face of a papal monarch who at first opposed and then condemned the national movement for unification certainly appears odd.

Perhaps the chief reason for such moderation was that the Italian clergy could not really be identified with any one particular class or political group in the nineteenth-century struggle. The papacy was of course opposed to unification in the way in which it came about, but there were probably more priests who supported the movement than opposed it. And probably most Italian clerics—including some popes—wanted unification; they disagreed only on the method.

Furthermore, the anticlerical statesmen of Italy were more perceptive in distinguishing between the myth and reality of clerical power. They seldom attacked the clergy head-on; when they did, they almost never implemented the laws they passed. There were fewer sweeping reforms, and property

143

confiscations occurred with many exceptions over an extended period of time. In addition, there was always respect for the person of the pope. The politicians knew the hold that papal allegiance had upon the Italian people. Popular anticlerical incidents were the exception rather than the rule; far more often the Romans turned out to cheer the pope, whatever the political atmosphere. Church leaders were also wise, and while there were great public condemnations, generally there was a tacit agreement, once the anticlericals had come to power, to allow them to secularize the state, provided they did so with moderation.

The issue of ultramontanism lacked strength in Italy. The issue of divided allegiance in a nationalistic sense was not raised. Practically the entire administration of the Church, from the pope and the curia down to the superiors of all religious orders, were Italians. Thus, although they may have opposed the state, they were part of the nation; the loyalties demanded by nationalism made no exception for those born and bred in the *patria.*

The lack of violent social anticlericalism, and, indeed, widespread nonviolent social anticlericalism, might be due to the fact that there was little desertion from the Church. If the Catholicism practiced by the Italian proletarians was purely nominal, it was no different from the practice of earlier centuries. Perhaps the force of religious ritual was greater among the Italian peasantry, and therefore they had a greater fear of antagonizing the clergy. Possibly the safety valve of emigration allowed potential social anticlericals to leave the country before they could act against the clergy. Possibly the love of display and formalism was too ingrained in the Italian psyche to countenance the forced departure of the papacy and all that the traditional Church signified.

*

The rather sparse Italian Enlightenment produced few anticlerical thinkers. Pietro Giannone pointed out that clericalism had ruined the Kingdom of Naples, and the playwright Vittorio Alfieri claimed that Catholicism was incompatible with freedom, but most thinkers shied away from such topics.[2] Of the states which made up Italy in the eighteenth century, Venice was the most anticlerical; there, clerical property was restricted and the clergy were subject to civil law. At the other extreme was Sardinia, where the clergy had a privileged position in state, society, and education. The cismontane reformers had met with varying degrees of co-operation and resistance (see chapter 7). In the Papal States, cutting across the peninsula, the city of Rome was under clerical administration, while the city of Bologna was under lay control. Inevitably, conflicts between the two caused trouble, and most observers could not fail to contrast the miserable administration of the Papal States with more enlightened governments elsewhere.

When the French Revolution broke out, many of the more clerical French priests fled to Italy. When Napoleon's army invaded Italy, a great deal of church property was confiscated and subsequently sold; in many instances, this property was not restored in 1815.[3] In addition, the French suppressed most of the regular clergy.

Napoleon established republican governments in Italy and gave them constitutions which emulated the French church-state settlement. He negotiated concordats with the papacy for the different republics. At first, he was not anxious to provoke the Italians to further conflict and generally avoided anticlerical activity, although some of his officials were anticlerical. However, when Napoleon abducted Pope Pius VII to France, both the clergy and laity rose up in opposition.

Priests and peasants led the opposition. Many of the groups they organized were distinctly clerical, opposing not only French control but French reforms as well. Whatever Italian anticlericalism existed was submerged in the opposition to the French. Among the secret societies organized were the *sanfedisti*, a distinctly clerical group in Naples, and the *carbonari*, to which many priests belonged and which had cells all over the peninsula.

When the French were expelled in 1814, Italy was restored to its status quo of 1789, with the exception of Venetia, which came under Austrian control. In Venetia and Lombardy, Austrian clergy were installed in power; since they were largely Josephist in their views, both the papacy and the Italian people had little use for them.

But the papacy was in no position to make an enemy of Austria. Fears of liberalism and memories of the Revolution led to the imposition of strict clerical rule in the Papal States, and Austria was looked upon by the clericals as a force for traditionalist restoration. All in the Papal States who had supported the French were forced out, the Inquisition was reestablished, the Roman Jews were forced back into the ghetto, and most French reforms were repealed, even many that were purely technological. Lay administrations everywhere, even in traditionally lay-controlled Bologna, were replaced by clerics. Similar clerical restorations occurred elsewhere in Italy. In Sardinia, ecclesiastical courts were reestablished, and students and teachers at the university were ordered to attend mass weekly and confess monthly or else lose their positions.

In 1817, a lay inspired anticlerical revolt in Macerata in the Papal States was put down harshly by papal troops; the brutality and the death sentences meted out simply encouraged more anticlerical conspiracies. By this time the *carbonari* had become predominantly anticlerical. Few priests belonged to the secret society any longer, and the *carbonari* were largely middle class in leadership and appeal. In 1820, they inspired and led a revolution in Naples where they proclaimed the Spanish Constitution of 1812 and suppressed the Jesuits. The Austrians were called in to restore the Neopolitan Bourbons.

In 1823, the papacy came firmly under the control of the *zelanti* with the accession of Leo XII. He condemned the *carbonari* and the other anticlerical secret societies. To counter the *carbonari,* the clericals encouraged the *sanfedisti* to ferret out anticlericals.

The accession of Gregory XVI in 1830 stimulated more anticlericalism. Shortly after his installation, a *carbonari* revolt broke out in Bologna. The Austrians moved in to put it down, and the Pope supported them. No action could have been better calculated to lose him the support of the Italian people.

Gregory's attitude, along with the growing desire for unification, posed a great problem, for any realistic unification would have to include the Papal States. Some leaders, such as Mazzini, were completely antisacerdotal and saw no recourse other than to do away with the papacy. Others tried to arrange a compromise. Known as the neo-guelphs, they had little use for Gregory, but they did see that a more liberal pope might accept their solution of a confederation of Italian states under papal leadership. In any event, they felt the papacy would have to come to terms with liberalism. Neoguelphs were prolific writers, and many became statesmen during the course of unification. Vincenzo Gioberti was the outstanding leader of this group, which included Cesare Balbo, Luigi Torelli, Leopoldo Galeotti, and Massimo d'Azeglio.

The priest Antonio Rosmini-Serbati was another important anticlerical. His most important work, *The Five Wounds of the Church* (1848), contended that one of the Italian clergy's main problems was their separation from the laity.[4] He proposed the clergy be selected by the bishops and the laity acting in concert, and that the bishops themselves be selected by the laity.

*

The election of a liberal pope in 1846 aroused everyone's hopes. Pius IX was a pope who could accept unification, perhaps even lead the movement, it was felt. He proclaimed amnesties for political prisoners and appointed commissions to study the feasibility of reforms in the Papal States. He was hailed everywhere by liberals and nationalists. This praise represented a great deal of wishful thinking, and realistic statesmen like Garibaldi and Cavour could not see how a papal confederation or even the temporal power of the papacy could be compatible with the existence of a unified Italian state.

The disillusionment came in 1848.[5] When the revolution broke out in France and spread to Austria, the Italians looked to Pius for guidance and leadership. But he refused to allow papal troops to join in the war to expel the Austrians, and immediately whatever hopes he had aroused were dashed. Overnight the unification movement became antipapal.

The Pope was also disillusioned. Having been forced out of Rome by an anticlerical uprising, he was in no mood to tolerate liberal reforms again, and once French troops restored him to Rome, he was transformed from the hope of the liberals to the hero of the reactionaries. Thereafter the lines were clearly drawn: the Pope would tolerate no schemes for the unification of Italy that threatened his lands, and the nationalists could see no way to unify Italy without the Papal States and Rome.

The anticlerical struggle in Italy thus became subordinate to the quest for unification. But the clergy were not completely unanimous in supporting the papal position; many desired unification, even if it meant confiscation of the Papal States. And, as the Pope became more reactionary in his political and theological statements, many sincere Catholics were antagonized, so that anticlericalism came to transcend the narrow sectarianism that it had developed in other countries. Arturo Jemolo comments, "By 1850 anti-Austrian feeling, national unity, representative government, and anticlericalism were closely associated in the minds of men representing every shade of political opinion."[6]

Every great intellectual, every great statesman was anticlerical. They were not antisacerdotalists. They were concerned about the papal problem and clericalism; beyond that they desired few restrictions upon the clergy. Count Cavour's formula of a "free church in a free state" was the ideal. Cavour understood it to mean that the clergy were to have no rights or privileges different from any other citizen in the state. He did not intend to persecute them, but rather to make every one equal in the eyes of the state.[7]

Cavour was the premier of Sardinia, and he promoted anti-clerical reforms in that state. The first major legislation in the 1850s was the Siccardi law which abolished the ecclesiastical court system and made the clergy subject to civil law. The law also required state approval for all land purchases by clergy. In 1854, the Rattazzi laws were passed to suppress all religious orders not devoted to teaching, preaching, or nursing, while no new orders could be established without state approval. The clergy's salaries (which had been paid since the turn of the century) were modified so that the bishops received less and the parish priests more. The property of the suppressed orders was to be sold to help pay for clerical salaries.

In the debates concerning these laws, Cavour maintained that the regular clergy were hampering the prosperity of the state; indeed, the prosperity of any nation was in inverse proportion to the number of regular clergy in that country. The bishops of Sardinia offered to pay the clerical budget if the law were not passed, and the King, Victor Emmanuel II, urged that the offer be accepted. Cavour would not budge and the law was passed.

The Pope condemned the laws, and the Archbishop of Turin refused to grant a church burial for the minister of agriculture on the grounds that the minister had supported the law.[8] The Archbishop was expelled by the government, another example of anticlerical feeling that the clergy's function is to minister, not to judge.

As unification progressed with the extension of the Kingdom of Sardinia-Piedmont, the Sardinian laws were extended to the newly incorporated parts of Italy, although with great moderation in those portions of the Papal States which were annexed. When Tuscany joined the new kingdom, the Archbishop of Pisa refused permission for his clergy to take part in national celebrations, and he was exiled from his see. There were some instances of extreme anticlericalism as societies were formed "for the emancipation of the clergy," but generally these were the exception rather than the rule.

In 1866 and 1867, the government began the confiscation of the secular clergy's lands, partly under pressure to settle the Austrian war debt. It was not, however, a wholesale confiscation; during the next three decades bits and pieces of clerical property were taken, but never so much at any one time that it provoked a massive clerical reaction. While there were complaints, there were no great disruptions of the national economy.

As Pius IX watched the Italian state grow and trespass more and more on his domains, he became more and more reactionary. He condemned the government for encroaching on the Papal States, which he defended as the patrimony of St. Peter, claiming that even he himself could not alienate them, for they did not belong to him. Most of the anticlerical politicians understood his position and tried to arrange a compromise, but Pius was adamant.

In addition, Pius became even more reactionary and clerical in theological matters. Some historians have claimed that he was under the influence of the Jesuit priest Taparelli, who had founded the newspaper, *La Civiltà Cattolica* and whose statements on authority and freedom leaned far in the direction of authority.[9] Certainly, the Syllabus of Errors (1864), most of whose anathemas were directed at various actions of the Italian government, did not help to bring about a compromise.

*

In 1858, one of the most celebrated clerical episodes in the entire history of the Church occurred. A Roman Jewish family, the Mortaras, employed a Catholic girl as a servant. When Edgardo, one of the Montara children, took ill, the girl secretly baptized the child. After the child recovered, she reported what she had done to her pastor, who then informed the Holy Office. Its officials, with the concurrence of the Pope, took Edgardo from his family and placed him in a Catholic foundling home. The principle applied was that the child, now a Catholic, would not learn his faith in a Jewish household. Even Napoleon III's intercession proved useless, and the Mortara child grew up permanently separated from his family. It was, in fact, a perfect example of clericalism: application of the principle, which was good, to a specific case where the effects were criminal.[10]

*

In 1870, the process of Italian unification was completed. When the Franco-Prussian War broke out, the French troops in Rome were called home, and an Italian army captured the city and proclaimed it the capital of Italy. The Pope retired to the Vatican, there to become the self-styled "prisoner of the Vatican." Before doing so, he hurled his last challenge to the world in the dogma of papal infallibility.

For the next half-century, the anticlerical struggle in Italy was dominated by the Roman Question.[11] Until 1929, all popes considered themselves prisoners of the Vatican and refused to recognize the Italian governments. The first two popes during this period—Pius IX and Leo XIII—repeatedly condemned the government and forbade Catholics to vote or run for national office. They tried to get the other European powers to pressure the Italian government to restore the Papal States. By this combination of pressure, condemnation, and Catholic political abstinence, they hoped to bring the Italian government to terms.

Instead, the government countered with anticlerical legislation, which was fairly easy to enact as long as Catholics obeyed the pope and refused to enter the chamber of deputies, so anticlerical was the majority in the chamber. There was no clerical party and no necessity to pass anticlerical legislation to keep the coalition together. As a result, little extreme legislation was passed, and even less was implemented. The anticlericals were mainly antipapal, but few opposed a particular pope. They feared the power of the papacy, but they respected the individual popes who held the office.

The government's first attempt to solve the Roman Question was the Law of Guarantees, passed in 1871.[12] This recognized the pope as sovereign ruler in the Vatican; he was promised an annual income in lieu of the lost revenues from the Papal States. The state renounced the right to nominate bishops, but it maintained the right of eminent domain over church property outside the Vatican.

Pius IX unhesitatingly responded with a condemnation of the law, although its terms were generally respected by the government. After the condemnation, the popes were not offered the annual income, and the government did maintain the privilege of approving bishops before allowing them to take possession of their sees; this latter practice provoked frequent conflict with the papacy, which in every instance was forced to accept the government's position. The government also began to legislate anticlerical reforms. As in France and Spain, the reasons advanced for anticlerical legislation were the same: the need for a secular school system that would reflect modern ideas, the need to place welfare work under state auspices for better distribution, and the need to suppress the special rights of the regular clergy in the name of political equality.

The Italian school system was not as highly centralized nor as highly developed as the French. Thus, aside from abolition of the chairs of theology in the universities, anticlerical educational activity was directed toward primary education. In 1871, the municipality of Rome made the teaching of religion in the state primary schools optional at the parents' request. This law was extended to all of Italy in 1878. Ten years later, teaching religion in the state primary schools was banned altogether.

As for the regular clergy, a series of laws was passed which eventually resulted in the suppression of most of the orders and the expropriation of their property. However, suppression simply meant that the order had no recognition at law; the regulars continued to live together in communities, but as members of "free associations." Furthermore, the expropriation did not extend to the houses of the heads of orders with an international membership resident in Rome.

The diocesan clergy became subject to military conscription, and the seminaries were ordered open to state inspection. All inhabitants of the Vatican except the pope were made subject to Italian laws and courts. Processions were banned, and in 1888 the Zanardelli laws made it a crime for the clergy to engage in politics or criticize the anticlerical laws; however, no one was ever arrested under this law.

Besides the expropriation of the regular clergy's property in 1890, the government seized the property of all charitable enterprises under church auspices and of the lay confraternities as well. In the debates on this law, Premier Francesco Crispi maintained that these organizations spent only one-tenth of their revenue on charity, the rest going for fireworks, processions, and the like. The state, he said, had the obligation to dispense charity equitably and efficiently.[13]

The only instance of popular anticlericalism occurred in 1881 when the body of Pius IX was moved to its final resting place and a mob threatened to throw the coffin into the Tiber. Popular anticlericalism in Italy tended to be spontaneous and sporadic. More irritating was petty governmental anticlericalism, stimulated to some extent by Freemasons. For example, in 1902, when the mayor of Rome formally congratulated Leo XIII on the occasion of the Pope's jubilee, Crispi dismissed him and appointed Ernesto Nathan, an anticlerical Jew, mayor. Nathan promptly invited the World Congress of Freethinkers to meet in Rome. He also staged the Rome exhibition of 1910, which the clerical newspaper, *La Civiltà Cattolica,* called "a frenzy of sectarian joy."[14]

Crispi, who professed a desire for a complete separation of church and state, catered to the vulgar anticlericals; he erected statues of Arnold of Brescia, Giordano Bruno, and —on the Janiculum, overlooking St. Peter's—one of Garibaldi. The symbolic intent was not lost on the Vatican.

But all of this activity was superficial; Catholicism was still very much a part of Italian life. The law banning religion in the state primary schools was revoked in 1908 and made optional at the parents' request. This revocation simply conformed to actuality. Even in 1911, when a law providing for the centralization of primary education was introduced, one of the arguments used was that most of the municipal communes had obviously not secularized the schools. Although the law was passed, there were so many exceptions that it was virtually nonoperable.

Even more interesting is the fact that the numbers of regular clergy actually increased between 1880 and 1900, despite the suppression laws.[15] Anticlericals who introduced divorce legislation could never muster enough support to pass the bills. The law abolishing tithes was so badly worded that priests could still legally claim them (although no one did); apparently, none of the anticlericals thought enough of it to change or reword the law.

In fact, the clergy and the politicians had reached a tacit agreement. The popes came to accept the fact of the state's existence, and the government did not implement the anticlerical laws harshly. And, despite public statements, there were generally cordial relations on a personal level between anticlerical politicians and popes.

There was reason for shrewd statesmen not to implement the laws. Aside from the adverse popular reaction such moves would evoke, there was the important consideration that as long as the papacy forbade Catholics to vote or run for national office, a clerical party could not be organized. Whereas in France, Spain, and Germany, anticlericals had to contend with powerful clerical parties and interests in the legislatures, in Italy the statesmen could get about the task of governing without having political opposition at every turn. Certainly, a by-product was the lack of violent anticlericalism, the kind frequently countenanced, if not spurred, by political anticlericals. As a result, Italy was spared the massive clerical-anticlerical struggle that could have ripped her national life asunder.[16]

*

The *Risorgimento* and the Roman Question stimulated a great deal of anticlerical thinking; indeed, in no other country was there such an abundance of relatively sophisticated intellectual anticlericalism.[17] The tone was set by Cavour's idea of "a free church in a free state"; the free state was viewed as the best instrument for creating a free church. Marco Minghetti, Bettino Ricasoli, and Carlo Boncampagni, all of them ministers in the new state, echoed the plea that the hold of the clericals upon the Church had to be broken. The only institution with enough power to do so was the state. Thus, they saw the state as an instrument of anticlerical reform, not to make the state supreme and despotic, but to make the Church free and responsive. Most were sincere Catholics and none descended to the petty vulgarism of many anticlericals in other countries, perhaps because of the personal respect they felt for the pope.

There were also secular anticlericals who were not Catholics but were also determined to eradicate clericalism in the Church in order to make it a free institution. The most important of these was Benedetto Croce, the thinker who had the greatest influence on the Italy of his age. He was the first to observe and point out the tacit agreement between the Vatican and the Quirinal that gave freedom to both. He was as harsh on the vulgar anticlericals, whom he claimed saw the hand of the Jesuits in everything, as he was on the vulgar clericals, who falsified history to exalt the clergy. His philosophical influence pervaded the entire intellectual atmosphere of Italy.

The anticlericals included a group of Catholics, founders of the demochristian movement in Italy, who wanted to organize Catholics into a strong progressive political party. Imbued with modern social ideas and determined to implement them to save Italy from the horrors of class warfare, they had to contend with the papal ban; they had to create a political organization without making it appear political. The founder and organizer of this movement was the priest Romolo Murri, who subsequently found himself involved in the modernist crisis and eventually left the priesthood.[18] Another was Antonio Fogazzaro, author of *Il Santo,* a famous anticlerical novel, also condemned along with the rest of the modernists. The best summation of the progressive ideological antiauthoritarian anticlerical stance is Tommaso Gallarati Scotti's speech to the demochristian organization in 1906, in which he said:

> I know that people from all walks of life will seek to brand us as rebels; I know that they will refuse to take account of our open profession of the Catholic faith, of the integrity of our lives, of the honesty of our words and deeds. . . . Rebels? Perhaps: words mean so little. But we are rebelling not against the Church's dogma, not against the hierarchical authority in its divine mission on earth, not against the prescribed forms of worship—we declare ourselves to be united in a single faith with the most ignorant old woman in Christendom—but against a false concept of authority which corrupts men's souls and seeks to penetrate even into the life of the nation, against a religious ignorance that invests profane, transient and conjectural things with the character of eternal truths, and would compel a people to observe outmoded and threadbare forms without permitting it that spontaneous development which alone can create new institutions and new forms of Christian civilization.[19]

*

The emergence of proletarian movements in Italy helped lead to a reconciliation of church and state and clericals and anticlericals. At first, however, some of the anticlericals tried to link socialist agitation with intransigent clericalism; both were enemies of the status quo, and they reasoned that both had cause to aid each other. Crispi, for example, claimed that the clergy were behind the anarchist agitation in southern Italy. The priests, he said, hoped that the combined pressure of the two would cause the state to fall, and the clericals, stronger than the anarchists, would be able to restore Rome to the pope.[20]

Soon, however, the anticlericals began to see that the clericals could aid them in the political struggle against the proletarians. The Italian middle class followed the same pattern as those in France and Spain: they began to view the clergy as a bulwark of law and order against anarchism and socialism. The clericals were also frightened, and they welcomed the advances of the middle class.

The sources of their fears, the socialists and anarchists, were actually no threat to the clergy. The socialists did not encourage violence against the clergy, and the anarchists were so few and so disorganized that even in the most poverty stricken areas of the country there was little agitation against the clergy. In fact, priests occasionally joined some of the more primitive anarchist movements.[21] Perhaps the anarchists retained the remnants of some fundamental fear —perhaps superstitious in origin—of the clergy. Possibly there was a fundamental respect, for the clergy were also at war with the state. Certainly the proletarian movements were not conspicuously any more anticlerical than those of the moderate middle class. Further, there is no evidence that the political anticlericals stirred up anticlericalism among the lower classes. Perhaps they understood, unlike the Spanish anticlericals, that clericalism was deeply ingrained in the popular mind and was so little a threat on the political level that the clergy might be useful allies in the class struggle.

By the turn of the century, the Vatican began to change its uncompromising stance. Leo XIII died in 1903 and was succeeded by Pius X, an instransigent clerical in many respects, but a realist in his understanding of the Italian situation. In 1904, he partially lifted the ban on Catholic voting by allowing the bishops to determine the rule for their own dioceses. The Pope wanted to allow Catholics to vote for the middle-class parties to prevent the socialists from coming to power.

The introduction of organized Catholic voting into national politics coincided with the debut of Giovanni Giolitti, the master parliamentary manipulator. Giolitti saw the possibilities of the Catholic vote, and he certainly did not want to introduce or implement anticlerical laws to offend Catholics, who in turn were not unhappy with Giolitti's stewardship of the Italian chamber. The tacit agreement was renewed:

Catholics supported Giolitti; he saw to it that new anticlerical
legislation was not introduced, and that the existing legislation was not harshly implemented. The clerical-anticlerical
struggle began to fade away.

*

When World War I broke out, the question of intervention
was raised. Generally, the anticlericals favored the Allies,
while the clericals were opposed to intervention. When Italy
finally did enter the war on the side of the Allies in 1915,
the Vatican maintained strict neutrality. The war had many
of the same effects in Italy that it had upon the struggle in
France: priests were conscripted and fought and were killed.
There were complaints from anticlericals that Pope
Benedict's peace plan favored the Central Powers, and there
were those who feared that an Austrian victory would lead
to a restoration of the Papal States. The foreign minister,
Sidney Sonnino, inserted a clause in the Secret Treaty of
London (in which Italy agreed to join the Allies in return for
large portions of Austrian territory) that the Roman Question
not be raised at the peace conference and that the pope not
be invited to attend.

After the war, Benedict completely lifted the ban on Catholic voting.[22] By this time, a Catholic party—the Popular party
—had been formed. It was led by a priest, Luigi Sturzo.
Sturzo wanted to avoid any question of clericalism and thus
he emphasized that his party was aconfessional and neutral
on the Roman Question. In fact, however, Sturzo was a priest
and could be silenced by Rome, and most of his strength lay
in the clerically directed vote. Any difference of opinion
between laymen and priests in the party was always settled
in favor of the clergy. The new socialist party leader, Palmiro
Togliatti, would have nothing to do with Sturzo, because he
considered the Popular party too open to clerical infuence
and too committed to bourgeois ideals, although actually
Sturzo held views close to the socialists on many economic
and social questions.

Sturzo himself was not an anticlerical. Indeed, he might

be called a neoclerical; he wanted to infuse the world with the spirit of a modern, socially progressive Christianity. He had every reason to be antipapal, especially after Pius XI broke the parliamentary power of the Popular party in 1924 by reaffirming the "traditional" papal ban on socialist-Catholic cooperation.[23] Even when he was sent into exile to London in order to allow for a settlement of the Roman Question, he restrained whatever anticlericalism he may have felt; his writings reveal none of the harsh antipapalism or even anticlericalism that Lamennais had exhibited.

One of the reasons the papacy withdrew its tacit support from Sturzo's party was that Benito Mussolini promised a settlement of the Roman Question favorable to the papacy. This was achieved in 1929 in the Lateran Accords. The Italian government recognized the pope as the sovereign of the Vatican and settled a cash indemnity upon him for the loss of the Papal States. In the concordat attached to the treaty, all of the anticlerical legislation was undone. Catholicism was to be taught in all schools in Italy; the clergy were to be salaried; the regular clergy could own property. In return, the state was allowed to exercise a primary veto in the appointment of the upper clergy.[24]

The Lateran settlement gave the pope a great deal. Some of the anticlericals in the chamber opposed it for this reason. The antifascist Catholics opposed it because it gave the regime prestige. But most of the clericals approved of the fascist dictator. They were pleased with the persecution of the liberals, and, in fact, Jemolo maintains that many of the clergy did more than support the state: they sanctified the fascist way of life.[25]

It would seem that under these circumstances Italy would be ripe for an anticlerical reaction when the regime fell in 1943. But there was none, and after 1945 Italy came to resemble a clerical state more so than at any time since the beginning of the nineteenth century.

One reason was that the clergy could not be singled out for collaborating with the regime, because most Italians had done likewise. Furthermore, there were enough priests who had supported the resistance to gain the grateful support of those who had fought the fascists. Certainly, it proved that the clergy were not a monolithic group of robots. In addition, the papacy had immense prestige during and immediately after the war; Pius XI had condemned fascism and nazism, and Pius XII had helped harbor resistance groups.

After 1943 there was a preoccupation with problems of much greater importance than the clerical problem. The communists were strong, and the ruling Christian Democratic government needed the support of the clergy. Neither the socialists nor the communists were willing to antagonize Catholic support by bringing up the clerical question. Pietro Nenni, the socialist leader, stated during the debates on the inclusion of the Lateran Accords in the new democratic constitution of 1946: "The smallest of agrarian reforms is of greater interest to me and my colleagues than the revision of the Concordat."[26] The communists also supported the inclusion of the Lateran Accords in an effort to gain Catholic support. Even when Pius XII intervened in the elections of 1948 by telling Catholics that a vote for the communists would be treated as a "grave sin," there were no charges of clericalism from the communists.

Thus, since 1945 Italy has remained a clerical state. The Church controls education; it has wide-ranging powers of censorship; up to 1970, it had prevented the enactment of a divorce law. The ruling Christian Democrats have never been willing to attack the clergy for any reason and have instead supported clericalism.

CHAPTER 12

Portugal

*Never wage war on religion, nor upon seemingly holy
institutions, for this thing has too great
a force upon the minds of fools.*

Francesco Guicciardini

THE DEVELOPMENT OF ANTICLERICALISM IN PORTUGAL BEARS
some resemblance to that in Spain.[1] The loss of empire, the
attempts to establish liberalism in the nineteenth century, the
republican experiment in the twentieth, the evolution of
landholdings—small in the north, large estates in the south
—in these respects Portuguese history closely parallels
Spanish.

There were, however, significant differences. For one
thing, the plight of the Portuguese poor was so overwhelming
that it presented too great an obstacle to the development of
social anticlericalism among the masses. Apparently, there is
a point at which the revolution of rising expectations helps
to create social anticlericalism; in Portugal that point was
never reached. The conditions of life were so mean and
miserable that the masses remained perfectly willing to accept
clerical domination; indeed, they probably would have been
lost without it and would have found a close substitute.

Furthermore, the clergy were comparatively unreformed.
The disciplinary decrees of the Council of Trent scarcely
touched Portugal. Most of the rural clergy still lived in
concubinage into the twentieth century. While this moral

lapse antagonized the middle-class citizens, the peasants probably looked with favor upon the arrangement. They sympathized with the priests, for the clergy's problems resembled theirs.

Nor had anything great ever been expected from the clergy. True, they had taken the same missionary risks that the Spanish clergy had in imperial days, but whereas the Spanish clergy had provided great moral and spiritual leadership as well, the Portuguese clergy had contributed little. They were powerful, of course, but they did not have the respect which leadership brings. The laity did not have a basis for comparison: their clergy had always been mediocre, and they expected nothing more.

Finally, the middle class in Portugal was extremely small in number and influence. Instead of following the lead of the Spanish middle class (which was very anticlerical), they tended to ape the British middle class with its ideal of moderation. There is no evidence that they ever stirred the proletariat to anticlerical action.

*

The cismontane policies of the Marquis of Pombal which resulted in the expulsion of the Jesuits came to an abrupt end with the death of King Joseph in 1777. His daughter, Maria I, and her son, the regent John VI, returned the nobility and the clergy to power and most of Pombal's reforms were undone. The anticlerical threat of the French Revolution also pushed the government to more clerical policies. Both crown and clergy used censorship to keep out the revolutionary literature (Pombal had encouraged the importation of Enlightened anticlerical literature) and, with the support of the Anglo-Portuguese alliance, maintained hostility to France throughout the revolutionary and Napoleonic period. When Napoleon invaded Portugal in 1808, the nation did not respond until the Spanish arose against the French, and only then did the clergy help support the anti-French rebellion. But this was a short-lived affair, for the British soon landed in Portugal and came to control the liberated portions of the country. At the one moment the clergy might have exercised national leadership, their efforts were cut short.

After the British drove out the French, middle-class Masonic lodges were formed, but they were of little immediate danger to the clergy. The Jesuits were invited to return, and despite the fact that the King, resident in Brazil since 1808, was the Grand Master of the Brazilian Freemasons, the population of Portugal was overwhelmingly rural, conservative, and clerical. They feared the British, not clerical domination.

In 1820, an anti-British revolution broke out, and the liberals, emulating the Spaniards, seized control of the country. With a new constitution and subsequent legislation, they abolished clerical privileges, suppressed some of the regular clergy, ordered the expropriation of clerical property, and abolished the Inquisition. Except for the last act, none of these laws was fully implemented, because a clerical reaction soon began against the small number of liberal anticlericals.

The leader of the clericals was King John's second son, Dom Miguel. When John died and his eldest son, Dom Pedro, was faced with a choice between ruling Brazil or Portugal, he opted in favor of the former and named his daughter Maria da Gloria Queen of Portugal. Miguel, with the support of most of the clergy, attempted to seize power. Miguelism, the movement generated by his supporters, resembled Spanish Carlism with its emphasis on pastoralism, clericalism, and regionalism. Miguel was named regent for his niece, to whom he was betrothed, and with power firmly in hand began a strict clerical regime. All the anticlerical legislation was abolished. Pedro was unhappy with this turn of events, and civil war broke out between his liberal supporters and the clerical Miguelists.

In 1833, Pedro returned from Brazil and defeated and forced Miguel into exile. His government began immediate anticlerical activity, apparently not so much for ideological reasons as for the practical purpose of weakening the Miguelists. An ecclesiastical reform commission was established, and the ministry dismissed all the clergy who had been appointed to their sees by Miguel. The Jesuits were again expelled, tithes were abolished, and the clergy were salaried. In 1834, Antonio de Aguiar, the minister of justice, suppressed all of the religious orders and confiscated their large property holdings. Since the secular clergy had already lost most of their landholdings earlier, these laws made the clergy completely dependent upon the state.

The clergy, in fact, came completely under the control of the state. The government assumed the right of appointment to all clerical positions to the extent that no priest could dispense the sacraments without crown permission. Any priest who wanted a benefice was forced to seek the approval of some government minister. Pope Gregory XVI was naturally displeased, and with the appointees of Miguel still claiming their sees, an incipient schism was averted only by compromise when in 1842 the government recognized Miguel's appointees in return for the papacy's recognition of the expropriation of the regular clergy's property as a *fait accompli.*

The crown still continued to exercise complete control over the clergy. The government took over the seminaries and abolished religion in secondary schools, although the primary schools were required to teach religion, and there was full freedom for the clergy to operate private schools. But even the redistricting of dioceses was done by the government, and religious confraternities were not allowed to exist without crown permission.

To what extent these laws affected the illiterate and poverty ridden masses is a matter of conjecture. There is one recorded instance of a clerical uprising in 1842. Premier Costa Cabral's sanitation law forbidding the burial of bodies in churchyards led to the "Maria da Fonte" uprising in northern Portugal. Obviously, the uprising climaxed an accumulation of grievances and probably disturbed traditional practices more than it did the people's faith, but the government was forced to retreat. Costa Cabral resigned, and the law was not enforced.[2]

By the middle of the nineteenth century, with the diocesan clergy completely under state control, the only outstanding problem between church and state involved the regulars, who, despite their legal suppression, continued to proliferate throughout the country. The government closed its eyes to much of this activity, for the regulars had always played a missionary role and were still needed to aid colonial administrators abroad. And, of course, suppression always created legal problems around the question of whether the orders could function as "free associations" or whether they must depart the country. In 1858, the issue was made public when the government questioned the establishment of a convent in Lisbon for the Sisters of Charity of France. The Cortes debated the problem and agreed that the nuns could remain if they renounced their allegiance to their French superior; they refused to do so and were dissolved. Finally, in 1886, the government concluded an agreement with the Holy See: the Vatican recognized the government's right to appoint the secular clergy in return for the right of the regular clergy to reestablish themselves.

These legal restrictions only hint at the appalling state of the Portuguese clergy, certainly the most unreformed in all Europe. With constant shortages, the ratio of clergy to laity was among the lowest in the world for any nominally Catholic country. The clergy were constantly vying for favors so they could secure the best benefices, preferably in the relatively cosmopolitan cities, away from the backward rural areas. They had little interest in intellectual or spiritual development. Their training in state controlled seminaries was inadequate and provided no protection against the liberal and secular ideologies that threatened them. The bishops remained a constant problem for the papacy. Pius IX repeatedly ordered the bishops to come to Rome to discuss issues; they always refused. When the First Vatican Council was held in 1869, only two from the entire Portuguese episcopate attended. It is no wonder that Pius was exasperated; he publicly referred to the Portuguese bishops as "dumb dogs."[3]

The clergy were, of course, deeply involved in politics, but aside from the ever present anticlerical clubs in Lisbon, there appeared to be no objection to their political role. Priests were frequently political agents for the government's parties in the countryside, and, on a more organized level, the Bishop of Viseu was a leader of the moderate party and once held a cabinet position.

Aside from the practical anticlericalism of the government and the hopeful anticlericalism of the liberals and republican reformers, most intellectuals directed their antipathy toward the clergy's role in history. The decline of the overseas empire provoked a debate on all national institutions, and this in turn provided the impetus for a literary renaissance in the late nineteenth century.

The anticlerical writers were generally positivists; they attributed the decline and decadence of the nation partly to the clergy. Two historians, Joaquin Oliveira Martins and Alexandre Herculano, stressed this. Socialist poet Antero de Quental used anticlerical themes on a more personal level. Certainly the most outstanding anticlerical writer was José María Eça de Queiroz, whose classic, *The Sin of Father Amaro*, was a bitter compendium of all the faults of the Portuguese clergy.[4] These men set the intellectual tone for a generation disappointed not only with the clergy but also with the monarchy, as one colonial disaster after another rocked the state.

The anticlerical mood and the inability of the state to solve the political, economic, and social problems of the nation led to the growth of a republican movement, heavily Masonic and anticlerical, in the larger towns of Portugal. Frustrated at every turn, reformers and urban proletarians turned to anticlericalism as a release for their tensions, despite the fact that the clergy were hardly a danger to anyone except themselves.

The first sign of anticlerical activity after the late nineteenth century hiatus came in 1901. A private family argument because the daughter of the consul to Brazil wished to become a nun against her father's wishes erupted into a public debate on the regular clergy. The government took action after the Lisbon offices of a Catholic newspaper were stoned. It ordered all regular houses to "secularize" (i.e., become free associations) or leave the country. Twelve orders accepted secularization, and the rest were ordered to leave. After a few months, the affair blew over, and most of the regulars returned or emerged from hiding.[5]

The anticlericals continued their agitation, and as national problems became even more severe, they demanded the suppression of the Jesuits. The last monarchist ministry closed the Jesuit houses in Lisbon, hoping that this would mollify the anticlerical republicans. The very next day, October 4, 1910, the monarchy fell and a republic was proclaimed.

*

The Republic rode in on a wave of anticlericalism.[6] The clergy again became the scapegoats for all national ills. The republican politicians, once faced with the fact of power and with the same insoluble problems as the monarchy had, found that the clergy were the only ones against whom they could take action with impunity. There were few who would defend the clergy, who undoubtedly needed reform. But, the ensuing anticlerical legislation was such a mixture of reform and continued state control that, as a solution to Portugal's clerical problem, it failed miserably. The only saving factor was that it did not lead to civil war, as happened in Spain.

Anticlerical reform became the province of the minister of justice, Afonso Costa, who publicly boasted that Catholicism in Portugal would disappear in a generation or two.[7] In the form of decrees and constitutional articles, Pombal's law suppressing the Jesuits and the 1834 law suppressing the other regulars were implemented. Religious instruction in the state schools was abolished, as were the chairs of theology in the universities. All of the clergy's property was taken from them, and church buildings were placed under the administration of a lay corporation. A commission was created to see to the implementation of these laws.

Significantly, there was little popular anticlericalism. The houses of a few of the orders were attacked, but apparently only under the provocation that they were monarchist centers and had been used as fortresses to fire upon the populace. A few priests were killed in the ensuing battles, and a number of regulars were arrested and imprisoned, but apparently the crowds were too apathetic to continue a sustained attack upon the clergy. It is also significant that these attacks occurred only in the larger towns of Portugal.[8]

The bishops and the Pope protested, and one bishop was deprived of his see by the government. There were other protests as well; foreign powers objected to the implementation of these laws in the Portuguese colonies, where most of the regular clergy were protected, as missionaries, by international convention. The republican anticlericals soon found that they had taken all the possible nonviolent action against the clergy that they could. The Republic was in grave difficulty, and more pressing problems, particularly those of national finance, began to command the ministry's attentions. Furthermore, when a miracle was reported at Fatima in 1917, there was such a groundswell of clerical support from the rural masses that wiser politicians decided to play down their anticlericalism. National unity was needed, and anticlericalism served only to alienate.

In 1918, after the first coup of Sidonio Paes, the military came to power. They dissolved the commission in charge of implementing the anticlerical laws. Then, in the 1920s, laws were passed allowing religious instruction in the state schools. When Antonio de Oliveira Salazar came to power as finance minister in 1928, the end of anticlericalism was in sight. Salazar's new constitution of 1933 rescinded most of the anticlerical laws, and a concordat with the papacy in 1940 provided for the legal return of the regular clergy and the subsidization of private church schools.[9]

Despite all of these church-state upheavals, Portugal has always been a clerical society. Ideological anticlericals have been few, if vociferous, and the practical anticlericalism of the governments, while restricting the clergy for political reasons, has been unable to break their dogmatic grip upon the masses of practicing Catholics. Even nominal Catholics have respected this hold, largely through the force of tradition.

CHAPTER 13

Colombia

*Archbishop—A Christian ecclesiastic of a rank
superior to that attained by Christ.*

H. L. Mencken

LATIN AMERICA PRESENTS A MICROCOSM OF THE ANTICLERI-
cal struggle. Practically every factor present in the European
conflict was present in Latin America under varying conditions and circumstances. There were, however, circumstances in Latin America's history which gave peculiar shape
to the development of anticlericalism in the New World.

One of these was the identification of the clergy with the
old regime—a foreign regime during the struggle for independence. Most of the higher clergy were *peninsulares*, native
Spaniards, and supported the Spanish crown in its attempts
to retain the colonies. Whereas in Europe there was no issue
of nationalism with the old regime, in Latin America the
upper clergy were supporting a foreign government, thereby
adding fuel to the anticlerical conflict.

This support for the Spanish crown was closely related to
the presence of foreign missionaries in Latin America
throughout the national period. Because of illiteracy and poor
economic and social conditions, there was a shortage of
vocations, which ultimately had to be made up by Spanish
and French missionaries in the nineteenth century and by
American clergy in the twentieth. This again raised the issue

of nationalism, which, although never extreme in Latin America, was nonetheless a part of the complexity of anticlericalism.

The shortage of native clergy was both cause and consequence of the high degree of nominal Catholicism in Latin America. Most of the anticlerical struggles were urban affairs; usually the hinterland was scarcely touched by the conflicts. The masses, largely Indian, practiced a mixture of their ancient religions and Catholicism, frequently at great variance with the Catholicism practiced in the larger cities and towns.

Two countries stand out as having had more profound anticlerical struggles than any of the other Latin American states. Colombia's and Mexico's conflicts overshadowed those in other countries. Their experience can serve to show the development of anticlerical struggles in the New World.[1]

*

The Spanish crown practiced cismontane anticlericalism in America to a degree unparalleled elsewhere in the New World. Through agreements with the sixteenth-century papacy, it came to have complete control over the Church. Every appointment, all of the tithes, and all communications with Rome were under the crown's control.[2]

The regular clergy were the crown's chief problem. They tended to be more independent than the diocesan priests, there were more of them, and they controlled the bulk of the Church's wealth in the New World. Indeed, so vast was their wealth that they were the main source of credit in colonial times. If landowners and merchants needed money they borrowed from the regulars; the lack of banks and other credit agencies indicates that these institutions were not needed as long as the regular clergy had a large supply of fluid wealth.[3] The regulars were also great landowners, for it was a common custom to will a portion of one's property to the clergy. It has been estimated that by the end of the eighteenth century at least half the land in New Spain (Mexico) was controlled by the clergy. The regulars owned most of this property.[4]

The crown tried to control them. As early as 1576, the

regulars were forbidden to acquire more property. The Bourbon regime of the eighteenth century forbade the construction or founding of new houses, decreed a moratorium on the entry of novices into the orders, and ordered the regulars not to interfere with the drawing up of wills. The culmination of this policy was the expulsion of the Jesuits from the Spanish Empire in 1767.

In 1804, the crown ordered the expropriation of property belonging to benevolent associations (which were controlled by the regulars), but both landowners and clergy protested, the former for fear of losing their source of credit, and the law was never implemented.

The anticlerical ideas of the Enlightenment had limited influence on Latin America. Crown and clergy exercised censorship, but foreign anticlerical literature was circulated. Enlightenment political theories were discussed among the educated classes; however, it is generally agreed that with or without the Enlightenment, the break with Spain would have occurred.[5]

*

When the struggle for independence began, Mexico and Colombia became the centers of anticlerical conflict. Both countries had been centers of viceregal authority in the colonial period, and were therefore more heavily influenced by Spain than were most other countries.

There were other reasons why Colombia became an anticlerical cockpit.[6] Despite endemic illiteracy, it had the most highly educated and literate middle and upper classes in all of Latin America. Issues were widely discussed, and the press was vigorous. Colombians tended to be issue oriented rather than personality oriented as were most other Latin Americans; other nations responded to strong men and dictators, but Colombians responded to abstractions and issues. As a result, ideological anticlericalism was more widespread. Because the press reported on events abroad, French anticlerical ideas were also discussed and understood by the literate and urbane Colombians. Most of the anticlericals freely quoted and exhibited a profound acquaintance with the ideas of the French Revolutions of 1789 and 1848.

Colombia was a stronghold of clericalism. Other countries depended upon foreign missionaries to supplement the native clergy, but Colombia was always able to supply the vast majority of its own priests. Furthermore, missionaries to Colombia were usually French rather than Spanish; their rigorous Jansenistic attitudes increased anticlerical tensions.[7] There was a higher degree of practical Catholicism. Even in the twentieth century, Colombia continued to have one of the highest ratios of priests per capita and the largest number of seminarians per capita. In their vigor, commitment, and mentality, the Colombian clergy resembled the Spanish clergy. This high degree of clericalism was a primary cause of the anticlerical conflict.

*

J. Lloyd Mecham in his monumental study of church-state relations in Latin America asserts that religion was not a factor in the revolutions for independence.[8] This is perfectly true in the sense that neither revolutionaries nor supporters of Spanish control wanted to do away with Catholicism. The revolutionaries demanded that Catholicism be the established religion in the new states, and few were in favor of the principle of toleration. All invoked the aid of the Church to their cause.

But there was anticlericalism in the revolution. Some of the lower clergy wanted a more equitable share of clerical wealth and resented the *peninsulares'* monopoly of bishoprics. The middle class wanted restrictions upon the regulars and particularly opposed the continuation of the Inquisition.

Although the vast majority of the Colombian clergy supported Simón Bolívar's independence movement, the higher clergy—Spanish born—backed the Spanish crown.[9] They frequently resorted to the principle of obedience to constituted authority in their appeal for support of the crown. Yet, this appeal to principle was shown to be false when circumstances in Spain changed. The original impetus for independence was the seizure of Spain by Napoleon in 1808. The bishops supported the crown against the revolutionaries, who claimed that the demise of the Spanish government had negated their dependence upon it. In 1814, the absolutist regime of Ferdinand VII was restored in Spain, and the bishops naturally supported this clerical regime. In 1820, Ferdinand's government was overthrown by the anticlerical liberals in Cádiz. Since the principle of obedience to constituted authority now meant support of an anticlerical government, the higher clergy shifted their support to the independence movement. This action had its effect upon the future development of anticlericalism by showing the bishops to be more concerned with political advantage than with principle.

By its actions the papacy likewise suffered a serious loss of prestige during these years. As various states declared independence, the new governments demanded the patronage powers of the Spanish crown. In Colombia, the government appealed to the Holy See for recognition of the transference of the patronage. Pope Pius VII was understandably hesitant, for he had no assurance that the new government was indeed independent; a change in fortunes might return the Spaniards to control with consequent repercussions. Pius did nothing at first. In 1816, two years after the Spanish restoration, when it appeared that Spain had regained effective control, he issued an encyclical calling upon the Latin Americans to recognize Spanish authority. When the Spanish anticlericals seized power in 1820 and the revolutions began again in Latin America, the Colombian bishops appealed for support for the independence movement. Pius declared his neutrality in 1822. A year later he died, and the same year the Spanish anticlerical regime was overthrown. The new pope, Leo XII, published an encyclical supporting Spanish control. By this time, however, the revolutions had been successful. The papacy's actions were understandable, faced as it was with the dilemma of supporting or denying the Spanish crown in very fluid circumstances. But the whole situation did little to increase the prestige of the papacy.[10]

Nor did the issue of the patronage. Bolívar sent Ignacio de Tejada to Rome to negotiate an agreement which would provide recognition of the principle that patronage had now devolved upon the successor to the Spanish crown, namely the government of Colombia. Not until 1833 did the papacy recognize the bishops appointed by the Colombian government, and not until two years later did it grant diplomatic recognition to the new state. Meanwhile, political anticlericals in Colombia took advantage of the clergy's embarrassment and the papacy's loss of prestige to begin anticlerical reforms.

*

In the first years after the success of the revolutions Colombian political anticlericalism was purely internal, untouched by antisacerdotalism or anti-Catholicism. It was aimed at clerical abuses. Three problems were singled out for attention: the patronage, the Inquisition, and the regular clergy.

Almost all Colombians were united in wanting the patronage powers formerly held by the Spanish crown. The issue of ultramontanism was not as important as the desire to gain independence from Spain and recognition from the papacy. They incorporated the principle in the Constitution of 1811, and in 1824 passed a law that clearly spelled out the patronage powers of the government.[11] The papacy did not accept this at first and refused to allow the consecration of new bishops nominated by the government. It was not until the pontificate of Gregory XVI, in 1833, that the papacy implicitly recognized the law of 1824. Thereafter, in one form or another, the government had control over the clergy.

The Inquisition was abolished in 1821, a measure that gained almost unanimous support in the congress. But the congress went on to legislate that the government would exercise its powers of censorship in accord with the rules of dogma, and it voted public funds for various church projects. The question of establishment was not acted on, but religious toleration was provided—for aliens, not Colombian citizens. These laws reveal that the government was not even moderately anticlerical.

President Simón Bolívar, although personally dedicated to

the principle of toleration and in favor of separation of church and state as it was practiced in the United States, felt that Colombians were not yet ready for such a radical step. A freethinker in his early years, he made a point of public attendance at religious functions.[12] His vice-president, Francisco de Santander, was more anticlerical and wanted some restrictions on the political activities of the clergy. Thus, when Bolívar was out of the country, Santander persuaded the congress to enact legislation against the regular clergy.[13]

Santander was concerned, as the Spanish crown had been, with the power and wealth of the regulars, as well as with their proliferation. In 1821, the congress suspended all religious houses with fewer than eight members, expropriated their property, and ordered the revenues to be spent for the support of education and charity. Schools and hospitals which fell under this law were exempt. In 1826, orders were forbidden to accept novices under the age of twenty-five.

In view of the harsher anticlerical precedents in France and Spain, it is a wonder that there was any clerical reaction at all. Bolívar was upset, however, and upon his return assumed dictatorial powers and suspended these laws. Apparently, he was concerned with clerical antagonism to the laws, and he had always felt the clergy were a force for law and order. He also decreed prohibitions upon secret societies, although this was largely directed against the Masonic supporters of Santander. Undoubtedly, anticlericals were also upset over the suspension of these relatively mild laws.

*

After Colombia was separated from Venezuela in 1831, clericalism and anticlericalism came to play a greater role in the political development of the country. The conflict was much like those fought elsewhere. The clergy supported the conservatives, chiefly landowners and usually centralists. The anticlerical liberals were urban, mercantile and normally regionalists or federalists. At times, the clerical-anticlerical issue was used by both conservatives and liberals to gain support, although it was frequently a subsidiary issue.

For the first two decades of Colombia's independence, the conservatives were in charge, and few anticlerical laws were passed. Occasionally mildly anticlerical governments came to power, but the clergy generally made few objections; all were appointees of the government, and any strong opposition came from the regulars.

The clergy were well represented in the new government. At first, the cabinet included an archbishop and the constitution of the new republic did not provide for religious toleration. The new president, Santander, however, wanted to continue his cismontane policies; he did not want to suppress the regulars, but rather to use the state's power to control them. His chief anticlerical action was to abolish clerical privileges and make the clergy subject to civil law.

Santander's successor, José Ignacio de Márquez, wanted to implement some of the milder anticlerical laws. In 1839, he abolished the exemptions from suppression (because of few members) enjoyed by the convents of Pasto, which, with the province of Antioquia, was a clerical stronghold. Although the Bishop of Popayán ordered obedience to the government, some of the clergy led the populace in a revolt against the law. Ultimately, Márquez had to send in troops to put down the rebellion.[14]

Otherwise, conservative rule was clerical. The Jesuits were invited to return to Colombia in 1844 for the first time since their expulsion in 1767. But by the late 1840s the conservatives began to lose support: they could not provide internal peace as the liberals began demanding a federal form of government. The liberals were stimulated by the French Revolution of 1848, and anticlericalism was one of the main facets of their program.

The reasons behind their anticlericalism were that the clergy were solidly allied with the conservatives and that the economic and political reforms which they considered necessary could not be implemented as long as the clergy continued to control large amounts of wealth and as long as they opposed federalism. Furthermore, with the increasing violence of Colombian political history, the clergy came to be the symbol of all that was wrong with the conservatives.

The liberals came to power in 1849. From 1850 to 1855 they legislated against the clergy. The Jesuits were again expelled, and control over the clergy was given to the municipal and state authorities. The tithes were annulled, the clergy were liable for trial in civil courts for offences of a purely ecclesiastical nature, and municipal councils were given the right to nominate all parish clergy. A national seminary was established under state control.

These laws were more radical than those which had been passed before, but they did not touch the main sources of clerical power, namely the regulars and clerical wealth. Despite this, the clergy protested vociferously, and the Archbishop of Bogotá and a number of other bishops and priests were expelled from the country.

In 1853, the congress passed an act of separation, formally disestablishing the Church. Although the document said that the state would cease to intervene in church affairs, particularly in the nomination of the clergy, the state still exercised control over them. As a corollary to the act of separation, the ownership of church buildings was given to all of the Catholics in a parish.

After 1855, the centralist-federalist conflict heightened, and in 1857 the conservatives returned to power. They had become federalists in order to protect themselves against the liberals, and the clergy had begun to talk of supporting federalism to secure "provinces of refuge" from anticlerical laws. With the conservatives in power, church buildings were returned to the clergy, and their right to own property was recognized. The Jesuits were also allowed to return.

In 1860, the liberals regained power and Tomás Mosquera was elected president. For the next seven years he devoted himself with single-minded determination to uprooting clericalism. His anticlericalism was that of the convert: his brother was the exiled Archbishop of Bogotá and he himself had been a leader of the conservatives. Now he had turned liberal and become radically anticlerical. He took the necessary steps to destroy the power of the clergy in Colombia.

From 1860 to 1867, under Mosquera, anticlerical legislation was enacted and implemented.[15] The Jesuits were once again expelled, no priest was allowed to exercise his office without the permission of the civil authorities, and various laws secularizing cemeteries and providing for civil marriage and divorce were passed. Clerics were forbidden to hold public office.

The major actions were the expropriation of the clergy's property and the suppression of religious orders. These laws effectively ended the power of the Colombian clergy to intervene successfully in secular affairs. From that time on they were dependent upon the state for their livelihood, or upon what support they could get from the faithful. This support could be considerable; like Spain and unlike most of the other Latin American states, the dogmatic grip of the clergy still remained, particularly in the clerical provinces.

The conservatives also relied upon the support of the clergy. Just as the liberals used anticlericalism to engender support for their political programs, the conservatives used clerical support to bring themselves back to power. After the failure of federalism, the conservatives returned in 1880 and the new president, Rafael Núñez, pursued a clerical policy. In a new constitution and a concordat negotiated with the papacy, the anticlerical legislation was abolished, although the expropriations were admitted as a *fait accompli*. The clergy were to be given compensation for their lost properties and granted financial subvention by the state. Regulars were allowed to return, and the right of the clergy to possess property in the future was recognized.

The concordat provided that the state would formally resume the powers of patronage to the extent that the government could submit nominations to the Vatican. Of considerable importance to the clergy was the provision that Catholicism would be taught in all state schools.

*

After the settlement of 1888, religious issues gradually died down.[16] The liberals came to accept the settlement, and more pressing issues could be attended to. The need for a stable plan of economic development, the growth of Colombian coffee as the chief export item, and the consequent inflations and depressions attendant upon a one-crop export economy absorbed the parties' attentions. Furthermore, the rise of proletarian political parties and unions forced the liberals and conservatives to rely more upon each other as middle-class parties to protect the status quo. The liberal-conservative tacit agreement was aptly characterized by the saying, "In Colombia, the Liberals are those who drink in public and pray in private; the Conservatives are those who pray in public and drink in private."[17]

Spiraling inflation in the 1910s and 1920s increased the misery of the Colombian masses and prompted some liberals to adopt the concept of the new welfare liberalism. In 1936, the liberal President Alfonso López pushed a program of social and economic reforms through the congress. These included a revision of the clerical laws. López' legislation was actually very mild—religious toleration, and some diminution of the clergy's influence in education; but the clergy were afraid, and they drifted into even greater dependence upon the conservatives and their spokesman, Laureano Gómez, a clerical who greatly admired the Spanish dictator Franco, the motivations of the Spanish *Falange*, and who promoted the traditional ideas of *hispanidad*, particularly the clerical notion that Catholicism was the core of Hispanic civilization.

López ultimately failed to implement his reform programs, and after he was voted out, President Eduardo Santos concluded a new concordat in 1942 which restored the Church's influence in public education. The Vatican agreed that all of the hierarchy had to be Colombian citizens, approved by the government. Nothing at all was said about the regular clergy, an indication that they no longer were a disruptive influence.

The educational issue was actually not as important as it was made out to be. In the nineteenth and twentieth centuries, the clergy had concentrated their educational efforts on the secondary-school system, so that by 1950 two-thirds of all the secondary schools in the country were operated by the Church.[18] The public-school laws actually affected only primary education, and since the clergy already exercised a great deal of influence among the illiterate and under-educated, they should not have been too concerned. Their secondary system was far better than the public system and heavily attended; presumably it would offset the mild secularism of the public primary schools.

*

Up to the twentieth century, indeed up to 1948, there was no indication of any social anticlericalism in Colombia. The masses, largely *mestizo* and Indian, had long looked upon the clergy as their protectors from the oppressive upper classes and the state, although, of course, this belief was not justified. But while the clergy exploited the Indians and *mestizos*, they helped relieve some of the oppression, and the ranks of the clergy were always open to the lower classes, even if at times only in the minor orders.

By the twentieth century, however, the proletarian parties began to offer their protection to the downtrodden, and a latent spirit of social anticlericalism developed. The clergy were seen as part of the ruling establishment, and when the establishment was attacked, the clergy would also be attacked.

In 1948, the reformist liberal spokesman Jorge Gaitán was assassinated during the Inter-American Conference being held in Bogotá. This touched off an uprising against the government and the ruling groups, which destroyed much of the city. During the *bogotazo*, churches were attacked, burned, and looted, and clergy were killed. During this wild rampage, banks, stores, and other symbols of the ruling establishment were also attacked.

It is difficult to tell how much social anticlericalism was involved in the *bogotazo*. There was no other incident of social anticlericalism in Colombian history, unlike in Spain, where church incendiarism had been a tradition. The *bogotazo* still awaits its social historian, but indications are that the clergy were attacked and the churches burned because they were seen as part of the establishment; they were not necessarily the primary target. Possibly the example of Spanish incendiarism led the mob to emulate those anticlerical actions without the actual anticlerical motivation. The *bogotazo* appears to have been an act of blind rage, motivated only by the nihilistic urge to destroy.[19]

Many of the clergy responded by joining in a counter-revolution, particularly as the violence spread to the rural areas. Colombia was actually in a state of civil war, and the clergy took part in it. But there was no formal statement by the clergy in support of the conservative cause, and priests throughout the country attempted to show their neutrality and their desire for pacification. It cannot be said that the clergy were for anything other than a restoration of law and order and they had no ideological axe to grind.

The clergy supported the regime of Laureano Gómez, who was elected president in 1949. Undoubtedly, his clerical ideas of *hispanidad* appealed to them. But they withdrew their support from Gómez when he exacerbated rather than halted the civil war, and they then supported the military strongman Gustavo Rojas Pinilla.

Social attitudes of the Colombian clergy changed in the mid-1950s. Many of the younger clergy began to play a more progressive social role, occasionally an extreme one, as in the case of the guerilla priest Camilo Torres.[20] Generally, the clergy became a vital force for social change, causing some degree of reactionary social anticlericalism, which spilled over into politics in the waning days of Rojas Pinilla's regime.

The clergy finally took a stand against the dictator, who was overthrown and replaced by a constitutional regime.

In the 1960s, the Colombian clergy remained a powerful group. The primitive social and educational levels in rural areas provided them with a continuing dogmatic hold. In the cauldron of Latin America, the clergy have a vital role to play; it may lead to anticlericalism if their role is not accepted by those who win the struggle.

CHAPTER 14

Mexico

*The moral worth of the clergy is always
proportional to the moral worth
of the people in whose
midst it lives.*

G. Desdevises du Dezert

NO OTHER NOMINALLY MAJORITY CATHOLIC COUNTRY HAS
experienced such extremes of anticlericalism as Mexico.
Other nations have had intense antireligious persecution, and
the majority Catholic countries behind the Iron Curtain have
had to deal with permanently antireligious regimes, but only
in Mexico have anticlerical laws spelled out in such detail
restrictions upon the clergy without actually forbidding them
the practice of their ministry.[1]

Two circumstances were responsible for this. One was the
vast economic and political power of the clergy. The Mexican
clergy's privileges and wealth in the nineteenth century
rivalled those of any other clergy in history since the
Reformation. There was no question that they had to be
stripped of their influence if reformers were to establish a
modern, secular state.

The other circumstance was the great vitality of Mexican
Catholics.[2] The large Indian population, which had early
adopted and integrated Catholicism into its ancient tribal
practices, was fanatically loyal to the Church and the clergy.

This strength pushed anticlerical reformers to extremes, because they could not shake the power of the clergy in the countryside. Only by the mid-twentieth century did the masses begin to support the middle-class politicians; still, the Mexican clergy had strength among the rural masses.

At the beginning of the nineteenth century, the Mexican clergy were undoubtedly the wealthiest in the world. Lucas Alamán, a clerical historian, claims that one-half of the productive real estate was held by them, and other reliable sources have estimated that over one-half of the houses in Mexico City itself were owned or held in mortgage by the clergy.[3] The rents from their lands, the tithes, and fees for performance of religious services all added up to make them wealthy and independent.

The clergy were not united in their response to the independence movement which broke out in 1808. The two most important leaders of the movement, Hidalgo and Morelos, were both priests, but the vast majority of the clergy were opposed to the break with Spain, and they gave the crown enough aid to stop the movement. Every instrument of clericalism—wealth, the Inquisition, the press—was used to promote the Spanish cause. This stance created an ample target for anticlericalism; but the clergy were much too strong to be attacked at this time.

In 1820, following the liberal anticlerical revolution in Spain, the Mexican clergy changed their position and demanded independence.[4] Their support made independence possible. The Plan of Iguala, the settlement which united revolutionary groups, had as one of its three cardinal points a guarantee for the security of the Church: there was to be no toleration for non-Catholics, and the clergy's rights (or *fueros*) were recognized. These included the right to be tried in clerical courts for all offenses and the state's protection for all clerical privileges. Patronage was the only problem between the new government and the clergy. Ultimately, appeal to Rome was made, and in 1831, Gregory XVI recognized the government's right to nominate candidates for the hierarchy.[5] However, since the government was largely in the hands of clericals, patronage was never the problem that it became in the other Latin American nations.

Mexican political life was dominated by two parties: the conservatives, landed, in favor of a centralized state, and supported by the clergy; and the liberals, moderately anticlerical and federalists. Freemasonry was a factor in the organization of both parties, but the conservatives were influenced by the less anticlerical Scottish rite. Furthermore, considering the clergy's power, the Masons really had little say in the running of the party.[6]

Liberal-party anticlericalism was purely political and practical during most of the first half of the nineteenth century. Whatever ideological motives may be ascribed to the anticlericals, the fact remains that their primary interest was a purely practical one—to defeat the conservatives by striking at their chief source of support, the clergy. Undoubtedly, there were a few liberals who were ideological anticlericals as well. The radical York rite of Freemasonry was a powerful influence upon the liberals, but it was primarily a vehicle for their anticlericalism, and after the first few years of independence Masonry ceased to be a factor. Clerical historians have made much of Masonic influence, but it seems likely that any party opposed to the conservatives would have to have been anticlerical, whatever vehicle was used.

During the 1820s the conservatives were split and the liberals assumed power. Since the president and congress were elected by the state legislatures, the liberals stayed in office much longer than their popular support merited. They made a timid attack on clerical control of education by creating secular schools in some of the states, but their success was too limited either to be effective or to rouse clerical anger. Problems with foreign nations and mounting war debts, along with the political adventurism of incipient *caudillos*, dominated the political scene. The clergy were secure and had no cause to take an active political role.

In 1833, Antonio López de Santa Anna was elected president. Santa Anna immediately retired to his country estate and turned his office over to the vice-president, Valentín Gómez Farías, a dedicated liberal. Gómez Farías saw his opportunity to make a frontal attack on the clergy and solve two problems: by confiscating clerical wealth he could pay off some of the government's debts, and the confiscations would also serve to weaken the clergy and the conservatives.

Thus, he initiated the first Reform.[7] The Reform of 1833 was relatively mild compared to the later ones. Public education, what little there was, was secularized. The government resumed the powers of patronage and exiled priests who objected. Tithes were abolished, and the government announced that it would no longer use civil compulsion to secure the observance of religious vows, meaning that an order could not appeal to the state to prevent one of its members from leaving.

The chief attack of the Reform of 1833 was directed at clerical landholdings. Congress legislated the secularization of the California missions and confiscated their property, which was to be divided among settlers and Indians. When some of the clergy began to sell their property in order to prevent the government from confiscating it, the government declared such sales illegal. Although the amounts realized from these confiscations were minimal, they roused the clergy to action.

Because the Reform had been directed against the military as well, the army and the clergy made common cause and overthrew the government. Santa Anna returned from his "vacation," suspended the laws, and exiled Gómez Farías. Santa Anna was hailed as the savior of the clergy and with their support gained considerable prestige. The elections of 1837 produced a conservative majority in the congress; the Reform of 1833 was formally abrogated.

Conservatives dominated the following two decades. Although dependent upon clerical support, the governments carried out some practical anticlerical policies. The reason was purely economic. Governmental debts had never been settled, and the conservatives, like the liberals, needed money. Church property beckoned. At first, conservative leaders asked the clergy for loans, but, when these were not forthcoming, they began to decree forced loans. Santa Anna, for example, returned to power in 1840, decreed the secularization of the California missions again. In 1846, with the beginning of the war with the United States, he ordered his ministers to issue letters of credit based on church property, and the following year, with Gómez Farías returned as vice-president, the congress passed a law authorizing loans secured on clerical property; the implementation of this law was prevented only by a large bribe from the clergy to Santa Anna.[8]

Clergy, by this time, were becoming fearful of a large scale confiscation of their property. The disastrous defeat by the United States created even more fiscal problems for the government, and the handwriting was on the wall. Thus, when the liberals won the elections of 1852, clergy led a revolt against the government and recalled Santa Anna to power in return for his promise that he would not confiscate clerical land. The liberals became even more convinced that the only way to destroy the clergy's power was to destroy their wealth. When popular dissatisfaction with Santa Anna rose to a pitch in 1854, they forced him out, seized power, and determined that the time had come to break the clergy.

*

The liberal revolution of 1854 ushered in the second Reform. It marked the liberals' coming of age, the transition from practical anticlericalism to ideological anticlericalism. Influenced by French anticlerical thought, they were determined to change the course of Mexican history.[9] The chief anticlericals were Melchor Ocampo, Sebastián Lerdo de Tejada, and Benito Juárez. Of the three, Juárez had the greatest determination; he was absolutely convinced that the only way to bring the benefits of democratic government to Mexico was to destroy the clergy's power. Although the 1854 revolution brought the *mestizo* close to power, Juárez himself was a full-blooded Indian. Trained in a seminary, he left before taking vows, and, through sheer native intelligence and will power, he became a lawyer. In 1854, he was named the minister of justice in the new liberal government. Juárez has been characterized by clericals as an irreligious atheist, but actually he had a deep sense of piety and was not antireligious or even anti-Catholic.[10]

In 1855, Juárez decreed a law restricting the jurisdiction of both military and ecclesiastical courts. The Juárez law provided that the ecclesiastical courts would have jurisdiction only over ecclesiastical crimes. This attack on their *fueros* so angered the clergy that they forced the resignation of the president and began to plot the overthrowal of the government. Before they were successful, a new radically anticlerical congress was elected.

The congress of 1856 formally adopted the Juárez law, and went on to adopt the law proposed by Miguel Lerdo de Tejada, the Lerdo law.[11] This was the greatest blow against clericals, for it struck directly at their source of power, their wealth. The Lerdo law prohibited the clergy from owning real property. Their property was to be put up for sale, with tenants given the first choice of purchase, and the proceeds from the sale turned over to the former owners. The aim of the Lerdo law was not only to destroy clerical power; it also provided for the sale of the common lands of the Indian villages. Lerdo's aim was threefold: to create a class of peasant proprietors, to help solve the state's fiscal problems from a tax on the sales, and to destroy the source of clerical power. He succeeded only in the last, for the land was purchased by wealthy speculators and foreigners, and the tax income from the sales was not large enough to settle the national debt. In retrospect, the forced sale of church property appears mild, especially in comparison to the outright confiscations in other countries.

The reaction to the Lerdo law was vociferous. The hierarchy and the Pope condemned it. Congress reacted in turn and produced more anticlerical laws: the Jesuits were once again expelled (they had returned during one of Santa Anna's clerical periods), the University of Mexico was closed because it was a clerical stronghold, and cemeteries were secularized. In 1857, the congress passed the Iglesias law, which prohibited the state from helping the clergy in the collection of fees and furthermore set a limitation upon the fees which they could charge for the performance of religious services. In addition, the congress ordered clergy to give their services freely to those who could not afford to pay.

All of these laws were included in the new Constitution of 1857, which also provided for the creation of a "free and laical" school system, prohibited state enforcement of compulsory observance of religious vows, prohibited the clergy from holding national political office (although it provided that they could vote), and officially abolished the state's use of the patronage power.

To legislate was one thing, to implement another. The fact was that the Reform of 1854 was carried out against the will of the majority of Mexicans.[12] Clerical reaction was not limited to the usual condemnations this time. They threatened excommunication for anyone who purchased church property and a number of clerical pamphlets called for an insurrection against the government. More to the point, they formed an alliance with the army (which was subject to antimilitary legislation in the 1854 Reform) and planned a revolt against the government.

This revolt was successful in 1857, and the clerical-military forces took over Mexico City. But unlike in earlier revolts, the defeated government did not surrender. Juárez went to Vera Cruz, where he set up a liberal government. With two governments contending for power, civil war broke out between clericals and anticlericals.

The War of the Reform was destructive. Whenever the liberal armies overran a clerical stronghold they sacked the churches and destroyed them. This was extreme political anticlericalism; its aim was to destroy actual clerical power and to erase the clergy's dogmatic grip on the minds of the Indians, but there were no social overtones to the Reform.

It was part of Mexico's bourgeois revolution and it brought the *mestizos,* not the Indians, to power.

In Vera Cruz, Juárez decreed more anticlerical laws. The clergy had taken the field of battle against his government; he therefore dealt harshly with them. He officially separated church and state, suppressed all the regular clergy, and nationalized all clerical property, real and intangible. This time the clergy were to get no proceeds from the sale of their lands. This broke the clergy's power, although Juárez was not able to enforce these laws until the war had been won.[13]

Mexico City was in the hands of the conservatives, who revoked the anticlerical laws and ordered church land returned to the clergy. But, as elsewhere, the process was irreversible; furthermore, large portions of clerical property had been purchased by foreigners who would not relinquish their newly bought lands. They sought their governments' protection, and this became part of the undoing of the clerical-conservative alliance.

In 1860, Juárez and the liberal army entered Mexico City after having defeated the conservative forces. He was able to implement many of his anticlerical laws, but he still did not realize enough from the sale of church lands to settle the national debt, a large amount principally owed to European countries which had purchased Mexican bonds. As a result, foreign armies were sent to force the collection of the debts.

Napoleon III of France was one of the prime movers of the Allied intervention in Mexico. Still a supporter of clericalism in France in order to keep the support of the French clericals, he was also supported by the Mexican clergy, who put aside whatever feelings of nationalism they had to hail Napoleon. The French took over the government, forced Juárez into the northern reaches of Mexico, and brought the clergy back to power. But the clergy, having lost much of their land by this time, were no longer the independent power they once had been. They could not force their will on the French; they wanted to return to the status quo of 1821. Napoleon, while not anticlerical, was resolutely opposed to a clerically dominated state.

Thus, the Napoleonic representatives refused to disturb the nationalization of clerical property; they revoked the law, but they did not demand the return of the already sold properties to the clergy. Neither did the new emperor, Maximilian of Habsburg, disturb the property confiscations when he arrived in Mexico to take the throne offered him by Napoleon.

Maximilian was a practical anticlerical in the Austrian fashion.[14] He wanted problems settled by a concordat with the papacy. He did not, however, come to a clear understanding with the Pope before he left for Mexico, and once there was unable to deal with the papal nuncio. His idea of a settlement was to recognize the status quo on church property and bring the clergy under the control of the state in cismontane fashion, meanwhile offering them a privileged position in the state. Since Pius IX could not agree with him, there was no settlement.

Maximilian had to rule without a concordat. He decreed religious toleration and confirmed the Juárez law limiting the ecclesiastical *fueros.* The clergy denounced him, and his regime lost its firmest base of support. By 1866, Maximilian had lost the support of Napoleon as well, and within a year he was defeated by Juárez' liberal army. This ended the War of the Reform. The liberals were solidly in power and were able to implement the Reform of 1854.

*

The reforms were a success. The power of the clergy had been broken, and they were now salaried by the state, transforming them from an independent to a dependent group. They had not lost all of their influence, of course, and in the rural areas large numbers of people still supported them; the Indians, particularly, had never developed anticlerical feelings.

Pressure eased after the War of the Reform. Juárez, in power as president, became less anticlerical: he asked the congress to restore to the clergy their right to vote. In 1874, when Sebastiàn Lerdo de Tejada became president, he asked the congress to pass enabling legislation to carry out the anticlerical reforms, and this was done: religion was no longer to be taught in the public schools, there were to be no religious acts outside the churches, and priests were not to wear religious garb outside the churches. The congress directed that disobedience of these laws would be a federal offense.

The unreasonableness of these laws in a country where religious processions were the lifeblood of rural folk and where public devotion to the Virgin of Guadalupe was more of a national than a church tradition soon became apparent. Most of the laws were never enforced. The clergy no longer played politics or took an active role in government, but they did not obey the laws, either.

The clergy reached a tacit agreement under Lerdo's successor, Porfirio Diáz, who became the dictator of Mexico from 1876 to 1911. The clergy counseled obedience to Díaz' regime and agreed not to foment or support revolts in return for Díaz' promise not to enforce the laws. Díaz was a Freemason and a professed anticlerical, but the clergy prospered.[15] They once again purchased land and came to control large amounts of capital wealth, while the regular clergy returned. Although they obeyed the law on the secularization of the public school system, the clergy began to build a private school system. None of the anticlerical laws was repealed or revoked. Díaz kept them on the books to threaten the clergy should they prove obstreperous, and occasionally he implemented them in minor matters, such as the expulsion of one group of regulars. But the clergy learned how far they could push and how much they could get away with. Sometimes Díaz allowed the state governors to enforce the anticlerical laws if they wished, and sometimes this was done on the local level.

As a result, in the popular middle-class mind, the clergy were identified with the Díaz regime, although they were far from that in actuality. The Indians accepted the clergy under any circumstances; in fact anticlericalism had probably brought the Indians and the clergy closer together, for both groups were civil outcasts. The official Díaz brain trust, the *científicos*, were positivist anticlericals, but they did not push Díaz to enforce the laws.

Reform movements against the corruption of the Díaz regime in the early 1900s seized upon anticlericalism as their theme. The formation of the new Mexican Liberal party by Camilo Arriaga and Juan Sarabia in San Luis Potosí was based upon an original appeal to anticlericalism, although this was quickly subsumed into demands for agrarian and social reform. The anarchist Ricardo Flores Magón used anticlericalism as one of his themes, but neither had the popular appeal of Spanish or French anticlericalism.[16]

*

When the Díaz regime was overthrown in 1911, the clergy were afraid.[17] Their identification with the regime, the unsettled nature of Mexican politics, and the possibility that the anticlerical laws would be implemented led them to organize a political party. In the long run, this probably did them more harm than anything. The early revolutionaries were not anticlerical, or at least did not attempt any anticlerical activity. Francisco Madero's plan for the overthrow of Díaz said nothing about the clergy, and he was too busy trying to stay in power to initiate any anticlerical reform. When he was overthrown by Victoriano Huerta with the support of the army, the clergy were pleased and supported the Huerta regime.

There was a natural reaction when Huerta was overthrown. The constitutionalists under Venustiano Carranza were determined anticlericals. They were angry with the clergy for having supported Díaz and Huerta, but their anticlericalism went beyond this: in this extremely complex political situation, they wanted to use anticlericalism to make political gains and to impress upon the Indians that the clergy were not possessed of supernatural powers. Thus, there was a great deal of persecution, particularly in the north, where much of the fighting took place. This violent political anticlericalism ranged from capturing and shooting priests to wanton destruction of religious objects (but little burning of churches). Destruction was widespread.

Curiously, there was little social anticlericalism. In Yucatan, where there had been some social anticlericalism in the nineteenth century, mainly because the class chasm was wider there than elsewhere, the revolutionaries sacked a church and set fire to religious objects which had been piled in the square in front of it.[18] But these were isolated instances. The one truly social revolutionary movement, that of Emiliano Zapata in Morelos, was devoid of any anticlericalism. His manifesto called for action against some of the higher clergy (along with practically everyone else), but there is no record of any overt anticlericalism among his followers.[19] Probably, the masses of Indians simply did not feel the clergy were their oppressors and therefore were not interested in the issues of anticlericalism.

But the constitutionalists—middle-class *mestizos*—were political anticlericals and, in the constitutional convention called to establish a basis for the new regime, wrote the most anticlerical constitution in history.

Aside from writing the 1854 Reform laws into the Constitution of 1917, the deputies prohibited the clergy from owning any property at all. All churches were to be under government supervision. Religious education of any sort was forbidden, in private schools as well as public, and to prevent any violations of this provision, no private religious primary schools were to be established. Private secondary schools operated by religious associations were permitted, but priests or religious were not allowed to teach in them. No political associations having a religious orientation were to be allowed, and priests and religious journals were forbidden to criticize the government.

The most stringent provision of the constitution gave the state legislatures the right to determine how many priests were to be allowed to function in each state. This was done at the insistence of the deputies from the more anticlerical states (the Yucatan deputies, for example, proposed that no priest be allowed to exercise his ministry unless he were married and over fifty years of age). No foreign clerics were to be allowed in the country. Infraction of any of the anticlerical provisions would be subject to summary justice; trial by jury was waived for such offenses.[20]

Carranza had not wanted so anticlerical a constitution, but

the deputies made it law. Significantly, the constitution was not enforced at first. Apparently, the anticlerical provisions had served the purpose of bringing the deputies together, but once having legislated, they did not demand implementation. Neither Carranza, who ruled until 1920, nor Álvaro Obregón, who was president to 1926, implemented the laws. Some of the state legislatures began limiting the numbers of clergy in their states, but, generally until 1926, the regime was too involved in consolidating its power to bother with anticlericalism. There were occasional instances of violence: bishops' homes were bombed, and even the national shrine of Guadalupe was the target of a bomb; but most of the time the clergy and the anticlericals made no trouble for each other. When Obregón was asked why he did not close the church schools, he replied that the state did not have enough schools to educate everyone and that it was better that children be taught by priests than not at all.[21]

All this came to an end in 1926 when Plutarco Elías Calles was elected president. Calles was more than anticlerical. He was anti-Catholic, and even before his election he announced his determination to implement the anticlerical laws. The clergy, for their part, gave him reason to do so; they issued a public protest against the Constitution of 1917. They had done so in 1917, but with the nonenforcement of the laws, matters had lain dormant. Why they provoked Calles (who admittedly needed little provocation) at this crucial moment is not known: perhaps they were testing the regime; perhaps fear of Calles led them to take the offensive; possibly the attitude of the more clerical Pope Pius XI encouraged them in their efforts.[22]

Calles ordered the anticlerical legislation put into effect. Religious schools were closed, foreign priests were ordered to leave the country, convents and monasteries were closed (which led to some rioting by clerical supporters), and the penal code was revised to provide specific penalties for violations of the law. Calles even tried to form a schismatic church, completely subservient to the state.

To enforce the limitation provisions, priests were ordered

to register with the government, and the state legislatures were told to determine the number of priests allowed. The number of clergy at that time was slightly over 3,000. The legislatures cut this to fewer than 1,000. In some states as few as five priests were authorized for the entire state. In the Federal District, there were 863,000 Catholics (admittedly most of them nominal); the number of priests allowed was cut from 289 to 90. Clearly, the clergy could not survive against this fanatical anticlericalism.

Their response was as extreme as the legislation. They ordered a suspension of all religious services in Mexico, and the churches were closed. Priests went into hiding into an underground church. The hierarchy complained to the president and congress, but their complaints went unanswered because, according to the constitution, they did not have "juridic personality." A clerical revolt, the Cristero movement, broke out in some of the provinces, and there was a great deal of violence done, both by the Cristeros and by the government in suppressing them. Bishops who complained were expelled, and President-elect Obregón was assassinated by a Cristero supporter.

After three years, and through American mediation, a new president, Emilio Portes Gil, reached a settlement with the clergy to the effect that nonregistered priests would be allowed to exercise their ministries. The suspension was lifted, and the churches were opened again in 1929. The Pope accepted the settlement and urged conciliation. But the clergy responded too openly to the settlement. Apparently they were unaware of the depth of anticlerical feeling among the politicians and the ruling classes. Catholic organizations were formed to provide for the education of Catholic children, and a great public celebration was held in 1931 to commemorate the four-hundredth anniversary of the miracle of Guadalupe.

The anticlerical politicians were determined to forbid these violations of the law, and the legislatures once again began limiting the number of priests. By 1935, fewer than 500 priests were authorized for all of Mexico—a nation with over 10,000,000 Catholics. In education, enabling legislation in

1934 provided that public education was to be organized to combat religious fanaticism and to promote socialism. Seminaries (which had been allowed under the Constitution of 1917) were expressly forbidden. In some of the states, teachers were required to take oaths that they were anti-Catholic and atheist in their beliefs. The clergy countered by ordering that no Catholic could in good conscience attend the public schools and began to organize illegal schools. There was violence: in the more clerical states, public-school teachers were murdered, in the anticlerical states, the police were sent in to break up the Catholic schools.

Conciliation came in 1936 after Lázaro Cárdenas was elected to the presidency. Cárdenas was anxious to undertake far-reaching economic and social reforms and he saw that the anticlerical conflict was divisive.[23] Thus, he announced that the government would enforce the laws with moderation, and the pressure was eased. The proof of the wisdom of Cárdenas' policy was seen in 1938 when he nationalized the foreign oil industry in Mexico and the clergy supported him.

Mexican politicians had finally come to the realization that anticlericalism breeds clericalism and that the clergy were really no longer a threat to the state. In 1940, when Manuel Ávila Camacho was inaugurated as president, he publicly announced that he was a Catholic. After 1940, the anticlerical laws were no longer enforced. The regulars returned and private schools were allowed. The government has not repealed the laws, but the clergy and Catholics have more freedom than at any time since the Revolution began.[24]

CHAPTER 15

Conclusion:
The End of Anticlericalism

*Every profession is a conspiracy
against the laity.*

G.B. Shaw

IT HAS FREQUENTLY BEEN OBSERVED THAT THE LAITY GETS
the clergy it deserves. Unquestionably, the laity have had
profound influence on the clergy. The clergy have been
recruited from the laity, have had lay upbringings, and there
has never been a period in the history of the Church that
the clergy have not been under some form of lay control,
either in the democracy of the early Church or under the
thumb of cismontane rulers. Even in the Middle Ages, the
clergy had lay patrons they had to please. The clergy have
always been dependent on lay contributions, lay support, and
lay cooperation.

Yet, on a very personal and private level, in areas which
historians have only begun to explore, the clergy's attitudes
were sometimes at great variance from the laity's. The
confessional, as Zeldin observes, has been a powerful source
of anticlericalism.[1] Priests with harsher, stricter, sometimes
more puritanical demands, could not help but antagonize
those who lived in a society that condoned forbidden

pleasures. This facet of the relationship between clergy and laity has been another point of tension in the anticlerical conflict.

*

Quite apart from specific criticisms made against the clergy's activities at any particular time, there has been a psychology of anticlericalism having to do with the clergy as a group.[2] As the visible representative of an institution, the individual cleric became the target of those who opposed the institution.

In this respect, anticlericalism is similar to other "anti" ideologies or feelings, like anti-Semitism, anti-Negro prejudice, anticommunism, and antimilitarism. In each case, the object of dislike is fairly easily identifiable: Negroes are black, communists are usually self-proclaimed, soldiers wear uniforms. In each case, the individual Jew, Negro, communist, or soldier is looked upon as the symbol of an entire race or institution. In anti-Semitic and anti-Negro prejudice the reasons can usually be found more easily in the hater than in the hated. In anticommunism and antimilitarism, unlimited ideology is often confused with limited aims: a communist may be a sincere social reformer and a soldier may be a sincere patriot. Anticlericalism shares a bit of both these rationales.

What all of these objects of dislike or hatred have in common is a sense of uniformity and distinction, although this sense is frequently mythical and imposed rather than real and innate. The clergy have been visible and identifiable representatives of an institution: they conform to a rule, their education (since Trent) has been standardized, and they wear a distinct garb.

The priest is really an outsider in any social group other than his own religious community. He is purposely set apart from the layman. He is distinct and therefore more likely to become an object of suspicion. The cleric belongs to a closed society, the fraternity of priests, a group that the layman can never hope to enter without becoming a priest himself. This privacy and closeness, which is unavoidable and necessary, creates anticlericalism, for it breeds suspicion. What the layman does not know he invents, and the myth is perpetuated.

But the clergy are distinct in a particular way that few other groups are. The cleric has to accept and act upon a higher and more rigid ethical and professional code than does the layman, whatever his profession. The moral demands of Christianity are difficult ones, yet the priest, because he has the special task of teaching and enforcing that moral code, must of necessity live up to it to a greater extent than does the layman. When he fails to do so, he falls much farther than does the layman: and since he is distinct, his moral lapse is more noticeable. While it may be a fact that no one can constantly practice what he preaches, few people are psychologically prepared to accept such a revelation about the clergy.

These high expectations are in part caused by the idealization of the clergy by the laity. Just as the anti-Semite has exaggerated notions of Jewish fiscal prowess and the extreme anticommunist believes the communist to be superhumanly and diabolically clever, so the extreme anticlerical idealizes the cleric to be a superior type of human being. Paradoxically, this idealization is a common characteristic of both extreme clericals and extreme anticlericals; the former entrust everything to the clergy because they believe them to be better judges than the laity, and the latter criticize the clergy for not being better than they actually are. In any event, all idols have the proverbial feet of clay, and the clergy are no exception.

Idealization contributes to the belief that there is something unnatural about the clergy. Although this sense of unnaturalness, like many other beliefs about the clergy, rests to a great extent upon myth and legend, it is nonetheless present. Priests are not thought of as sharing the pleasures of the common man. They fast, they are celibate, they constantly compare everything to a supernatural ideal—this is not the way laity live. Nuns in particular seem to be singled out as otherworldly, probably because motherhood is so much a part of the feminine psyche and function.

Celibacy is considered to be the most unnatural aspect of the clergy. Celibacy strikes at the very root of human nature. The desire for sexual pleasure and the psychological grasp at immortality that children provide are probably among the most fundamental human needs, yet these the clergy voluntarily deny themselves. Whether necessary or not, clerical celibacy serves to widen the separation between clergy and laity.

The clergy are subject to the temptation of all professionals —arrogance. Anticlericals find it easy to manufacture a stereotype of snobbishness and condescension. The clergy are particularly prone to these because they have so many more professional functions, and the cleric frequently makes the case that his supernatural powers and tasks are vastly more important than any mundane ones the laity might have. On the other hand, there is the stereotype of the obsequious priest, one who constantly humbles himself and makes himself anxious to please. Often treated as an object of contempt in literature, he appears to strike a pose of false humility. Certainly, given these alternative poses, the clergy's task is not and has not been an easy one.

*

If the psychology of anticlericalism considers the clergy members of a group rather than as individuals, in fact, they have usually acted as an institutional group, as officers and representatives of an institution. Like officers in the military, bureaucrats in government, and intellectuals in academe, they have sought to protect their privileges and to extend their power against those who have threatened them, or against the day that they would be threatened. Like other professionals and officers, they have used fair means and foul to garner power; and they cannot be condemned out of hand for doing so, because foul means were used against them as well. Their mistakes were the professional mistakes of identifying their own interests with the interests of the institution as a whole.

Such behavior is a common occurrence in almost any facet of institutional relations.

All institutional groups are threatened with change, because most base their position on the stability of the status quo. Some of these groups adjust to change more readily than others. For the clergy, adjustment has been particularly difficult because practically all change has heralded the advance of the secular revolution. This movement struck directly at the most basic clerical power—dogmatic prestige—and every change meant a lessening of that power.

The clergy themselves were susceptible to change, but clerical institutions were not. The consolidation and incorporation of the Church, the bureaucratization of the Tridentine reforms, all these made clerical institutions frozen and impervious to change. But it must be said that the clericals who opposed change were perfectly correct in their assessment of the danger to their institutional power; each small advance of the secular revolution threatened the entire structure of their power. In placing their struggle against secularism and change in the starkest terms imaginable as a struggle between good and evil, they were simply practicing good institutional policy. The clergy can be faulted for many things, but not for the lack of perception of the immense and unalterable damage the secular revolution could have upon their position.

The clergy differed from other institutional groups in another way. They had to tread the narrow line between precept and practice. In their sermons they preached the Christian ideals of humility, poverty, and charity; but as an institution they could not survive by practicing such precepts. Militarists propound bellicosity and aggressiveness and in this sense are true to their institution. But the clergy had to preach virtues that they could not practice, or could practice only in the confines of contemplative life.

The regular clergy made an attempt to answer this criticism. The foundation of contemplative orders in the Middle Ages demonstrated that the clergy could practice what they preached; and violations of their rule always generated greater anticlerical criticism than that directed against the diocesan clergy. But the contemplatives did not make any attempt to live in this world. When orders such as the Franciscans were founded, they tried to live the ideals preached in the gospels, and their initial attempts were successful in preventing anticlericalism. But, as with all institutions which want to survive, they also eventually had to compromise with the world and thus came in for their share of criticism. In the sixteenth century the Jesuits were founded, not so much to combat change, but rather to serve the Church by adapting to change. This attitude earned them a barrage of criticism from all quarters, particularly from the new anticlericals who wanted a less adaptable clergy.

The problem posed by precept and practice had another aspect: the difficulty of knowing when to participate in the affairs of this world. The constant theme of nineteenth-century anticlericals was that the clergy should stay in their churches, attend to matters of faith, and stay out of politics. Indeed, most classic definitions of clericalism refer to it as the clergy's intrusion into politics. Yet, in the twentieth century the clergy were criticized precisely for not intervening in what the nineteenth-century anticlericals would have called "secular" affairs. The demands from modern liberals that the clergy concern themselves with the problems of poverty, racism, and war would have astounded the nineteenth-century participants in the anticlerical struggle, and they would not have comprehended Rolf Hochhuth's condemnation of Pius XII for not speaking out against the persecution of the Jews during the Second World War.[3] Anticlerical liberalism has come full circle. It is one of the ironies of history that the modern, socially activist clergy are actually neoclerical and are now criticized by reactionary social anticlericals, who in a true sense are the heirs of the nineteenth-century liberal anticlericals; while modern liberals who want the clergy involved in the world have the nineteenth-century clericals as their intellectual predecessors.

*

The criticisms of anticlericals have been barometers of the age, the chief anticlerical complaints at any time have reflected the main concerns of that age. But one should not think of most anticlericals as malicious malcontents. Anticlericals have played a vital role within the Church by reminding the clergy of their duties and by maintaining the tension that has had much to do with producing the vitality and dynamism of Christianity. Furthermore, they recognized the dangers of clericalism and were willing to stake their lives (and souls) in the struggle against it. Certainly not only the history of the Church, but the Church itself would be poorer today without the constant constructive criticism of anticlericals.

Unfortunately, anticlericalism as a movement was sometimes dominated by those who practiced a bogus anticlericalism designed to use the clergy as scapegoats to cover up other problems. The history of parliamentary anticlericalism is replete with examples. Frequently seizing on valid issues, anticlericals sometimes distorted them out of proportion to the dangers they posed and thus unwittingly contributed to the continuation of clericalism itself. In addition, many anticlericals were not perceptive to the shifts in the power of the clergy. When the clergy lost much of their wealth in the nineteenth century, anticlericals were not aware that criticism no longer served the function it had when clericalism had been a valid problem.

*

Anticlericalism died in the mid-twentieth century. The success of the secular revolution, eroding the clergy's dogmatic power, killed it. Even before the Second Vatican Council, political anticlericalism had ceased to be an issue in all but the most primitive countries. The social activism of many of the younger clergy put an end to social anticlericalism; although, it created reactionary social anticlericalism among those who object to this neoclericalism, this is not a progressive ideology and lacks vitality.

Religious issues today concern doctrine more than discipline, and dissent reflects this concern. In a sense, the end of anticlericalism is the result of the shift in emphasis of dissent. The Church has always been faced with dissent of one kind or another. In the primitive and medieval Church, dissent was focused on dogma. The doctrinal heresies of the Arians and the Manicheans consumed the energies of the early Fathers of the Church, but there were few problems with the clergy as clergy.

By the beginning of the twelfth century, dissent focused on the clergy, continuing in intensity to the early twentieth century. But today dissent is no longer anticlerical; it is again dogmatic. Catholicism's main problems are no longer the method of belief, but belief itself. The clergy, in general, lead the new criticism, but the issues they raise are no longer the main concern of Catholics.

Certainly the events surrounding the pontificate of Pope John XXIII and the early sessions of the Second Vatican Council had much to do with destroying the last vestiges of the clergy's dogmatic power. Perhaps Pope John and the Vatican theologians simply recognized the secular revolution's success; perhaps they unwittingly contributed to it; perhaps in the long run they contributed to the formation of a new kind of clergy that will successfully meet modern needs. It is too early to tell.

Anticlericalism has been almost uniquely a problem relevant only to Roman Catholicism. Other Christian religions have not had the problem to the same degree of intensity. If an overbearing and authoritarian clergy have been the main cause of anticlericalism, then Lutheranism and early Calvinism do not bear this out. Perhaps the Reformation doctrine of the priesthood of all believers so characterized Protestantism that anticlericalism was an impossible ideology to develop. As for non-Christian religions, there is no more authoritarian and priest-ridden religion than Hinduism, yet there has been no evidence of anticlericalism among the untouchables.

Perhaps it is tension that makes anticlericalism. The practical and the ideal, the possible and the impossible, the attainable and the unattainable have been the poles of tension that have created much of the conflict. This tension has provided Christianity with much of its dynamism as well. Perhaps in the ultimate analysis only dynamic religious creeds can breed anticlericalism, and the very conflict may be a chief source of Christianity's vigor.

NOTES

NOTES TO CHAPTER 1

1. See Brian Tierney, *The Crisis of Church and State, 1050-1300* (Englewood Cliffs, N.J., 1968) for a discussion of Boniface's struggle with Philip the Fair of France and for the text of the bull.

2. The term *clericalism* was not coined until the mid-nineteenth century; *anticlericalism* did not come into general use until the turn of the twentieth. Léon Gambetta made the term famous with his remark on the floor of the chamber of deputies on May 4, 1877: "Le cléricalisme—voilà l'ennemi!" (cited in Adrien Dansette, *Religious History of Modern France*, trans. J. Dingle [New York, 1961], I, 349). For the etymology of the terms, see E. Magnin, "Anticléricalisme," *Dictionnaire de Sociologie* (Paris, 1938), I, 935-936.

3. "Clericalism and Anti-Clericalism," *Encyclopedia of Religion and Ethics* (Edinburgh, 1910), III, 690. Encyclopedia treatment of the terms is weak; Whittuck's article is very penetrating considering its age. There is a superficial article by C. Berthelot du Chesney in the *New Catholic Encyclopedia* (New York, 1967), I, 618-620, but none in the original *Catholic Encyclopedia* (New York, 1907). The *Enciclopedia Cattolica* (Vatican City, 1948) briefly mentions clericalism but not anticlericalism. The *Grand Larousse* (Paris, 1960) and the *Grande Enciclopedia Portuguesa e Brasileira* (Lisbon and Rio de Janeiro, n.d.) have short articles, but there is nothing in the German encyclopedias, the Spanish *Enciclopedia Universal Ilustrada* (Madrid, 1928), the *Enciclopedia Italiana* (Rome, 1949), or the *Brittanica* (Chicago, 1968). Magnin's article in the *Dictionnaire de Sociologie* is useful, as is J. Lecler, "Anticléricalisme," *Catholicisme: Hier, Aujourd'hui, Demain*, ed. G. Jacquemet (Paris, 1947), I, 633-638.

4. Little work has been done on the history of anticlericalism. Joseph N. Moody, *The Church as Enemy: Anticlericalism in Nineteenth Century French Literature* (Washington, 1968), and Joan Connelly Ullman, *The Tragic Week: A Study of Anticlericalism in Spain, 1875-1912* (Cambridge, Mass., 1967), although both dealing with specific areas, have extremely useful insights into the general problem. Among other works, J. Salwyn Shapiro, *Anticlericalism: Conflict Between Church and State in France, Italy, and Spain* (Princeton, 1966), is weak and amounts to little more than an inadequate study of church-state relations. Alec Mellor, *Histoire de l'Anticléricalisme Française*

(Paris, 1966), is too narrow, but is useful for Freemasonic anticlericalism. John Devlin, *Spanish Anticlericalism* (New York, 1966), is a literary study. The older works, such as Emil Faguet, *L'Anticléricalisme* (Paris, 1906), and Victor Giraud, *Anticléricalisme et Catholicisme* (Paris, 1906), serve only to reveal the anticlericalism of their authors. The most helpful general history of the Church for any study of anticlericalism, although weak on the nineteenth and twentieth centuries, is Henri Daniel-Rops, *A History of the Church of Christ*, trans. various scholars, 9 vols. (Garden City, N.Y.: Doubleday, Image Books, 1960-67). Luigi Sturzo, *Church and State*, trans. B. B. Carter (Notre Dame, 1962), has good insights.

Useful articles include: Guillaume de Bertier de Sauvigny, "French Anticlericalism Since the Great Revolution: A Tentative Interpretation," *Historical Records and Studies*, XLII (New York: United States Catholic Historical Society, 1954), 3-21; Charles Taylor, "Clericalism," *Cross Currents* X (Fall 1960): 327-336; J. Lecler, "Origines et Evolution de l'Anticléricalisme," *Etudes* CCLIII (May 1947): 145-164; Frederick E. Flynn, "Clericalism, Anti-Clericalism," *Commonweal* LVIII (Apr. 17, 1953): 43-47; Joseph H. Fichter, "Anticlericalism in the American Catholic Culture," *The Critic* XXI (Feb.-Mar. 1963): 11-15.

5. Moody, *The Church as Enemy*, pp. 4-11, has a discussion of limited and unlimited anticlericalism in France.

6. See the discussions of the problem of authority in John L. McKenzie, *Authority in the Church* (New York, 1966), and Ives Simon, *Nature and Functions of Authority* (Milwaukee, 1940).

7. The great French historian Ernest Lavisse phrased this approach better than anyone: "To be secular [*laïque*]...is not to make the best of ignorance about anything. It is to believe that life is worth the trouble of being lived, to love life, to refuse to look upon the world as a vale of tears, to deny that tears are necessary and providential.... It is not to leave consoling the sorrowful to a judge seated outside of this life: it is to join battle with evil in the name of justice" (cited in Yves Congar, *Lay People in the Church: A Study for a Theology of the Laity*, trans. D. Attwater [Westminster, Md., 1957], p. 19).

NOTES TO CHAPTER 2

1. Jeffrey B. Russell, *Dissent and Reform in the Early Middle Ages* (Los Angeles and Berkeley, 1965), is uncontestably the best study of medieval dissent; see pp. 246-247 for his argument that dissent did not occur where external pressure was too great.

Two good histories of the medieval Church are Jean Daniélou and Henri Marrou, eds., *The Christian Centuries* (New York, 1964–) and Hubert Jedin and John Dolan, eds., *Handbook of Church History* (New York, 1965–). See also Jeffrey B. Russell, *A History of Medieval Christianity* (New York, 1968), for an excellent interpretative essay. Henri Pirenne, *A History of Europe from the Invasions to the XVI Century*, trans. B. Miall (New York, 1955), has many penetrating insights.

2. See R. E. Roberts, *The Theology of Tertullian* (London, 1924).

3. See W. H. C. Frend, *The Donatist Church* (London, 1952).

4. The most complete statement of Pelagius' views can be found in Robert F. Evans, *Pelagius: Inquiries and Reappraisals* (New York, 1968).

5. In this context, it is interesting to observe that the Eastern Orthodox clergy never became targets of anticlericalism to the extent the Roman clergy did; they also were a married clergy and continued to be so after the Roman Church began to enforce clerical celibacy.

6. J. Lecler, *The Two Sovereignties: A Study of the Relationship Between Church and State* (New York, 1952), pp. 108-127, and Karl Morrison, *Tradition and Authority in the Western Church* (Princeton, 1969), have good discussions of the problems caused by overlapping jurisdictions.

7. Very little is known about Charles' confiscations, but most historians agree that he had no ideological bias. See D. Herlihy, "Secularization of Church Property," in *New Catholic Encyclopedia*, XIII, 40.

8. D. Herlihy, "Church Property on the European Continent, 701-1200," *Speculum* XXXVI (1961): 81-105, details the extent of clerical landholdings.

9. In 1075, Gregory VII issued the *Dictatus Papae*, a strong condemnation of lay control. Innocent III maintained in a number of statements and letters the primacy of the papacy in temporal matters. See Brian Tierney, *Crisis of Church and State*, pp. 49, 131-136.

10. See Russell, *Dissent and Reform*, pp. 125-151, for a full discussion of the reactionary anticlericals.

11. Russell, *Dissent and Reform*, pp. 114-117, tells of the "religious eccentricity" that accompanied the strange journey of a huge boat on wheels pulled by weavers from Inda to Sint Truiden.

12. Russell, *Dissent and Reform*, pp. 102-108.

13. Russell, *Dissent and Reform*, pp. 111-113; and Walter L. Wakefield and Austin P. Evans, eds., *Heresies of the High Middle Ages* (New York, 1969), pp. 72-73, for Ralph the Bald's account of Leutard.

14. Russell, *Dissent and Reform*, pp. 45-46, and Wakefield and Evans, *Heresies*, p. 23.

NOTES TO CHAPTER 3

1. George W. Greenaway, *Arnold of Brescia* (Cambridge, 1931), is a good biography. See also Russell, *Dissent and Reform*, pp. 96-100, and the contemporary accounts in Wakefield and Evans, *Heresies*, pp. 146-150.

2. Useful works for studying the twelfth-century anticlerical revolt are:

Russell, *Dissent and Reform*; Wakefield and Evans, *Heresies*; Gordon Leff, *Heresy in the Later Middle Ages*, 2 vols. (Manchester, 1967); and Norman Cohen, *The Pursuit of the Millenium* (New York, 1961).

3. Pirenne, *A History of Europe*, pp. 238-242.

4. Leff, *Heresy in the Later Middle Ages*, I, 14-15, discusses the effects of centralization and incorporation.

5. Wakefield and Evans, *Heresies*, p. 25.

6. See the ideas and impact of Joachim of Fiore in Cohen, *Pursuit of the Millenium*, pp. 99-103.

7. Russell, *Dissent and Reform*, pp. 230-241, argues this point convincingly against Cohen's emphasis on the social roots of dissent: "Far from having any social program, their concern was with the enhancement of the purity of individuals. The Church as an institution was condemned, not because of its social role, but because its frequent state of corruption seemed to obstruct the individual's path to God."

8. Daniel-Rops, *History of the Church of Christ: Cathedral and Crusade*, I, 170.

9. See the contemporary accounts of Tanchelm in Wakefield and Evans, *Heresies*, pp. 97-101; also Russell, *Dissent and Reform*, pp. 56-68.

10. Contemporary accounts of Henry are in Wakefield and Evans, *Heresies*, pp. 107-117; see also Russell, *Dissent and Reform*, pp. 68-78.

11. Wakefield and Evans, *Heresies*, pp. 118-121, has a contemporary account; see also Russell, *Dissent and Reform*, pp. 68-78.

12. On Clement and Ebrard see Russell, *Dissent and Reform*, pp. 78-81; on Albero, pp. 86-89; and pp. 84-89 on the Cologne anticlericals.

13. For contemporary accounts of the Waldensians, see Wakefield and Evans, *Heresies*, pp. 200-241.

14. For the dispute within the Franciscan Order, see Leff, *Heresy in the Later Middle Ages*, I, 51-255.

15. Jedin and Dolan, *Handbook of Church History*, IV, 355-358.

16. Jedin and Dolan, *Handbook of Church History*, IV, 271, 358-359.

17. For the conflict between Philip and Boniface and the texts of the bulls, see Tierney, *Crisis of Church and State*, pp. 172-192.

18. Ernst Kantorowicz, *Frederick the Second, 1194-1250* (New York, 1957), pp. 615-616, 618-619. See also Cohen, *Pursuit of the Millennium*, pp. 103-107.

NOTES TO CHAPTER 4

1. Daniel-Rops, *History of the Church of Christ: Cathedral and Crusade*, II, 367-370, details some of the effects of the plague in the fourteenth century.

2. A catalogue of these abuses can be found in practically any history

of the Protestant Reformation. Among more recent studies, John P. Dolan, *History of the Reformation: A Conciliatory Assessment of Opposite Views* (New York, 1966); A. G. Dickens, *Reformation and Society in Sixteenth-Century Europe* (London, 1966); and Hans J. Hillerbrand, *Men and Ideas in the Sixteenth Century* (Chicago, 1969), are excellent works.

3. See Walter Ullman, *The Origins of the Great Schism* (London, 1948), and Brian Tierney, *Foundations of the Conciliar Theory* (Cambridge, 1955).

4. Willson H. Coates, Hayden V. White, and J. Salwyn Shapiro, *The Emergence of Liberal Humanism* (New York, 1966), I, 3-44, is a clear summary of the meaning and practice of pre-Reformation humanism. For a contrasting view see John C. Olin, ed., *Christian Humanism and the Reformation* (New York, 1965), and Charles E. Trinkhaus, *In Our Image and Likeness* (Chicago, 1970).

5. Jedin and Dolan, *Handbook of Church History*, IV, 426-443.

6. Most of the clerics placed in hell by Dante typified the targets of the twelfth-century anticlericals. See *The Divine Comedy*, Carlyle-Wickstead translation (New York, 1932).

7. See the examination of Erasmus' ideas in Johan Huizinga, *Erasmus and the Age of the Reformation* (New York, 1957).

8. More's *Utopia* contains no evidence of anticlericalism.

9. See Daniel-Rops, *History of the Church of Christ: The Protestant Reformation*, I, 289-293.

10. Marsiglio felt that "the priesthood should be concerned with the care of souls, not judging men" (Dickens, *Reformation and Society*, p. 21). This also is a modern anticlerical notion.

11. Leff, *Heresy in the Late Middle Ages*, II, 494-707, is excellent on Wycliffe and Hus.

12. Ralph Roeder, *The Man of the Renaissance* (New York, 1958), pp. 3-130, is an interesting study of the Florentine reformer.

13. Roland Bainton, *Here I Stand* (New York, 1955).

14. George H. Williams, *The Radical Reformation* (Philadelphia, 1962), is good on the Anabaptists.

15. Dickens, *Reformation and Society*, pp. 22-28.

16. See Philip Hughes, *The Reformation in England*, 3 vols. (New York, 1950-54), and the stimulating study by Peter Heath, *The English Parish Clergy on the Eve of the Reformation* (London, 1969).

NOTES TO CHAPTER 5

1. A. G. Dickens, *The Counter Reformation* (New York, 1969), and H. Outram Evennett, *The Spirit of the Counter-Reformation* (Cambridge, 1968), are both excellent works on this period. Philip Hughes, *Under God and the Law* (Oxford, 1949), has a good understanding of the clerical temperament.

2. Dickens, *Counter Reformation*, p. 128. Hubert Jedin, *A History of the Council of Trent*, 2 vols. (New York, 1947), is a fine study of the formation of the decrees.

3. Dickens, *Counter Reformation*, p. 101.

4. James Broderick, *The Origin of the Jesuits* (New York, 1940) and *The Progress of the Jesuits* (New York, 1947) are worthwhile studies, as is Thomas J. Campbell, *The Jesuits*, 2 vols. (New York, 1921).

5. Dickens, *Counter Reformation*, p. 82, points out that the success of the Jesuits was not in their alleged robotlike performance, but rather in the fact that the Jesuit superiors gave suitable tasks to men of great ability.

6. See Daniel-Rops, *History of the Church of Christ: The Catholic Reformation*, I, 91-93.

7. Georgio di Santillana, *The Crime of Galileo* (Chicago, 1955), is a masterpiece of historical detection and understanding.

8. "Giordano Bruno," *Encyclopaedia Brittanica*, 13th ed. (London, 1926), IV, 686-687.

9. See Henry Kamen, *The Rise of Toleration* (New York, 1967), pp. 139-145, and "Hugo Grotius," *Encyclopaedia Britannica*, 13th ed. (London, 1926), XII, 621-623.

10. Dickens, *Counter Reformation*, p. 132.

NOTES TO CHAPTER 6

1. Peter Gay, *The Enlightenment: An Interpretation*, vol. I: *The Rise of Modern Paganism* (New York, 1968) is an outstanding work. Also useful is Paul Hazard, *European Thought in the Eighteenth* Century, trans. J. L. May (Cleveland, 1963).

2. See E. E. Y. Hales, *Revolution and Papacy* (Garden City, N.Y., 1960), pp. 296-297.

3. Gay, *The Enlightenment*, pp. 336-357.

4. Gay, *The Enlightenment*, p. 149.

5. Paul Hazard, *The European Mind, 1680-1715* (Cleveland, 1963), pp. 102-105.

6. Baron de Montesquieu, *The Spirit of the Laws*, trans. T. Nugent (London, 1823), I, 229-230; II, 127-128.

7. Voltaire's writings fill many volumes. Gay, *The Enlightenment*, and Hazard, *European Thought*, both have excellent evaluations of his anticlerical thought and influence.

8. See "Supplement to Bougainville's 'Voyage,'" in Denis Diderot, *Rameau's Nephew and Other Works*, trans. J. Barzun and R. H. Bowen (Garden City, N.Y., 1956), pp. 187-239.

9. A. N. de Condorcet, *Sketch for a Historical Picture of the Progress of the Human Mind*, trans. J. Barraclough (New York, 1955), p. 137.

10. On the English anticlericals see Janet Griffin, *Anticlericalism Among the English Deists* (St. Louis, 1969).

11. Raymond Carr, *Spain, 1808-1939* (Oxford, 1966), p. 45.

12. Gay, *The Enlightenment*, pp. 372-373.

13. See Daniel-Rops, *History of the Church of Christ: The Church in the Eighteenth Century*, pp. 314-317.

NOTES TO CHAPTER 7

1. Sturzo, *Church and State*, pp. 314-365, is good on the cismontanes.

2. Charles III of Spain while practicing cismontane anticlericalism prayed daily and had Spain consecrated to the Sacred Heart of Jesus.

3. Sturzo, *Church and State*, p. 328.

4. For the French struggle in the eighteenth century see Adrien Dansette, *Religious History of Modern France*, I, 3-37.

5. "The clergy retained enough of the old persecuting spirit to disgust the laity, but not enough to crush dissent." *The Cambridge Modern History* (London, 1907), VIII, 56.

6. Newman C. Eberhardt, *A Summary of Catholic History* (St. Louis, 1962), II, 365.

7. John Lough, *An Introduction to Eighteenth Century France* (New York, 1960), p. 102.

8. Richard Herr, *The Eighteenth Century Revolution in Spain* (Princeton, 1958), pp. 11-36, is excellent on the regalist attempts in Spain. See W. Eugene Shiels, *King and Church* (Chicago, 1961), for the *patronato*.

9. Harold Acton, *The Bourbons of Naples* (London, 1956), pp. 31, 58, 110.

10. Mary Clare Goodwin, *The Papal Conflict with Josephism* (New York, 1938), is the best work on Josephism.

11. Daniel-Rops, *History of the Church of Christ: The Church in the Eighteenth Century*, p. 294.

12. Francis Hanus, *Church and State Under Frederick II* (Washington, 1944), p. 95.

13. Hales, *Revolution and Papacy*, pp. 58-60.

14. Hales, *Revolution and Papacy*, pp. 64-65.

15. On Pombal and the Portuguese cismontanes, see Marcus Cheke, *Dictator of Portugal: A Life of the Marquis of Pombal* (London, 1938).

16. There is no comprehensive study of the suppression of the Jesuits. A brief account can be found in Hales, *Revolution and Papacy*, pp. 11-44.

NOTES TO CHAPTER 8

1. The subject of Freemasonry awaits its historian.

2. Nothing has been written on social anticlericalism; however, much useful information for understanding it can be found in Gerald Brenan, *The Spanish Labyrinth* (Cambridge, 1952); E. J. Hobsbawm, *Primitive Rebels* (New York, 1959); James Joll, *The Anarchists* (Boston, 1964); George Woodcock, *Anarchism* (Cleveland, 1962); and Neil J. Smelser, *Theory of Collective Behavior* (New York, 1963).

3. Brenan, *Spanish Labyrinth*, p. 190.

4. Kenneth Scott Latourette, *Christianity in a Revolutionary Age*, vol. I: *The Nineteenth Century in Europe* (New York, 1958), pp. 238-242.

5. On the demochristian movement, see Michael Fogarty, *Christian Democracy in Western Europe* (Notre Dame, 1957).

6. On modernism, see John J. Heaney, *The Modernist Crisis: von Hügel* (Washington, 1968), pp. 219-234, and Émile Poulat, *Histoire, dogme et critique dans la crise moderniste* (Tournai, 1962).

7. On the first four popes listed see Hales, *Revolution and Papacy*. On Pius IX the best biography is E. E. Y. Hales, *Pio Nono* (Garden City, N.Y., 1962). There is no adequate biography of Leo XIII. On the last four popes, see the interesting study by Carlo Falconi, *The Popes in the Twentieth Century* (Boston, 1967).

8. See George Rudé, *The Crowd in History, 1730-1848* (New York, 1964), pp. 135-147.

9. Cited in Theodore Zeldin, ed., *Conflicts in French Society: Anticlericalism, Education and Morals in the Nineteenth Century* (London, 1970), p. 10.

10. On Ireland, see Edward R. Norman, *The Catholic Church and Ireland in the Age of Rebellion* (Ithaca, 1965), and Emmet Larkin, "The Devotional Revolution in Ireland, 1850-75," *American Historical Review* LXXVII, no. 3 (June 1972): 625-652; on Poland, see W. F. Reddaway, ed., *The Cambridge History of Poland* (Cambridge, 1941).

11. On Austria, see Josef Wodka, *Kirche in Ostrreich* (Vienna, 1959).

12. On Belgium, see H. Vander Linden, *Belgium, The Making of a Nation* (Oxford, 1920), and H. Pirenne, *Histoire de Belgique*, VII (Brussels, 1948).

13. On Germany, see Hajo Holborn, *A History of Modern Germany*, 3 vols. (New York, 1959-1970), and Gunther Lewy, *The Catholic Church and Nazi Germany* (New York, 1964).

14. On the United States, see Robert D. Cross, *The Emergence of Liberal Catholicism in America* (Cambridge, Mass., 1958), and John Tracy Ellis, *American Catholicism* (Chicago, 1956).

NOTES TO CHAPTER 9

1. Moody, *The Church as Enemy*, is an excellent study of French anticlerical literature.

2. On French anticlericalism in general see Bertier de Sauvigny, "French Anticlericalism . . ."; Dansette, *Religious History*; Mellor, *Histoire*; Magnin, "Anticléricalisme"; and André Latrielle, *Histoire du Catholicisme en France* (Paris, 1957).

3. A useful work for the anticlericalism of the Revolution is Alphonse Aulard, *Christianity and the French Revolution* (London, 1927). For the eighteenth-century background see R. R. Palmer, *Catholics and Unbelievers in Eighteenth Century France* (Princeton, 1939); John McManners, *French Ecclesiastical Society Under the Ancien Regime* (Manchester, 1960); and Charles A. LeGuin, "An Anti-Clerical Bureaucrat in Eighteenth Century France: Jean-Marie Roland," *Catholic Historical Review* LI, no. 4 (Jan. 1966): 487-502. An outstanding recent work is John McManners, *The French Revolution and the Church* (New York, 1970).

4. Daniel-Rops, *History of the Church of Christ: The Church in the Eighteenth Century*, pp. 73, 86.

5. Rudé, *The Crowd in History*, p. 50.

6. George Rudé, *The Crowd in the French Revolution* (London, 1959), p. 66.

7. Rudé, *French Revolution*, p. 66.

8. Dansette, *Religious History*, I, 77.

9. See Donald M. Greer, *The Incidence of Terror During the French Revolution: A Statistical Interpretation* (Cambridge, 1953), pp. 161-166, on the number of priests killed in the Revolution. Stanley Loomis, *Paris in the Terror* (Philadelphia, 1964), has a good description of the September massacres.

10. Dansette, *Religious History*, I, 114.

11. On Napoleon's views, see E. E. Y. Hales, *Napoleon and the Pope* (London, 1960).

12. Sturzo, *Church and State*, p. 382.

13. On the Restoration, see Guillaume de Bertier de Sauvigny, *The Bourbon Restoration* (Philadelphia, 1967), and Stanley Mellon, *The Political Uses of History: A Study of Historians in the French Restoration* (Stanford, 1958). For the nineteenth century, and on a personal and provincial level, see Zeldin, ed., *Conflicts*.

14. Theodore Zeldin, "The Conflict of Moralities: Confession, Sin and Pleasure in the Nineteenth Century," in Zeldin, ed., *Conflicts*, p. 30. Zeldin says that a map showing surviving Jansenists and anticlerical hostility would be very similar.

15. Roger Magraw, "The Conflict in the Villages: Popular Anticlericalism in the Iserè (1852-1870)," in Zeldin, ed., *Conflicts*, pp. 170-171.

16. Dansette, *Religious History*, I, 91.

17. Mellon, *Political Uses*, p. 131.

18. Mellon, *Political Uses*, p. 142.

19. Mellon, *Political Uses*, pp. 168 ff.

20. Dansette, *Religious History*, I, 215. There are two good biographies of Lamennais: Peter N. Stearns, *Priest and Revolutionary* (New York, 1967), and Alec Vidler, *Papacy and Prophecy* (New York, 1954).

21. Philip Spencer, *Politics of Belief in Nineteenth-Century France* (London, 1954), pp. 17-21.

22. On 1848 see Jacques Droz, "Religious Aspects of the 1848 Revolutions in Europe," in Evelyn M. Acomb and Marvin L. Brown, eds., *French Society and Culture Since the Old Regime* (New York, 1966), pp. 133-148.

23. On Proudhon, see Henri de Lubac, *The Un-Marxian Socialist*, trans. R. E. Scantlebury (New York, 1948), and Barbara Hughes, *Anticlericalism in the Writings of Pierre-Joseph Proudhon* (St. Louis, 1972).

24. Cited in Zeldin, ed., *Conflicts*, p. 218.

25. Cited in Dansette, *Religious History*, I, 265.

26. Cited in Dansette, *Religious History*, I, 279.

27. On the myth and substance of anticlericalism caused by the Falloux law, see Robert Anderson, "The Conflict in Education: Catholic Secondary Schools (1850-1870): A Reappraisal," in Zeldin, ed., *Conflicts*, pp. 51-93. On the Jesuit schools, see John W. Padberg, *Colleges in Controversy* (Cambridge, Mass., 1968).

28. Magraw, in Zeldin, ed., *Conflicts*, p. 175.

29. On the Third Republic, see D. W. Brogan, *The Development of Modern France, 1870-1939* (New York, 1966), 2 vols.

30. Cited in Dansette, *Religious History*, I, 321.

31. On the Commune see Alistair Horne, *The Fall of Paris: The Siege and the Commune* (New York, 1965), and Frank Jellinek, *The Paris Commune of 1871* (New York, 1965).

32. Evelyn M. Acomb, *The French Laic Laws, 1879-1899* (New York, 1941), p. 116. See also Mildred Headings, *French Masonry Under the Third Republic* (Baltimore, 1949).

33. Dansette, *Religious History*, II, 38.

34. Acomb, *French Laic Laws*, has a complete summary of this legislation.

35. Dansette, *Religious History*, II, 98.

36. Cited in Dansette, *Religious History*, I, 347.

37. On this period, see Malcolm O. Partin, *Waldeck-Rousseau, Combes and the Church: The Politics of Anticlericalism, 1899-1905* (Durham, 1969).

38. On the inter-war years see Brogan, *Development of Modern France*, II, 639-644.

39. On the controversy with *Action Française* see Eugen Weber, *Action Française* (Stanford, 1962), and Harry W. Paul, *The Second Ralliement* (Washington, 1967).

NOTES TO CHAPTER 10

1. Works on modern Spain that offer some insights into the anticlerical struggle are: Carr, *Spain*; E. Allison Peers, *Spain, the Church and the Orders* (London, 1945); Brenan, *Spanish Labyrinth*; A. Ramos Oliveira, *Politics, Economics and Men of Modern Spain, 1808-1946*, trans. T. Hall (London, 1946); Devlin, *Spanish Anticlericalism*; Ullman, *Tragic Week*; José M. Sánchez, *Reform and Reaction: The Politico-Religious Background of the Spanish Civil War* (Chapel Hill, 1964).

2. On the "two Spains," see Jaime Vicens Vives, *Approaches to the History of Spain*, trans. J. C. Ullman (Berkeley, 1967), and the concluding chapter of Herr, *Eighteenth Century Revolution*.

3. Marcelino Menéndez y Pelayo, *Historia de los Heterodoxos Españoles* (Madrid, 1933), VII, 514-515.

4. On Godoy, see Richard Herr, "Good, Evil, and Spain's Rising Against Napoleon," in Richard Herr and Harold T. Parker, eds., *Ideas in History* (Durham, 1965).

5. Gabriel Lovett, *Napoleon and the Birth of Modern Spain*, 2 vols. (New York, 1965), is excellent on the period from 1808 to 1814.

6. For the texts of all the Spanish constitutions, see Arnold Verduin, ed., *Manual of Spanish Constitutions, 1808-1931* (Ypsilanti, Mich., 1941).

7. Of the many histories of the Inquisition, Henry Kamen, *The Spanish Inquisition* (London, 1965), is the best.

8. Carlism, like Freemasonry, awaits its historian.

9. Brenan, *Spanish Labyrinth*, p. 43.

10. Jaime Vicens Vives, *An Economic History of Spain*, trans. F. López Morillas (Princeton, 1969), pp. 626-638, lists the laws and amounts of land involved in the *desamortización*.

11. The Marxist historian Ramos Oliveira in *Politics, Economics and Men*, pp. 55-61, gives a penetrating analysis of the consequences of the *desamortización*.

12. C. A. M. Hennessy, *The Federal Republic in Spain* (Oxford, 1962), is the only solid work dealing with any aspect of this period.

13. Brenan, *Spanish Labyrinth*, pp. 188-192, presents the best picture of the anarchists as social anticlericals. Novelist José María Gironella in *The Cypresses Believe in God* (New York, 1955) captures the character and actions of all Spanish anticlericals—political and social—far better than any historian.

14. See Sánchez, *Reform and Reaction*, pp. 49-50.

15. Devlin, *Spanish Anticlericalism*, details the anticlerical thinking of the major Spanish writers. See also John B. Trend, *The Origins of Modern Spain* (Cambridge, 1934).

16. The Barcelona events are discussed and documented in Ullman, *Tragic Week*.

17. On the King, see Vicente Pilapil, *Alfonso XIII* (New York, 1969).

18. On the Second Republic, see Sánchez, *Reform and Reaction*; Gabriel Jackson, *The Spanish Republic and the Civil War, 1931-1939* (Princeton, 1965); Richard A. H. Robinson, *The Origins of Franco's Spain: The Right, the Republic and Revolution* (Pittsburgh, 1970).

19. Cited in Sánchez, *Reform and Reaction*, p. 149.

20. The best study of the homicidal and incendiary anticlericalism during the Civil War is Antonio Montero Moreno, *Historia de la Persecución Religiosa en España, 1931-1939* (Madrid, 1961).

NOTES TO CHAPTER 11

1. Works useful for studying the anticlerical struggle in Italy are: Denis Mack Smith, *Italy, A Modern History* (Ann Arbor, Mich., 1959); Arturo C. Jemolo, *Church and State in Italy, 1850-1950*, trans. D. Moore (Oxford, 1960); George Martin, *The Red Shirt and the Cross of Savoy* (New York, 1969); Hales, *Pio Nono*.

2. On Alfieri, see Martin, *Red Shirt*, pp. 53-59.

3. See the studies cited in Alan J. Reinerman, "The Napoleonic Suppression of Italian Religious Orders and Sale of Their Property: Studies since 1960," *Catholic Historical Review* LVII, no. 2 (July 1971): 290-297.

4. See Mario Sancipriano, *Il Pensiero Politico di Haller e Rosmini* (Milan, 1968).

5. One of the best accounts of the 1848 Revolution in Italy is in Priscilla Robertson, *The Revolutions of 1848* (New York, 1960).

6. Jemolo, *Church and State*, p. 6.

7. On Cavour, see William R. Thayer, *The Life and Times of Cavour*, 2 vols. (Boston, 1911).

8. Jemolo, *Church and State*, p. 11.

9. Jemolo, *Church and State*, pp. 13-14.

10. See E. H. Flannery, "Mortara Case," *New Catholic Encyclopedia*, IX, 1153, and B. W. Korn, *American Reaction to the Mortara Case* (Cincinnati, 1957).

11. On the period after 1870, the best work is D. A. Binchy, *Church and State in Fascist Italy* (Oxford, 1941).

12. On the early disputes, see S. William Halperin, *Italy and the Vatican at War* (Chicago, 1939).

13. Jemolo, *Church and State*, p. 67.

14. Jemolo, *Church and State*, p. 111.
15. Smith, *Italy*, p. 223.
16. On this point see Benedetto Croce, *A History of Italy 1871-1915*, trans. C. M. Ady (Oxford, 1929), pp. 65 ff.
17. Jemolo, *Church and State*, and S. William Halperin, *The Separation of Church and State in Italian Thought from Cavour to Mussolini* (Chicago, 1937), give examples.
18. On Murri see Martine Hundelt, *Romolo Murri and the First Christian Democratic Party in Italy* (St. Louis, 1964).
19. Cited in Jemolo, *Church and State*, p. 120.
20. Jemolo, *Church and State*, p. 81.
21. Hobsbawm, *Primitive Rebels*, p. 100.
22. On the period after 1918, see Richard A. Webster, *The Cross and the Fasces* (Stanford, 1960).
23. This ban had never been extended to the German Center Party and its frequent parliamentary alliances with the German Social Democrats.
24. Binchy, *Church and State in Fascist Italy*, has the most complete account of the making of the Lateran Accords.
25. Jemolo, *Church and State*, pp. 182-277.
26. Jemolo, *Church and State*, p. 293.

NOTES TO CHAPTER 12

1. Little has been written on Portuguese religious history. Useful works for understanding the anticlerical struggle are: Richard Pattee, *Portugal and the Portuguese World* (Milwaukee, 1957); Charles Nowell, *A History of Portugal* (New York, 1952); Fortunato de Almeida, *Historia de Igreja em Portugal*, 4 vols. (Coimbra, 1922); Miguel de Oliveira, *Historia Eclesiastica de Portugal* (Lisbon, 1958); Manuel Ferrandis and Caetano Beirao, *Historia Contemporáneo de España y Portugal* (Barcelona, 1966), pp. 627-847.
2. Nowell, *History of Portugal*, p. 196.
3. Orazio M. Premoli, *Contemporary Church History* (London, 1932), p. 176.
4. No student of anticlericalism should miss this work. See the translation by Nan Flanagan (New York, 1962).
5. Pattee, *Portugal*, p. 181, and James MacCaffrey, *History of the Catholic Church in the Nineteenth Century* (Dublin, 1910), p. 392.
6. On the Republic, see Pattee, *Portugal*, pp. 186-191; Jesús Pabón, *La Revolución Portuguesa*, 2 vols. (Madrid, 1941); and Vicente de Braganza-Cunha, *Revolutionary Portugal, 1910-1936* (London, 1937).
7. Pattee, *Portugal*, p. 188.
8. On violence against the Jesuits, see Luis G. d'Azvedo, *Poscrits* (Tournai, 1912).

9. On the Salazar period, see Hugh Kay, *Salazar and Modern Portugal* (New York, 1970).

NOTES TO CHAPTER 13

1. The best single study for understanding anticlericalism in Latin America is J. Lloyd Mecham, *Church and State in Latin America*, rev. ed. (Chapel Hill, 1966). Also useful is Fredrick B. Pike, ed., *The Conflict Between Church and State in Latin America* (New York, 1964).

2. The best study of the patronage power is Shiels, *King and Church.*

3. Clarence Haring, *The Spanish Empire in America* (New York, 1947), pp. 191-192. See also, Asunción Lavrin, "The Role of the Nunneries in the Economy of New Spain in the Eighteenth Century," *Hispanic American Historical Review* XL (1966): 371-393.

4. Haring, *Spanish Empire*, p. 191.

5. See Karl Schmitt, "The Clergy and the Enlightenment in Latin America: An Analysis," *The Americas* XV (1959): 381-391.

6. Mecham, *Church and State*, pp. 88-98, 115-138, is the best survey of the Colombian struggle.

7. Zeldin, ed., *Conflicts*, p. 21.

8. Mecham, *Church and State*, pp. 42-43.

9. David Bushnell, *The Santander Regime in Gran Colombia* (Newark, Del., 1954), p. 196.

10. The history of papal relations is in Mecham, *Church and State*, pp. 61-87.

11. The texts of all the Colombian constitutions are in William M. Gibson, *The Constitutions of Colombia* (Durham, 1948).

12. For Bolívar's views, see Gerhard Masur, *Simón Bolívar* (Albuquerque, 1948).

13. Bushnell, *Santander Regime*, is the best work on this period.

14. Mecham, *Church and State*, p. 119.

15. Mecham, *Church and State*, pp. 123-124, on Mosquera's reforms.

16. John D. Martz, *Colombia: A Contemporary Political Survey* (Chapel Hill, 1962), is the best work on modern Colombia.

17. Cited in Vernon Fluharty, *The Dance of the Millions* (Pittsburgh, 1957), p. 49.

18. Mecham, *Church and State*, p. 137.

19. Martz, *Colombia*, and Fluharty, *Dance of the Millions*, both have accounts of the *bogotazo.*

20. A substantial literature has grown up about Torres. See Germán Guzmán, *Camilo Torres*, trans. J. D. Ring (New York, 1969).

NOTES TO CHAPTER 14

1. General works useful for understanding the anticlerical conflict in Mexico are: Henry Bamford Parkes, *A History of Mexico* (New York, 1960); Leslie Byrd Simpson, *Many Mexicos* (Berkeley, 1952); Charles C. Cumberland, *Mexico, The Struggle for Modernity* (New York, 1968); Mecham, *Church and State*, pp. 340-415; especially, two volumes by Wilfrid H. Callcott, *Church and State in Mexico, 1822-1857* (Durham, 1926), and *Liberalism in Mexico, 1857-1929* (Stanford, 1931). The recent work of Jan Bazant, *Alienation of Church Wealth in Mexico*, ed. and trans. by M. P. Costeloe, is a mine of information and corrects the impressions of earlier writers.

2. The cause of much of this vitality can be found in colonial times: see Robert Ricard, *The Spiritual Conquest of Mexico*, trans. L. B. Simpson (Berkeley, 1966). Also useful on the colonial background is Nancy M. Farris, *Crown and Clergy in Colonial Mexico, 1759-1821* (London, 1968).

3. Lucas Alamán, *Historia de Méjico* (Mexico, 1849), I, 67. See also Michael P. Costeloe, *Church Wealth in Mexico* (Cambridge, 1967). Bazant, *Alienation of Church Wealth*, p. 13, claims that by 1850 the Church owned less than one-fourth of the national wealth.

4. See James M. Breedlove, "Effect of the Cortes, 1810-1822, on Church Reform in Spain and Mexico," in Nettie Lee Benson, ed., *Mexico and the Spanish Cortes* (Austin, 1966).

5. Mecham, *Church and State*, pp. 79-86, details papal-Mexican relations.

6. Callcott, *Church and State*, pp. 56-59.

7. The details of the first Reform can be found in Callcott, *Church and State*, pp. 90-101.

8. Mecham, *Church and State*, p. 357.

9. French intellectual influence has always been greater than Spanish in modern Latin America.

10. The best biography of Juárez, along with the details of the second Reform, is Ralph Roeder, *Juárez and His Mexico*, 2 vols. (New York, 1957).

11. The excellent study by Frank A. Knapp, Jr., *The Life of Sebastián Lerdo de Tejada* (Austin, 1957), gives details of the Lerdo law. Bazant, *Alienation of Church Wealth*, has statistics and details on the loss of clerical property from 1856 to 1875.

12. Mecham, *Church and State*, p. 364.

13. Callcott, *Liberalism*, pp. 22-39, describes Juárez' reforms.

14. Egon Caesar Corti, *Maximilian and Charlotte of Mexico*, 2 vols. (New York, 1928), is the best study of Maximilian.

15. See Karl M. Schmitt, "Catholic Adjustment to the Secular State: The Case of Mexico, 1867-1911," *Catholic Historical Review* XLVIII, no. 2 (July 1962): 182-204.

16. James D. Cockcroft, *Intellectual Precursors of the Mexican Revolution, 1900-1913* (Austin, 1968), p. 96.

17. On the Mexican Revolution, see Stanley R. Ross, *Francisco I. Madero, Apostle of Mexican Democracy* (New York, 1955), and Charles C. Cumberland, *Mexican Revolution: Genesis Under Madero* (Austin, 1952).

18. Callcott, *Liberalism*, p. 245. On nineteenth-century Yucatan, see Nelson Reed, *The Caste War in Yucatan* (Stanford, 1963).

19. There are no instances of anticlericalism recorded in the authoritative John Womack, Jr., *Zapata and the Mexican Revolution* (New York, 1969).

20. See E. V. Niemeyer, "Anticlericalism in the Mexican Constitutional Convention, 1916-1917," *The Americas* XI, no. 2 (July 1954): 31-49.

21. Cited in Mecham, *Church and State*, p. 389.

22. There is a vast amount of polemical literature on the conflicts of the 1920s and 1930s; nothing objective has been written. Graham Greene's novel *The Power and the Glory* (New York, 1946) gives some insight into the problem.

23. On Cárdenas, see William Townsend, *Lázaro Cárdenas, Mexican Democrat* (Ann Arbor, 1952).

24. See Howard Cline, *Mexico: Revolution to Evolution, 1940-1960* (New York, 1963).

NOTES TO CHAPTER 15

1. Zeldin, ed., *Conflicts*, pp. 48-50.

2. There are no studies of the psychology of anticlericalism; however, recent sociological studies of the role of the clergy are useful. See Joseph H. Fichter, *Priest and People* (New York, 1965), and *Religion as an Occupation* (Notre Dame, 1961); David O. Moberg, *The Church as a Social Institution* (Englewood Cliffs, N.J., 1962); Andrew Greeley, *Religion and Career* (New York, 1963).

3. See Hochhuth's play, *The Deputy*, trans. R. and C. Winston (New York, 1964), and the valuable collection edited by Eric Bentley, *Storm Over the Deputy* (New York, 1965).

WORKS CITED

ACOMB, EVELYN M. *The French Laic Laws, 1879-1899.* New York, 1941.

ACTON, HAROLD. *The Bourbons of Naples.* London, 1956.

ALAMÁN, LUCAS. *Historia de Méjico,* I. Mexico, 1849.

ALMEIDA, FORTUNATO DE. *Historia de Igreja em Portugal.* 4 vols. Coimbra, 1922.

D'AZVEDO, LUIS G. *Poscrits.* Tournai, 1912.

BAINTON, ROLAND. *Here I Stand.* New York, 1955.

BAZANT, JAN. *Alienation of Church Wealth in Mexico.* Edited and translated by M.P. Costeloe. Cambridge, 1971.

BENTLEY, ERIC, ED. *Storm Over the Deputy.* New York, 1965.

BERTHELOT DU CHESNEY, C. "Anticlericalism." In *New Catholic Encyclopedia,* I, 618-620. New York, 1967.

BERTIER DE SAUVIGNY, GUILLAUME DE. *The Bourbon Restoration.* Philadelphia, 1967.

————. "French Anticlericalism Since the Great Revolution: A Tentative Interpretation." In *Historical Records and Studies, XLII, 3-21. New York: United States Catholic Historical Society, 1954.*

BINCHY, D. A. *Church and State in Fascist Italy.* Oxford, 1941.

BRAGANZA-CUNHA, VICENTE DE. *Revolutionary Portugal, 1910-1936.* London, 1937.

BREEDLOVE, JAMES M. "Effect of the Cortes, 1810-1822, on Church Reform in Spain and Mexico." In *Mexico and the Spanish Cortes,* edited by Nettie Lee Benson. Austin, 1966.

BRENAN, GERALD. *The Spanish Labyrinth.* Cambridge, 1952.

BRODERICK, JAMES. *The Origin of the Jesuits.* New York, 1940.

————. *The Progress of the Jesuits.* New York, 1947.

BROGAN, D. W. *The Development of Modern France, 1870-1939.* 2 vols. New York, 1966.

BUSHNELL, DAVID. *The Santander Regime in Gran Colombia.* Newark, Del., 1954.

CALLCOTT, WILFRID H. *Church and State in Mexico, 1822-1857.* Durham, 1926.

————. *Liberalism in Mexico, 1857-1929.* Stanford, 1931.

Cambridge Modern History. Edited by A. W. Ward, G. W. Prothero, and S. Leathes. VIII. London, 1907.

CAMPBELL, THOMAS J. *The Jesuits.* 2 vols. New York, 1921.

CARR, RAYMOND. *Spain, 1808-1939.* Oxford, 1966.

CHEKE, MARCUS. *Dictator of Portugal: A Life of the Marquis of Pombal.* London, 1938.

CLINE, HOWARD. *Mexico: Revolution to Evolution, 1940-1960.* New York, 1963.

COATES, WILLSON H.; WHITE, HAYDEN V.; and SHAPIRO, J. SALWYN. *The Emergence of Liberal Humanism.* 2 vols. New York, 1966.

COCKCROFT, JAMES D. *Intellectual Precursors of the Mexican Revolution, 1900-1913.* Austin, 1968.

COHEN, NORMAN. *The Pursuit of the Millennium.* New York, 1961.

CONDORCET, A. N. DE. *Sketch for a Historical Picture of the Progress of the Human Mind.* Translated by J. Barraclough. New York, 1955.

CONGAR, YVES. *Lay People in the Church: A Study for a Theology of the Laity.* Translated by D. Attwater. Westminster, Md., 1957.

CORTI, EGON CAESAR. *Maximilian and Charlotte of Mexico.* New York, 1928.

COSTELOE, MICHAEL P. *Church Wealth in Mexico.* Cambridge, 1967.

CROCE, BENEDETTO. *A History of Italy 1871-1915.* Translated by C.M. Ady. Oxford, 1929.

CROSS, ROBERT D. *The Emergence of Liberal Catholicism in America.* Cambridge, Mass., 1958.

CUMBERLAND, CHARLES C. *Mexican Revolution: Genesis under Madero.* Austin, 1952.

————. *Mexico, The Struggle for Modernity.* New York, 1968.

DANIÉLOU, JEAN, and MARROU, HENRI, eds. *The Christian Centuries.* New York, 1964–.

DANIEL-ROPS, HENRI. *A History of the Church of Christ.* 9 vols. Garden City, N.Y.: Doubleday, Image Books, 1960-67.

DANSETTE, ADRIEN. *Religious History of Modern France.* Translated by J. Dingle. 2 vols. New York, 1961.

DANTE ALIGHIERI. *The Divine Comedy.* Carlyle-Wickstead translation. New York, 1932.

DEVLIN, JOHN. *Spanish Anticlericalism.* New York, 1966.

DICKENS, A. G. *The Counter Reformation.* New York, 1969.

————. *Reformation and Society in Sixteenth-Century Europe.* London, 1966.

DIDEROT, DENIS. "Supplement to Bougainville's 'Voyage' " in his *Rameau's Nephew and Other Works.* Translated by J. Barzun and R. H. Bowen. Garden City, N.Y., 1956.

DOLAN, JOHN P. *History of the Reformation: A Conciliatory Assessment of Opposite Views.* New York, 1966.

DROZ, JACQUES. "Religious Aspects of the 1848 Revolutions in Europe." In *French Society and Culture Since the Old Regime,* edited by Evelyn M. Acomb and Marvin L. Brown. New York, 1966.

EBERHARDT, NEWMAN C. *A Summary of Catholic History.* 2 vols. St. Louis, 1962.

EÇA DE QUEIROZ, JOSÉ MARÍA. *The Sin of Father Amaro.* Translated by Nan Flanagan. New York, 1962.

ELLIS, JOHN TRACY. *American Catholicism.* Chicago, 1956.

EVANS, ROBERT F. *Pelagius: Inquiries and Reappraisals.* New York, 1968.

EVENNETT, H. OUTRAM. *The Spirit of the Counter-Reformation.* Cambridge, 1968.

FAGUET, EMIL. *L'Anticléricalisme.* Paris, 1906.

FALCONI, CARLO. *The Popes in the Twentieth Century.* Boston, 1967.

FARRIS, NANCY M. *Crown and Clergy in Colonial Mexico, 1759-1821.* London, 1968.

FERRANDIS, MANUEL, and BEIRAO, CAETANO. *Historia Contemporáneo de España y Portugal.* Barcelona, 1966.

FICHTER, JOSEPH H. "Anticlericalism in the American Catholic Culture." *The Critic* XXI (Feb.-Mar. 1963): 11-15.

————. *Priest and People.* New York, 1965.

————. *Religion as an Occupation.* Notre Dame, 1961.

FLANNERY, E. H. "Mortara Case." In *New Catholic Encyclopedia,* IX, 1153. New York, 1967.

FLUHARTY, VERNON. *The Dance of the Millions.* Pittsburgh, 1957.

FLYNN, FREDERICK E. "Clericalism, Anti-Clericalism." *Commonweal* LVIII (Apr. 17, 1953): 43-47.

FOGARTY, MICHAEL. *Christian Democracy in Western Europe.* Notre Dame, 1957.

FREND, W. H. C. *The Donatist Church.* London, 1952.

GAY, PETER. *The Enlightenment: An Interpretation,* vol. I: *The Rise of Modern Paganism.* New York, 1968.

GIBSON, WILLIAM M. *The Constitutions of Colombia.* Durham, 1948.

GIRAUD, VICTOR. *Anticléricalisme et Catholicisme.* Paris, 1906.

GIRONELLA, JOSÉ MARÍA. *The Cypresses Believe in God.* New York, 1955.

GREELEY, ANDREW. *Religion and Career.* New York, 1963.

GREENAWAY, GEORGE W. *Arnold of Brescia.* Cambridge, 1931.

GREENE, GRAHAM. *The Power and the Glory.* New York, 1946.

GREER, DONALD M. *The Incidence of Terror During the French Revolution: A Statistical Interpretation.* Cambridge, Mass., 1953.

GRIFFEN, JANET. *Anticlericalism Among the English Deists.* St. Louis, 1969.

GOODWIN, MARY CLARE. *The Papal Conflict with Josephism.* New York, 1938.

GUZMÁN, GERMÁN. *Camilo Torres.* Translated by J. D. Ring. New York, 1969.

HALES, E. E. Y. *Napoleon and the Pope.* London, 1960.

———. *Pio Nono.* Garden City, N. Y., 1962.

———. *Revolution and Papacy.* Garden City, N. Y., 1960.

HALPERIN, S. WILLIAM. *Italy and the Vatican at War.* Chicago, 1939.

———. *The Separation of Church and State in Italian Thought from Cavour to Mussolini.* Chicago, 1937.

HANUS, FRANCIS. *Church and State Under Frederick II.* Washington, 1944.

HARING, CLARENCE. *The Spanish Empire in America.* New York, 1947.

HAZARD, PAUL. *The European Mind, 1680-1715.* Cleveland, 1963.

———. *European Thought in the Eighteenth Century.* Translated by J. L. May. Cleveland, 1963.

HEADINGS, MILDRED. *French Masonry Under the Third Republic.* Baltimore, 1949.

HEANEY, JOHN J. *The Modernist Crisis: von Hügel.* Washington, 1968.

HEATH, PETER. *The English Parish Clergy on the Eve of the Reformation.* London, 1969.

HENNESSY, C. A. M. *The Federal Republic in Spain.* Oxford, 1962.

HERLIHY, D. "Church Property on the European Continent, 701-1200." *Speculum* XXXVI (1961): 81-105.

———. "Secularization of Church Property." In *New Catholic Encyclopedia,* XIII, 40-42. New York, 1967.

HERR, RICHARD. *The Eighteenth Century Revolution in Spain.* Princeton, 1958.

———. "Good, Evil, and Spain's Rising Against Napoleon." In *Ideas in History,* edited by Richard Herr and Harold T. Parker. Durham, 1965.

HILLERBRAND, HANS J. *Men and Ideas in the Sixteenth Century.* Chicago, 1969.

HOBSBAWM, E. J. *Primitive Rebels.* New York, 1959.

HOCHHUTH, ROLF. *The Deputy.* Translated by R. and C. Winston. New York, 1964.

HOLBORN, HAJO. *A History of Modern Germany.* 3 vols. New York, 1959-70.

HORNE, ALISTAIR. *The Fall of Paris: the Siege and the Commune.* New York, 1965.

HUGHES, BARBARA. *Anticlericalism in the Writings of Pierre-Joseph Proudhon.* St. Louis, 1972.

HUGHES, PHILIP. *The Reformation in England.* 3 vols. New York, 1950-54.

———. *Under God and the Law.* Oxford, 1949.

HUIZINGA, JOHAN. *Erasmus and the Age of the Reformation.* New York, 1957.

HUNDELT, MARTINE. *Romolo Murri and the First Christian Democratic Party in Italy.* St. Louis, 1964.

JACKSON, GABRIEL. *The Spanish Republic and the Civil War, 1931-1939.* Princeton, 1965.

JEDIN, HUBERT. *A History of the Council of Trent.* 2 vols. New York, 1947.

JEDIN, HUBERT, and DOLAN, JOHN, eds. *Handbook of Church History.* New York, 1965 .

JELLINEK, FRANK. *The Paris Commune of 1871.* New York, 1965.

JEMOLO, ARTURO C. *Church and State in Italy, 1850-1950.* Translated by D. Moore. Oxford, 1960.

JOLL, JAMES. *The Anarchists.* Boston, 1964.

KAMEN, HENRY. *The Rise of Toleration.* New York, 1967.

———. *The Spanish Inquisition.* London, 1965.

KANTOROWICZ, ERNST. *Frederick the Second, 1194-1250.* New York, 1957.

KAY, HUGH. *Salazar and Modern Portugal.* New York, 1970.

KNAPP, FRANK A., JR. *The Life of Sebastián Lerdo de Tejada.* Austin, 1957.

KORN, B. W. *American Reaction to the Mortara Case.* Cincinnati, 1957.

LARKIN, EMMET. "The Devotional Revolution in Ireland, 1850-75." *American Historical Review* LXXVII, no. 3 (June 1972): 625-652.

LATOURETTE, KENNETH SCOTT. *Christianity in a Revolutionary Age,* vol. I: *The Nineteenth Century in Europe.* New York, 1958.

LATRIELLE, ANDRÉ. *Histoire du Catholicisme en France.* Paris, 1957.

LAVRIN, ASUNCIÓN. "The Role of the Nunneries in the Economy of New Spain in the Eighteenth Century." *Hispanic American Historical Review* XL (1966): 371-393.

LECLER, J. "Anticléricalisme." In *Catholicisme: Hier, Aujourd'hui, Demain,* edited by G. Jacquemet, I, 633-638. Paris, 1947.

————. "Origines et Evolution de l'Anticléricalisme." *Etudes* CCLIII (May 1947): 145-164.

————. *The Two Sovereignties: A Study of the Relationship Between Church and State.* New York, 1952.

LEFF, GORDON. *Heresy in the Later Middle Ages.* 2 vols. Manchester, 1967.

LEGUIN, CHARLES A. "An Anti-Clerical Bureaucrat in Eighteenth Century France: Jean-Marie Roland." *Catholic Historical Review* LI, no. 4 (Jan. 1966): 487-502.

LEWY, GUNTHER. *The Catholic Church and Nazi Germany.* New York, 1964.

LOOMIS, STANLEY. *Paris in the Terror.* Philadelphia, 1964.

LOUGH, JOHN. *An Introduction to Eighteenth Century France.* New York, 1960.

LOVETT, GABRIEL. *Napoleon and the Birth of Modern Spain.* 2 vols. New York, 1960.

LUBAC, HENRI DE. *The Un-Marxian Socialist.* Translated by R. E. Scantlebury. New York, 1948.

MACCAFFREY, JAMES. *History of the Catholic Church in the Nineteenth Century.* Dublin, 1910.

MCKENZIE, JOHN L. *Authority in the Church.* New York, 1966.

MACK SMITH, DENIS. *Italy, A Modern History.* Ann Arbor, 1959.

MCMANNERS, JOHN. *French Ecclesiastical Soceity under the Ancien Regime.* Manchester, 1960.

———. *The French Revolution and the Church.* New York, 1970.

MAGNIN, E. "Anticléricalisme." In *Dictionnaire de Sociologie,* I, 935-36. Paris, 1938.

MARTIN, GEORGE. *The Red Shirt and the Cross of Savoy.* New York, 1969.

MARTZ, JOHN D. *Colombia: A Contemporary Political Survey.* Chapel Hill, 1962.

MASUR, GERHARD. *Simón Bolívar.* Albuquerque, 1948.

MECHAM, J. LLOYD. *Church and State in Latin America.* Rev. ed. Chapel Hill, 1962.

MELLON, STANLEY. *The Political Uses of History: A Study of the Historians in the French Restoration.* Stanford, 1958.

MELLOR, ALEC. *Histoire de l'Anticléricalisme Française.* Paris, 1966.

MENÉNDEZ Y PELAYO, MARCELINO. *Historia de los Heterodoxos Españoles.* Madrid, 1933.

MOBERG, DAVID O. *The Church as a Social Institution.* Englewood Cliffs, N. J., 1962.

MONTERO MORENO, ANTONIO. *Historia de la Persecución Religiosa en España, 1931-1939.* Madrid, 1961.

MONTESQUIEU, BARON DE. *The Spirit of the Laws.* Translated by T. Nugent. 2 vols. London, 1823.

MOODY, JOSEPH N. *The Church as Enemy: Anticlericalism in Nineteenth Century French Literature.* Washington, 1968.

MORRISON, KARL. *Tradition and Authority in the Western Church.* Princeton, 1969.

NIEMEYER, E. V. "Anticlericalism in the Mexican Constitutional Convention, 1916-1917." *The Americas* XI no. 2 (July 1954): 31-49.

NORMAN, EDWARD R. *The Catholic Church and Ireland in the Age of Rebellion.* Ithaca, 1965.

NOWELL, CHARLES. *A History of Portugal.* New York, 1952.

OLIN, JOHN C., ed. *Christian Humanism and the Reformation.* New York, 1965.

OLIVEIRA, MIGUEL DE. *Historia Eclesiastica de Portugal.* Lisbon, 1958.

PABÓN, JESÚS. *La Revolución Portuguesa.* 2 vols. Madrid, 1941.

PADBERG, JOHN W. *Colleges in Controversy.* Cambridge, Mass., 1968.

PALMER, R. R. *Catholics and Unbelievers in Eighteenth Century France.* Princeton, 1939.

PARKES, HENRY BAMFORD. *A History of Mexico.* New York, 1960.

PARTIN, MALCOLM O. *Waldeck-Rousseau, Combes and the Church: The Politics of Anticlericalism, 1899-1905.* Durham, 1969.

PATTEE, RICHARD. *Portugal and the Portuguese World.* Milwaukee, 1957.

PAUL, HARRY W. *The Second Ralliement.* Washington, 1967.

PEERS, E. ALLISON. *Spain, the Church and the Orders.* London, 1945.

PIKE, FREDRICK B., ed. *The Conflict Between Church and State in Latin America.* New York, 1964.

PILAPIL, VICENTE. *Alfonso XIII.* New York, 1969.

PIRENNE, HENRI. *Histoire de Belgique.* VII. Brussels, 1948.

———. *A History of Europe from the Invasions to the XVI Century.* Translated by B. Miall. New York, 1955.

POULAT, ÉMILE. *Histoire, dogme et critique dans la crise moderniste.* Tournai, 1962.

PREMOLI, ORAZIO M. *Contemporary Church History.* London, 1932.

RAMOS OLIVEIRA, A. *Politics, Economics, and Men of Modern Spain, 1808-1946.* Translated by T. Hall. London, 1946.

REDDAWAY, W. F., ed. *The Cambridge History of Poland.* Cambridge, 1941.

REED, NELSON. *The Caste War in Yucatan.* Stanford, 1963.

REINERMAN, ALAN J. "The Napoleonic Suppression of the Italian Religious Orders and the Sale of Their Property: Studies since 1960." *Catholic Historical Review* LVIII, no. 2 (July 1971): 290-297.

RICARD, ROBERT. *The Spiritual Conquest of Mexico.* Translated by L. B. Simpson. Berkeley, 1966.

ROBERTS, R. E. *The Theology of Tertullian.* London, 1924.

ROBERTSON, PRISCILLA. *The Revolutions of 1848.* New York, 1960.

ROBINSON, RICHARD A. H. *The Origins of Franco's Spain: The Right, the Republic and Revolution.* Pittsburgh, 1970.

ROEDER, RALPH. *Juárez and His Mexico.* 2 vols. New York, 1957.

———. *The Man of the Renaissance.* New York, 1958.

ROSS, STANLEY R. *Francisco I. Madero, Apostle of Mexican Democracy.* New York, 1955.

RUDÉ, GEORGE. *The Crowd in the French Revolution.* London, 1959.
––––––. *The Crowd in History, 1730-1848.* New York, 1964.
RUSSELL, JEFFREY B. *Dissent and Reform in the Early Middle Ages.* Los Angeles and Berkeley, 1965.
––––––. *A History of Medieval Christianity.* New York, 1968.
SÁNCHEZ, JOSÉ M. *Reform and Reaction: The Politico-Religious Background of the Spanish Civil War.* Chapel Hill, 1964.
SANCIPRIANO, MARIO. *Il Pensiero Politico de Haller e Rosmini.* Milan, 1968.
SANTILLANA, GEORGIO. *The Crime of Galileo.* Chicago, 1955.
SCHMITT, KARL M. "Catholic Adjustment to the Secular State: The Case of Mexico, 1867-1911." *Catholic Historical Review* XLVIII, no. 2 (July 1962): 182-204.
––––––. "The Clergy and the Enlightenment in Latin America: An Analysis." *The Americas* XV (1959): 381-391.
SHAPIRO, J. SALWYN. *Anticlericalism: Conflict Between Church and State in France, Italy, and Spain.* Princeton, 1966.
SHIELS, W. EUGENE. *King and Church.* Chicago, 1961.
SIMON, IVES. *Nature and Functions of Authority.* Milwaukee, 1940.
SIMPSON, LESLIE BYRD. *Many Mexicos.* Berkeley, 1952.
SMELSER, NEIL J. *Theory of Collective Behavior.* New York, 1963.
SPENCER, PHILIP. *Politics of Belief in Nineteenth-Century France.* London, 1954.
STEARNS, PETER N. *Priest and Revolutionary.* New York, 1967.
STURZO, LUIGI. *Church and State.* Translated by B. B. Carter. Notre Dame, 1962.
TAYLOR, CHARLES. "Clericalism." *Cross Currents* X (Fall 1960): 327-336.
THAYER, WILLIAM R. *The Life and Times of Cavour.* 2 vols. Boston, 1911.
TIERNEY, BRIAN. *The Crisis of Church and State, 1050-1300.* Englewood Cliffs, N.J., 1968.
––––––. *Foundations of the Conciliar Theory.* Cambridge, 1955.
TOWNSEND, WILLIAM. *Lázaro Cárdenas, Mexican Democrat.* Ann Arbor, 1952.
TREND, JOHN B. *The Origins of Modern Spain.* Cambridge, 1934.
TRINKHAUS, CHARLES E. *In Our Image and Likeness.* Chicago, 1970.
ULLMAN, JOAN CONNELLY. *The Tragic Week: A Study of Anticlericalism in Spain, 1875-1912.* Cambridge, Mass., 1967.

ULLMAN, WALTER. *The Origins of the Great Schism.* London, 1948.

VANDER LINDEN, H. *Belgium, The Making of a Nation.* Oxford, 1920.

VERDUIN, ARNOLD, ed. *Manual of Spanish Constitutions, 1808-1931.* Ypsilanti, Mich., 1941.

VICENS VIVES, JAIME. *Approaches to the History of Spain.* Translated by J. C. Ullman. Berkeley, 1967.

———. *An Economic History of Spain.* Translated by F. López Morillas. Princeton, 1969.

VIDLER, ALEC. *Papacy and Prophecy.* New York, 1954.

WAKEFIELD, WALTER L., and EVANS, AUSTIN P., eds. *Heresies of the High Middle Ages.* New York, 1969.

WEBER, EUGEN. *Action Française.* Stanford, 1962.

WEBSTER, RICHARD A. *The Cross and the Fasces.* Stanford, 1960.

WHITTUCK, C.A. "Clericalism and Anti-Clericalism." In *Encyclopedia of Religion and Ethics* III, 690-695. Edinburgh, 1910.

WILLIAMS, GEORGE H. *The Radical Reformation.* Philadelphia, 1962.

WODKA, JOSEF. *Kirche in Ostrreich.* Vienna, 1959.

WOMACK, JOHN, JR. *Zapata and the Mexican Revolution.* New York, 1969.

WOODCOCK, GEORGE. *Anarchism.* Cleveland, 1962.

ZELDIN, THEODORE, ed. *Conflicts in French Society: Anticlericalism, Education and Morals in the Nineteenth Century.* London, 1970.

INDEX